Robert Moffat Webb

Moffat Jack was my
Godfather — a relative.

LIFE AND LETTERS OF STOPFORD BROOKE

BY LAWRENCE PEARSALL JACKS
M.A., HON. LL.D. AND D.D.
PRINCIPAL OF MANCHESTER COLLEGE, OXFORD

"Thy voice is on the rolling air;
I hear thee where the waters run."

VOLUME I

NEW YORK
CHARLES SCRIBNER'S SONS
1917

PRINTED BY
WILLIAM CLOWES AND SONS, LIMITED,
LONDON AND BECCLES, ENGLAND.

All rights reserved

PREFACE

In this Biography I have endeavoured to let Stopford Brooke reveal himself. Such description as I have attempted is chiefly intended to define the field of vision, and the most I can hope to have achieved is to have left his self-revelation unimpaired. I have built a frame round the picture, of which the lines and colours are his own.

The thanks I owe to those who have helped me in this work are, in the main, family debts; but they are exceptionally great, and I cannot refrain from mentioning them.

To Miss Cecilia Brooke, and to Miss Angel Brooke, the surviving sisters of Stopford, and to the Reverend Arthur Brooke, his surviving brother, I am indebted for access to a vast amount of correspondence, for permission to make use of the early diary of their mother—a very sacred document—and for much personal information, without which some of the earlier chapters could not have been written.

My brother-in-law, Mr S. W. Brooke, and my eldest sister-in-law, Miss Honor Brooke, have read the whole in manuscript or proof, helping me to correct the proportions where they seemed to be faulty, and confirming me at many points of essential importance where I wished for collateral support. The spirit in which they have helped me has been an echo of the large-heartedness of their father, who knew the difficulties of treating a great subject, and gave encouragement where it was needed.

To another sister-in-law, Miss Evelyn Brooke, the devoted companion of her father during the last period of his life, my debt, which is also the reader's, is assuredly very great. She has given me access to the diaries and letters of which she was left the custodian; and in this she has been followed by her five sisters, who have placed their father's letters in my hands, not excepting many which relate to matters far too sacred for publication.

Among the family claimants on my gratitude the chief place must be given to my wife, the fourth daughter of Stopford Brooke, who has written out the whole text from my dictation, and suffered no word to pass unchallenged which, in her judgment, might leave a wrong impression on the reader's mind. It is to her that I would dedicate the book. Without her the biography of her father could not have been written by me.

Lastly, I have had the advantage of being able to consult, from time to time, the wide experience and ripe judgment of Viscount Bryce. His close friendship with Brooke covered a period of forty years, from middle life to the end. Lord Bryce has helped me to feel, however far I have fallen short in presenting it, the deepening beauty of the old age of Brooke, a feature which gives a peculiar significance to the earlier phases of his life and may almost be said to furnish the key to the whole.

Other helpers I have had whose names will be found at the head of the published letters. The best return I can make for their kindness is to say that, in my judgment, the friends of Brooke have been guided by a just view of his character in allowing so much that was intimate in his correspondence to see the light. He was the soul of candour, and open as the day—a man who had the courage and strength to be himself under all conditions and in all relationships.

Although I have been greatly helped in the manner indicated, the responsibility is entirely my own if any part of my work is unworthy, as the whole may well be, of Stopford Brooke. I have had to contend throughout with the difficulties which always attend the presentation of the greater by the less. From this cause faults must inevitably arise; and for these I crave the indulgence of the reader.

OXFORD, *July*, 1917.

CONTENTS

BOOK I
EARLY LIFE IN IRELAND

CHAPTER		PAGE
I.	Ancestry and Parentage	1
II.	Mother and Son. Boyhood. 1832–1850	15
III.	Trinity College, Dublin. 1851–1856	39
IV.	Vocation	54
V.	To London. 1857	73

BOOK II
CURATE: CHAPLAIN: BIOGRAPHER

VI.	First Curacy: Marriage. 1857–1858	86
VII.	Kensington. 1859–1863	113
VIII.	The Quest for Knowledge	137
IX.	Berlin. 1863–1865	152
X.	St James' Chapel. 1865–1866	172
XI.	The Life of F. W. Robertson. 1865	192

BOOK III
THE BROAD CHURCHMAN

XII.	Queen's Chaplain. Holidays. A Bereavement. 1866–1870	210
XIII.	Events and Opinions. Letters to his Wife. 1870–1875	244
XIV.	The Death of Mrs Stopford Brooke. 1874	274
XV.	Bedford Chapel. 1875–1880	284

BOOK IV
PROPHET AND POET

XVI.	Secession from the Church of England, 1880	309
XVII.	Letters to his Children. 1872–1881	332

ILLUSTRATIONS

		TO FACE PAGE
1.	BROOKE IN 1884 . . . *Frontispiece to Vol I.*	
2.	THE MOTHER OF BROOKE IN YOUTH AND AGE . . .	30
3.	BROOKE IN 1857	80
4.	MRS STOPFORD BROOKE	158
5.	BROOKE IN 1876	286
6.	BROOKE AT THE TIME OF HIS SECESSION	320

LIFE AND LETTERS OF STOPFORD BROOKE

BOOK I

EARLY LIFE IN IRELAND

CHAPTER I

ANCESTRY AND PARENTAGE

"I have the old belief of reincarnation, and it is more than probable that I began as a very primeval, arboreal person, and have been of all tribes, of all nations and climates, and have seen a hundred civilizations in my time. . . ."—(*Diary*, December 7, 1898.)

"This place is called Brunnen, which means Brookes. It is the source of our family. . . . Three brooks sprang out of the earth to hail the fourth. These three brooks still remain in the Rütli meadow, but the fourth flowed away and came to Ireland, and we are its sole descendants."—(Letter to a Daughter, 1884.)

STOPFORD AUGUSTUS BROOKE was born on November 14, 1832, in the rectory of Glendoen, near Letterkenny, Co. Donegal, of which parish his maternal grandfather, the Rev. Joseph Stopford, D.D., Fellow of Trinity College, Dublin, was then rector. His father, Richard Sinclair Brooke, was the curate.

The genealogy of the Irish Brookes can be clearly traced as far back as 1668, or somewhat earlier; but prior to that date the line has not been established a physician. It is through Alexander, who married a Miss Young, of Lahard, that the line of descent comes down to Stopford Brooke.

Alexander appears to have had three children, of whom the eldest, again William, born in 1720, became rector of Granard in Co. Longford. He was a friend of Maria Edgeworth's. This William was living in 1808, and is thus described by his grandson, Dr Richard Brooke—

"I can still retain a vision of an old gentleman with a silvery wig, a shovel hat and gold spectacles, who was very much at my father's house, and called me grandson. This was old William Brooke, formerly a scholar of Trinity College, and at this time rector of the large union parish of Granard, Co. Longford, in which county he possessed a fair property in Abbeylara, and a pretty residence, entitled Firmount, within a few miles of Edgeworthstown."

The line passes on through the eldest son of the rector of Granard, yet another William Brooke (1769–1829), a well-known Dublin physician of his day and President of the Irish College of Physicians, who erected a monument to his memory in St Thomas' Church, Marlborough Street, Dublin. At a date I have not been able to ascertain, but presumably about 1790, he married Angel Perry, niece and heiress of Colonel Richard Graham. Dr Richard Brooke was their son.

The ancestry of Angel Perry, the grandmother of Stopford Brooke, is of great interest. Through her father, who was of Welsh descent in another line, she was the great-granddaughter of Hector Graham, of Leix Castle and Culmaine, descended in the direct line from Fergus Graeme, of Mote Netherby, in Liddesdale, to whom Queen Mary granted the Augmentation Arms of "the Oke Branch" in the shield, for services rendered to Henry VIII., presumably on Flodden field. His grandson, Sir Richard Graham, one of Queen Elizabeth's knights, routed the Earl of Ormond at Aherlow in 1597, in recognition of which he was presented by the Queen with the Vallery crown. Through him the line of descent comes down to Angel Perry.

The characteristics of the Grahams of Liddesdale, from whom Stopford Brooke was thus descended, are familiar to all readers of Sir Walter Scott. They were of a "fierce and irrepressible audacity in overleaping or breaking down every obstacle which lay in the way of their achieving their ends." Camden says "they were very famous among the Borderers for their great valour. They were able to raise at any time a troop of 400 horse for a raid upon England." Fuller remarks of them "they are amongst the wonders more than the worthies of England. They dwell on the borders of either kingdom, but obey the laws of neither. They are a nest of hornets; strike one and they all stir about your ears."

The most notorious member of the Graham family established in Ireland was Hector Graham,[1] who flourished in the early decades of the eighteenth century. He had large estates in Queen's County, together with Leix Castle in Armagh, Derrymore and Racomber in Galway and Culmaine in Monaghan. The latter estate was inherited by Angel Perry, from her uncle, Sir Richard Graham, and passed from her into the possession of the Brooke family, where, in part, it still remains.

We now turn to the maternal side. The mother of Stopford Brooke was Anna, the beautiful daughter and only child of the Rev. Joseph Stopford, the rector of

---

[1] Many particulars concerning Hector Graham, and the connexion of his family with Ireland, are found in an article in the third series of Sir Bernard Burke's "Vicissitudes of Families," p. 129.

Conwall and Letterkenny. At the time of her marriage in 1831 to Richard Brooke, Anna was eighteen years of age. It was a romantic and impetuous wooing, of which in after years Mr and Mrs Richard Brooke told many a story to their children. For some time after the marriage the young couple lived with Dr and Mrs Stopford—whose maiden name was Anne Campbell—in the rectory at Glendoen, where, as I have said, Stopford Brooke was born. Two trees, still living, were planted in the rectory grounds to commemorate his birth.

In 1903, Stopford Brooke, then seventy-one years of age, visited his birthplace, of which the description shall be given in his own words.

"Fate gave us a charming day on which to see my birthplace. The sun never ceased to illuminate it, and the congregation of white clouds that listened to the light and air, and the low hills of this well-tilled country, through which a slow river flows among oak, ash and willow, answered the beauty of the sky with a beauty of their own. We drove to Glendoen, passing the Boyd's place—Ballymacool—well-known to me from my mother's diary. The beeches that bordered the road were well-bred, like very cultured people, not huge, but more various in bough, branch and stem than any others I remember. We drove past the rectory with one glimpse of the house then . . . over the oldest bridge in Donegal, where the river ran dark and amber under thorns and alder, and back to the rectory. My grandfather built the house, an honest square standing firm on a rise of ground. A garden, with roses and flowers and grass smooth as a young man's cheek, surrounded it. Quiet, retired, and well cared for was its aspect. The two tall firs, which were planted on the day of my birth, stand on either side of the drive—and are perhaps the noblest object in Ireland ! . . . We had tea in the drawing-room, where my Father first pressed and kissed my Mother's hand, and where he was accepted at last. We saw the dining-room, the library, the bedrooms, and tried to imagine in which of them I was born. We saw the Glen where these ancient days of love were so often passed, and where my Father and Mother stood so often in close embrace. . . . (He then goes to the church at Letterkenny, which he finds, unlike the neighbouring R. C. Cathedral, locked and barred.) I could not get in to see the place where my Grandfather and Father preached, where my Mother was married and churched, and where I was baptized. And I went down the hill, half wishing in petulant thought that I had been born a Roman Catholic."

Dr Joseph Stopford, the grandfather here mentioned, was the son of James Stopford (born 1732) and grandson of Joseph Stopford, Bishop of Cloyne and successor to Bishop Berkeley. By the marriage of James Stopford with Anne Wray the family was connected with the Wrays of Wray Castle, Co. Donegal. Earlier marriages of the Wrays connect it with the Gores and the Hamiltons.

The family of Stopford has been traced back to a Saxon freeman named Wulric, also of Cheshire, who was allowed to retain his lands in that county at the time of the Norman Conquest. His descendant became Baron de Stockport in the reign of Henry II., and "Stockport" appears to have been the original form of the name. Later on the family acquired estates in Lancashire. There are said to be numerous Stopfords in the neighbourhood of Manchester at the present day.

The first Stopford to settle in Ireland was a soldier in Cromwell's Irish army about 1649, and is described as a "republican fanatic." Large migrations to Ireland from Cheshire and Lancashire took place at this period and the picturesque suggestion has been made that possibly ancestors of Stopford Brooke, in both branches,

VOL. I.

"went over in the same boat." The republican fanatic acquired estates in Wexford, and his grandson was created Earl of Courtown in 1762, the political principles of the family having previously changed to the high Tory side. His daughter Anne—"the sly Nancy of Courtown" immortalized by Swift—married her cousin, the Bishop of Cloyne mentioned above. This pair were the great-great-grandparents of Stopford Brooke.

The family of Stopford is noted for its longevity and for the tendency to cousin marriages, which reappears in every generation. The family motto is "Patriae Infelici Fidelis;" this, however, does not refer, as many have supposed, to Ireland, but to England at the time of the Parliamentary War. The name figures largely in the history of the Irish Church, and is continually found in the record of both services down to the present day.[1]

The details of these pedigrees reveal several interesting facts to the student of heredity, and throw some light on the complex personality of Stopford Brooke. English, Irish, Scotch and Welsh elements mingled in his ancestry. It was an ancestry of clergymen, doctors, soldiers and landowners, and in some of its remoter roots, of wild, masterful men whose blood was quick with elemental force. Both on the Brooke and on the Stopford side the clerical element strongly preponderates in the later branches.

All this reappeared in Stopford Brooke. The elemental and the ideal were co-present in him to the end of his long life; he was Christian, Greek and Goth; and it is a remarkable circumstance, upon which I shall say more in its proper place, that when he was advanced in years he created the myth of an elemental being, without soul

[1] I am indebted for most of this information to Mr Francis Stopford, the Editor of *Land and Water*.

or conscience, whose presence he could summon at will, and who was undoubtedly the projection of some power felt by him to be stirring in the depths of his nature. Some of his characteristics might well have belonged to Fergus Graeme of Netherby. His massive frame, his flashing and commanding presence, his audacities of speech and action, his joy in life, the swift transitions by which he would pass from the resolve to the deed might be transferred, by a slight effort of imagination, to a Border chieftain of the sixteenth century. It is conceivable that the independence of mind and love of liberty which marked his career as a mid-victorian preacher had their roots in long-buried generations, and were not without affinities to a very different form of latitudinarianism.

We see, moreover, how deeply rooted in the soil of Ireland was the life whose development we are to follow, and we are prepared to learn how strongly its spirit was moulded by Irish traditions, Irish manners, and the soft beauty of the Irish landscape. The ancestors of Stopford Brooke were owners of land, of flocks and of herds; they lived close to nature and breathed the open air; the blue mountains, the rushing waters, the green spaces of Ireland were before them; they administered justice in Irish courts, they tended the sick in Irish villages; they bore arms in Irish quarrels; they preached the Word of God to six generations of Irishmen. Stopford Brooke was, in essentials, a surprising personality, and only one land in the world could have produced him—the land where the inevitable happens seldom, and the impossible happens every day. His temperament, his intellect, his imagination, his tenderness, his manners were predominantly Irish, and the genius of his native land remained with him to the closing years of his long life. He was, however, an Irishman who loved England. "One ought not," he writes in his diary for 1899, "if Irish, to live in England and abuse the country which gives him shelter."

Dr Richard Brooke, the father of Stopford, was a distinct, powerful and commanding personality, deeply revered by his children and friends, and greatly honoured as a clergyman of the Irish Church. He had a wonderful charm of manner, wide knowledge, a full memory, great vigour of mind and body, an endless flow of varied conversation; ready in wit, quick in observation, large of heart. He was a classical scholar of no mean order and a well-grounded theologian, ardent in the ministration of the Word and beloved of the poor. He has left a vivid revelation of himself, and an interesting record of the circles in which his long life was passed, in his two volumes of "Recollections of the Irish Church."

He was, moreover, a devoted lover of literature, especially of poetry, and this gave a width to his interests and a beauty to his style not common among the Irish clergy of his time. He published some volumes of poems, and a novel, "Parson Annaly." Even those who never knew him personally, like the present writer, may easily picture him through characteristics of his which reappeared unmistakably in one or other of his four sons, and through the abundant memories retained in the family circle of a personality so lovable and full of spiritual fire. He died in 1882.[1]

In Mrs Richard Brooke a cultivated mind was united to a moral nature of fine simplicity; hers was the charity that thinketh no evil and never faileth. Her

[1] A noble tribute to his memory, written by Stopford Brooke, appeared in the *Irish Ecclesiastical Gazette* for August 19, 1882.

gracious and beautiful presence, her dignity of mind, her deep piety, her love of all things pure and of good report are evident alike in the records which remain of her girlhood, and in the letters which passed between her and her children when she had passed into the quietude of old age. There are letters written to her during the closing years of her life by Stopford, then himself an old man, which tell a moving tale of tender and reciprocal love maintained to the very last. The diaries of her early married life, of which I have seen a large portion, present us with the picture of a fine nature heroically facing the daily struggle to bring up a family of eager and gifted children on inadequate means. I have before me a book of her early sketches executed with a firmness of touch and intuitive grasp of the beautiful which show the source of much that was characteristic in the genius of Stopford Brooke. There is also a Hebrew Grammar written out in an exquisite caligraphy, by Mrs Brooke before her marriage—a significant light on the ideals that were cultivated in an Irish country rectory in the early decades of the nineteenth century. From girlhood to extreme old age, the life of this gentle lady was consistently spent in the service and love of others. In this also it was a foreshadowing of the character and message of her son. From his father he inherited his vigour of mind and body, his commanding presence, his gaiety, his wit, his fluency of tongue; from his mother, self-forgetfulness and a childlike heart.

So deeply intertwined was the life of Stopford Brooke with that of other members of his family that no account of him would be complete without some mention of them. With his two brothers, William and Edward, his relations remained constant and close until the death of the first in 1907, and of the second in 1909. Of the hundreds of letters from which selection has to be made, by far the largest number are addressed to William, who was a barrister, and held for many years the office of Chief Clerk to the Lord Chancellor of Ireland. Edward was in the Army; he distinguished himself as an officer of Engineers in the Maori War of 1864, and rapidly rose to the rank of Major-General, on which rank he retired in 1886. In childhood, youth and age the three brothers were as one; hand in hand they had trotted behind their mother as she went about her household tasks, they had played the same pranks in boyhood, shared the same friendships, studied in the same college, read the same books, discussed the same pictures. In later life they delighted to recall the common memories of their romantic youth. Seated side by side in their father's church at Kingstown, they turned their heads at the same moment to answer the smile of the fair damsel who beamed upon them from the gallery, and when an hour later they met her promenading on the Kingstown pier, off came the three hats at a single swoop. Whenever it was possible in earlier or later life for the three to be together, together they were; and to none of the three was any company so welcome as that of the other two. Often have I seen them in their later life, kindling a new radiance on each other's presence, bantering wit, reviving old memories, discussing the things of beauty in which all three took an equal delight, or devising together some scheme for helping the poor or adding to the happiness of their mother's or their sisters' lives. In matters of opinion they were greatly divided: Stopford was radical, latitudinarian, and a Home Ruler; William, like his father, was conservative in politics, and a convinced follower of the old ways in religion. But this made no difference either to the warmth of their mutual affection or to the admiration which each entertained for the character of the others. They were wonderfully alike, and as wonderfully different. In stature they marked the same height and bore themselves with a similar carriage, and being all three handsome men, in youth as well as in age, there may be some truth in the legend that the young ladies of Kingstown were captivated by the trio as by an undivided personality, and became greatly confused in their subsequent discriminations. Yet there was no mistaking where nature had bestowed her richest gifts. In all that makes the charm of an Irish gentleman they were equals, but in spiritual fire and force Stopford was evidently supreme.

William Brooke was a man of deep sagacity and knowledge of affairs. The lively sense of humour, and the love of poetry and of the fine arts, common to the family, were joined in him with a firm judgment and a logical mind. As a wise counsellor and a penetrating critic his advice was constantly sought by his elder brother, in whose life he played no inconsiderable part.

Edward, though the least worldly of men, had also seen much of the world. His chief quality, in which all the rest were summed up, was his power of winning the affections of those with whom he came into contact; and this he did by means of which the Irish character alone seems to possess the full secret. Wearing a gravity which was half real and half assumed, and modest almost to a fault regarding his own merits, he was one of those rare men in whose presence pretentiousness of all kinds, especially intellectual pretentiousness, instantly vanishes. "Your high forehead, sir, makes me afraid of you," was his remark, spoken in a deep and solemn voice, on being introduced to a person who had won some reputation as a thinker and was taking himself too seriously in consequence. In putting down the self-conceit of superior persons, and that without giving them offence, he had a genius which I have seen equalled in no other man. The stiffest of starch surrendered to his charming drollery or to his delightful irrelevance. Mr Podsnap himself would have been unable to resist him. And with all this he was a lover of order and method, a stern critic of slovenly detail, a good mathematician, an excellent judge of pictures, a gallant soldier, and a very humble follower of Christ. Of the sunshine that fell continually on the life of Stopford Brooke no small part came from his brother Edward, whom, needless to say, he deeply loved.

Such were the relations of the three brothers. I mention them thus early because it is necessary to understand from the outset that Stopford Brooke was a multiple personality, not merely in the sense that he combined the gifts of many men—though that also is true—but because the life of his family was essentially a part of himself. This interpenetration with the family life extended to every member of the circle, and if fully set out would require me to speak of his surviving brother, the Rev. Arthur Brooke, the rector of Slingsby in Yorkshire, and of his four sisters, of whom two are now living—to say nothing of his children, nor of his grandchildren, in every one of whom he was deeply interested to the last.

CHAPTER II

MOTHER AND SON. BOYHOOD

"... I have seen my mother and had a good time with her, and I am all the better for that within, whatever may befall me without. She has been charming, like a fairy in a shepherd story in an 18th century French tale, one of those old fairies who have strange reminiscences and suggestions of extreme youth which flash now and then from lip and eye and cheek, and who, in the end of the story, put off their old age like a robe and step out with a wand and a delicate figure, and a lovely robe, and golden hair and eyes of the dawn, and are called Violante or Gloriette or some such elfin name.—(Letter to the Revd Arthur Brooke, September 27, 1891.)

"My mother's eyes are as bright and her ways as simple, gentle, high-bred, living and eager, as of old. She seems to have refined away all that is of earth, except love, and to belong to the spirits made perfect. I bade her goodbye with fear and care. So little, so very little, touches fine human porcelain at this age into death.—(*Diary*, October 1 and 3, 1899.)

On the death of Dr Joseph Stopford in 1833 Richard Brooke, with his wife and infant son, left Glendoen Rectory to take up another curacy at Abbeyleix, in Co. Meath. Three years later he was appointed Chaplain of the Mariners' Church, Kingstown, a position which he retained until 1862. The earliest memories of Stopford Brooke begin with the Kingstown period. The following extract from a letter to one of his children in 1874 gives us a characteristic example :—

"I am in Ireland now, a green country you may have seen on the map. I was born in it, and in a place not very far from here. Can you fancy me a tiny little boy, with long light, curly hair, and smiling like an angel when I was good. And oh! how good I was, you can't think, especially when I was let to do what I liked. I used to make palaces out of mud in the path at the back of the house, and fill them with gold and silver boys and girls and with little dogs who had diamonds for eyes, and at the end of whose tails there was a star. Your grandmother used to tell me it was all nonsense, but I knew better; and I often see, when I am asleep and become, in my dreams, a little child again, one of my dear tiny golden boys walking by very grandly like a fine gentleman and nodding to me in a stately way, and with him a little black dog with silken hair, diamond eyes, and a star on the tip of his tail. It lights up the whole dream, I can assure you. I sometimes wish I were back again in the time when I was a small boy and thought that mud pies were palaces, but I cannot get back there, and I must be content to have children, and not to be a child."

A diary of Mrs Richard Brooke, covering the years between 1837 and 1847, has been preserved from which we may reconstruct, with little effort of imagination, the environment of Brooke's childhood. Much of the diary is concerned with the anxieties involved in the bringing up of a large family on very narrow means, anxieties which were then more formidable than now, for that was an age when infant mortality ran high, when disease played havoc with young children, and when a mother looking round upon her babes on New Year's Day might well doubt, as Mrs Brooke often doubted, whether they would all be alive at the end of the year. Along with the daily record of the children's health and of other worldly cares, there is a current of religious musing, and of self-examination, in the characteristic vein of evangelical piety as it flourished in the early decades of the nineteenth century. Of references to events in the great world there is little, which is not surprising in a diary of this kind; though faint echoes of them are occasionally heard, as when the followers of O'Connell take to noisy demonstrations in the neighbourhood of the Mariners' Church, or when the spectres of famine and cholera begin to stalk abroad in the land. Plainly it was in the nursery that Brooke first learnt of the troubles of Ireland, and things learnt in the nursery are apt to be long remembered.

When Richard Brooke began his ministry at the Mariners' Church his salary was £100 a year, and many are the indications in the diary of the bitter struggle with poverty which the young mother had to face. "I never felt at such a non-plus." "We are in the midst of poverty and ourselves penniless." "My heart is very low. . . . I feel a desolation reigning round me. . . . Oh what happy hours were mine in Donegal—dear, dear my native place. . . . How I sometimes long for wings to fly away and find an ark. . . . There are not many sunny spots on earth. . . . Was it of God our coming to Kingstown? . . . But I must not repine at my present lot." One day she looks in the glass and sorrowfully writes down, "I am growing old. Twenty-seven to-day."

There was much sickness among the children, and Stopford seems to have been the chief sufferer. Again and again his life was in peril, and the cry of Mrs Brooke's agony, as she watched beside the wasted form and listened in fancy to the beating of the wings of death, rises almost audibly from the page. "It is a heart-break," she cries, "to see this dear one so maimed. . . . It is a lash to pride. We used to think so much of him—his health, his beauty." One night as he lay tossing in fever "he rolled his large and lovely eyes upon her," and said, "it is my *clay* which is in pain."

I have a wreath of daisies on my head made by him. . . . They are now withering. He said he made it for me because he loved me. . . . Oh! Oh!" And the handwriting, usually firm, begins to scrawl over the sheet.

Gleams of sunshine break out from time to time. Let Stopford recover his health, looking once more "like a young Jupiter," and the high spirits of Mrs Brooke know no bounds. Behold her riding on horseback "up Shady Avenue," or off with the children to Dromore "whose gray walls echo to the shouts of their over-bursting spirits." And there are matters for yet deeper satisfaction. When the great storm of 1839 swept over Dublin and the roof was blown off their house she lies in bed "listening to dear Stopford so sweetly repeating hymns and trying to compose me by reminding me of Papa's sermon in which he had exhorted us to be satisfied!" "I am sure he has a feeling for religion and a cultivated conscience. 'Mama,' he said, 'You are the best of all.'" And "one evening when I was telling him about the wanderings of the children of Israel he became thoughtful and I saw an expression on his face I had never seen before." Again (1838), "Here we are sitting at our round table. Stopford reading, he is becoming most studious . . . the little mind so active, he is so fond of books." "At times he shows pleasing traits of character. For instance, the other day he asked me for fourpence I owed him, and he ran up to the town, came back and poured some sugar candy and lozenges, which he had bought for her, on Nannie's bed." Other "pleasing traits" are recorded. At the end of a very gloomy day, when the world seemed so dark to poor Mrs Brooke that she had begun to doubt whether "the fabric of nature" would hold out much longer, "I pinned a rose to his little bed and he kissed my hand and said—

with another roll of those large and lovely eyes, 'Mama, do not fret, and I will make you laugh.'"

There are many details in the diary which, as we dwell upon them, grow into pictures. We can visualize the hard work and the hard fare of the Rev. Richard Brooke. We see him increasing in eloquence and evangelical power, until the Mariners' Church is crowded to the doors, and another hundred pounds or so added to the pittance with which he began. Whatever danger threatens the household, whatever misfortune befalls it, there is instant recourse to prayer, and due thanksgivings for deliverance when the cloud has passed. If a tempest devastates the town, if the neighbourhood is roused by an alarm of robbers, if Willy comes home with his finger half cut off—comforting texts are quoted, appropriate sermons called to mind, and hymns said or sung. A profound piety is apparent, united with natural affection in a single stream: as we may see in the tragic episode of the cut finger, when Richard, as he kneels beside the bed, is so overcome with emotion that he breaks down in the midst of his prayer "and cannot get on." Now and then we get a glimpse of less lovable personalities. There is a narrow-minded Archdeacon who lays a ban on the prayer-meetings—"which have done so much good." There are various worldly men, "bulls of Bashan," by whom the good minister is sorely let and hindered in his preaching of the Gospel. There is an ungrateful brother clergyman who owes to Richard his first introduction to the lady of his choice ("one of the twins—but not the one we like, thank goodness"), but who, when Richard, with a bad cough, and otherwise beset and encumbered, asks for a little help with the work of the Home Mission, cruelly declines, and leaves his benefactor to go trapsing about

Ireland in midwinter—yes, right across 'that lonely bog between Portarlington and Monastereven, where even now the precious good man presumably is.' Indignation, however, is not characteristic of Mrs Brooke. She prefers to write of "the dear, kind friends" who are gathering round them; of the de Vescis, of the Fitzpatricks and of Mrs O'Reilly, "that clever, piquant person whom I like."

Mrs Richard Brooke, who thought herself old at twenty-seven, lived to the great age of ninety-one, retaining the full use of her faculties, a venerable and gracious figure. She died in 1903, Stopford being then seventy-one. It might almost be said that mother and son grew old together; and since the bond between them remained to the end essentially as it was in the days when she pinned roses to his little bed, the following letters, an echo from his childhood, may fitly be introduced at this point.

"April 16, 1894.

"DEAREST MOTHER,—I was delighted to hear from you that you liked the bag, and would wear it for my sake. It is entirely the fashion here in London for all serene and handsome old ladies to have a silver-mounted bag hanging at their side, and who more serene and handsome a lady than you could be in this world? Therefore I took pains that it should be no common or modern production, but a veritable old and dainty thing which I laid at your feet. And I drew myself the pattern of the velvet bag, and chose the silk for the inside, so that it should be all filled with my loving thoughts of you, and worthy, not of you, for it is not worthy enough of you, but worthy of my admiration of your life, and of all of you.

"If a book called 'Tennyson' arrives at your address in a few days, it is your son's last production, and is sent to you by him. You may not like part of the

Introduction, but skip what you don't like. The rest of the book will, I hope, give you some pleasure."

"November 2, 1901.

". . . Bother old age, say I. Next year I shall be seventy—fancy that! And you ninety! On the whole we are remarkably well preserved, both of us, and are a credit to the universe. We can't expect to be young, more's the pity, but I wish you were young again, and riding Lightfoot[1] through the glades of Erin. It would be fortunate for Erin."

"November 16, 1901.

"Thank you so very much, my dearest Mother, for one of the tenderest and loveliest letters I have ever received from you. . . . It was full of your gracious sweetness and charm. A beautiful soul breathed through every word. You see I am so old now that I think I understand and feel you in your old age better than I did before. Seventy years is not far from ninety. After seventy twenty years makes no difference. We bring our years into our minds as a tale that is told. And on the whole your life has been a happy one and so has mine. I hope I shall be as gay and fresh and good as you are if ever I get to your age. But it is difficult to live so long, and without a great hope and faith such as make the strength of age, it would be lonely within. So much to look back on, and so far, so very far away. I do not remember myself in the ancient days, and indeed I look forward with infinite pleasure at times."

"March 30, 1902.

". . . Let me congratulate you with all my heart on the infinite cleverness you have shown in reaching the age of ninety. Well done! And how happy it is for others that you have given so much pleasure and goodness for ninety years to all who have loved you—to

[1] A beautiful mare which belonged to Mrs Brooke when she was a girl. The animal was brought to Kingstown, where it chiefly served to remind Mrs Brooke of vanished joys. It is often mentioned in her diary.

three full generations. It is a splendid record, and no one can be more delighted than I that you have lived to bless us all, and to tell us how unselfish a life can be lived."

"March 30, 1903.

". . . I have just sent off the last batch of the 'Liber Studiorum'[1] to Ireland. My poor walls look very denuded and unhappy. I hope they will look well in Dublin, and that they will interest the Irish. It will give me great pleasure to see them all some day and renew my friendship with them. And I like that far better than leaving them in my will and never seeing them in their new place. It is true I might come back and see them in spirit, but I trust I shall have something better and more interesting to do."

A large and united family; four brothers and four sisters; some eager, others dreamy, all lovers of beauty; cultivated, high bred and very poor; a home saturated with the spirit of evangelical piety; much reading of the Bible and many religious exercises; the father a fervent minister of the Irish Church, with a turn for poetry; the mother, a gentle, saintly soul; the table talk mainly of literature; and with all this abundance of wild spirits, and a tendency both in young and old to look on the romantic side of life—such was the home from which the genius of Stopford Brooke received its earliest impulse. The conditions were present which make religion a habit, there was varied food for intelligence and imagination, and there was much to prompt the spirit of discovery.

"My father," says Brooke, in 1907,[2] "waked us every morning with snatches from the *Lay*, from *Marmion*, and the *Lady of the Lake*, and the day was

[1] He made a gift of these, which were all "first states," during his lifetime to the Irish National Gallery.
[2] "Studies in Poetry," p. 58.

haunted with their charm. We learnt for ourselves more than half of the poems. Wherever we played or walked on the hills or by the sea, Scott taught us to build up tales of war and love round the scenery of places, and to fill them with romantic adventures."

The strict theology and small stipend of Richard Brooke, who waked his sons in this musical manner, were no barrier to the geniality of his disposition and the breadth of his literary tastes. He is described, when off duty, as "bubbling over with fun," at the least provocation, and often, since he is Irish, with no provocation at all. His knowledge of the English poets includes Byron and Shelley, whom he reads with fervour tempered by discrimination. Being a man of expansive soul and fluent tongue he does not keep these things to himself. The names of the poets are household words; their works are copiously quoted round the table and discussed in the daily walks, and a general murmur of versification pervades the house. The "wanderings of the Israelites" are not neglected; but these are mainly Sunday themes handled, as we have seen, by Mrs Brooke, with excellent moral effect. The "young Jupiter" is attentive in both departments, but, on the whole, prefers Childe Harold to the Pentateuch. He marks the shelf in his father's library where the more attractive literature is stored away, presumably out of reach; chooses his moment, mounts a chair, and enjoys himself thoroughly with "Manfred" and "The Vision of Judgment" until returning footsteps warn him to desist. One day he is discovered devouring a forbidden volume of Scott, on which, as on all novels, a severe embargo has been placed—a rule that would not have been necessary unless there had been novels at hand, and a disposition to read them among the younger members of the family. The reprimand was severe, but the effect of it was transitory. The first literary production of Stopford Brooke was an article on "The Growth of the Novel," written at the age of twenty-three; while in later life he read every novel he could lay his hands on, and had an extraordinary memory of their plots.

Tales of travel formed no inconsiderable part of the literature favoured in the early home of Brooke; and there are indications that the world of adventure, as well as the world of poetry, was opened to him by his father. He used to say that Millais' picture of "The Boyhood of Raleigh" reminded him of himself in those days. There is an early sketch of his before me, a strange medley of fancies, which seems to have been inspired by stories of distant lands: there is a pearl-diver and his boat, an octopus making ready to attack the diver, an albatross hovering overhead, a sea serpent and a Bedouin Arab—and in the midst a representation of Absalom hanging by his hair from a tree, executed in a manner not quite respectful to Holy Writ.

There is another name famous in the world of letters, and more famous then than now, with which he must have been familiar from earliest boyhood. This was Henry Brooke (1706–1783), author of "The Fool of Quality," a mystical book, abounding in bold religious speculation, which Charles Kingsley greatly admired. Henry Brooke was the acknowledged genius of the family. Richard Brooke knew every word of his writings and honoured them, their advanced tendency notwithstanding, and there is little doubt that Stopford read "The Fool of Quality" as soon as he was able to understand it. Thus from the first dawnings of his reflective intelligence he was in contact with the broad and daring mind of one who bore his own name and sprang from the same stock. To the end of his life he retained a high admiration for the work of Henry Brooke and acknowledged an influence derived from his writings.

The Brookes had abundance of friends in Kingstown and the neighbourhood, among whom are found the names of many families of Huguenot descent—Trench, Lefroy, L'Estrange, de Vesci, La Touche. Most important, in view of its future consequence, was their friendship with the Fitzpatricks (the family name of Lord Castletown) of Granston Manor, Co. Meath, with whom the connexion began when Richard Brooke was curate at Abbeyleix in the early thirties. The Fitzpatricks were in touch with the leaders of the Broad Church movement, and it was at their house that Brooke as a boy met F. W. Robertson, in 1847. There also, in 1856, he had a more fateful meeting—with Emma Beaumont, who two years afterwards became his wife. Of the influence of Lady Castletown (then the Hon. Mrs. Fitzpatrick) on his future career more will be said in the proper place. When Lady Castletown died in 1899 Brooke wrote in his diary, "A hundred memories come back to me . . . her interest in all I read, her passion for fine poetry . . . my first rides and the wild gallops at Lisduff. There I first read the Arabian Nights. . . . I might fill this book with recollections."

The first school attended by Brooke was that of the Rev. Christopher Eade, "in Shady Avenue." From this he was removed in 1844 to another, kept by Dr Stacpoole, which is described as "the best private school in Kingstown," whatever that may imply. A few floating legends, mostly of escapades, with a precise detail here and there of a silver medal or of "an excellent report," exhaust the contemporary record of his schooldays in

Kingstown. And there is the following reminiscence in his diary for June 22, 1898:—

"Visited Kingstown. All the way to Dalkey on the top of the tram I told stories of the places we passed. There was the road I used to run home on at five minutes a mile lest I should be locked out. There was the house I used to visit every day, being in love with V. W. Her brother became Commander-in-chief in India. There was Sandy Cove over every rock in which I had climbed. There was Dalkey Castle and the ruined church where I once went at midnight to see the ghosts. There was Dalkey Island, where I used to love to fish and round which I have often rowed. . . . I visited all my old haunts. Then I roamed through the tiny garden [of the old home] and tried to remember more than I could."

In 1847 the dangers which continually threatened his life in childhood were passed. At the age of fifteen, Brooke has grown "into a tall, well-knit and singularly handsome boy," with a noble head and a mass of waving hair, hardy for games and exercise, but highly strung and quickly sensitive to the influences of his environment, both physical and mental.

To those who were watching him, and they were many, signs had appeared which gave rise to hopes and expectations of great things to come. In particular his uncle, William Brooke, Master in Chancery, a solid, judicious man of various culture, saw the promise of the boy and the need of a broader education than Kingstown could provide. A spell of discipline, moreover, would do him no harm. For a romantic young Irishman, whose wings needed a little trimming, what better place could be found than an English boarding school?

The school chosen was the Kidderminster Grammar School, a foundation incorporated under the Charter granted to Kidderminster in 1636 by Charles I., of which

KIDDERMINSTER GRAMMAR SCHOOL 27

the Headmaster was then the Rev. Samuel Cockin, M.A., an Oxford Honours man and a good Greek scholar. There were about forty boys in the school, most of whom came from Kidderminster or from the neighbouring counties. Among his schoolfellows I note the names of Edward Bradley ("Cuthbert Bede"), the author of "Verdant Green," Charles Edward Matthews, the well-known Alpinist and author of the "History of Mont Blanc," and R. B. Girdlestone, afterwards Canon of Christ Church and Principal of Wycliffe Hall. Another well-known name, occurring a few years earlier, is that of George Simcox, the editor of Thucydides.

"Three times a day," writes "Cuthbert Bede," "[the pupils] went down [from Mr Cockin's house, in the outskirts, to the school] at 7 a.m. till 8.30; at 10 till 12.30, and at 2 till 4 p.m.; and on winter mornings the institution of school before breakfast was very trying to all concerned. We found the schoolroom cheerless and cold, the fire just lit in the stove, and some candles to illuminate dimly the dreary scene. As soon as we got in we had to repeat from memory twenty-five lines of Vergil or Horace; and then to puzzle our heads with a Greek play, until the welcome time came to dismiss us to our well-earned breakfast."

"Mr Cockin was a born teacher," says Mr C. E. Matthews, "a very thorough master in teaching from a sound foundation. There was no attempt to teach science; there were no playing-fields; no gymnasium; and no organized recreation of any kind. They played hockey in the churchyard and cricket in Habberley Valley. They caught butterflies in 'The Devil's Spadeful,' and some love of nature was implanted in their minds as they wandered through the Forest of Wyre, or watched the glint of the sunlight on the silver Severn as it swirled under the woods at Ribbesford."

Another old boy, Mr Richard Grove, writes, "We had no playground except the small area of the churchyard on the south side, or front, of the [Parish] Church. . . . In this small space before school began and at the usual play-time at 10.30 in the morning and 3 in the afternoon we played all the games in existence at that time . . . rounders, marbles, prisoners' base, cutter and flyer, leap-frog, bullock and bear, and French and English. Some of these games were very rough indeed, and ofttimes ended in a general melée like an Irish faction-fight, and no inconsiderable amount of danger to our clothes and our persons resulted."

From the letters written home by Brooke it is evident that the education given was liberal, at least for those days. The classics, of course, had the chief share of attention; but time was also devoted to the study of English; there was some reading of general history and literature, and a reasonable latitude was allowed to the older boys in following their own tastes. They were taught to write good English prose, and encouragement was given to the writing of English verse. When the new buildings were opened by the Bishop of Worcester in 1847, we read that " Stopford Brooke attracted much notice by the recitation of a poem on 'The Farewell of Charles I. to his Children,' a foretaste of his future literary fame."[1] This was a portentous event about which he writes to his mother, "Perspiration breaks out at the very idea . . . I am in a great funk." On the whole he was fortunate in his school companions, and, except for the home-sickness which never left him, the two years at Kidderminster were happy. Sometimes, indeed, he would date his letters from " the Jail," or " the Convent," or " the Desert," but these epithets, in fairness to the Rev. Samuel Cockin, must be taken in

[1] For this and much else in the above information I am indebted to the " History of Kidderminster Grammar School " (1903), by Dr H. de B. Gibbins.

the comparative sense, for they are invariably followed by references to "the dashing waters of the Bay," or to glorious days at Dalkey Island, or to "the long evenings in the parlour," or to "the dear, dear faces of home"—things which it is not in the nature of boarding schools to provide, and over the absence of which affectionate boys will continue to mourn until the last boarding school is no more.

A large number of Brooke's schoolboy letters have been preserved, from which a few extracts will be given. Those who remember him in the later phases of his life will recognize at once the spirit and the voice which speak to us in these early outpourings of himself. There is the same openness and spontaneity; the same hunger of imagination; the same devotion to nature, extending even to details, such as his passion for moving water;[1] the same affection for kindred and friends; the same wish to be remembered; the same demand for constant communication with those whom he loved. We may even note the beginnings of a characteristic which he shared with Robertson of Brighton—his tendency to seek sympathy from women and his dependence on that sympathy for the impulse which sustained him in arduous work. We find him, even here, in constant correspondence with his girl friends, complaining bitterly if "Bessie" forgets to write to him, and asking his mother, with a charming frankness, if she thinks he may begin writing to "Mary"; noting with some alarm —also in a letter to his mother—that Henry Brooke has been seen walking with "Flora," promising himself no doubt to set that right as soon as the holidays begin.

[1] "For the Poet thought that the place of the revealing of poetry was always by the brink of water." His father used to quote this from an Irish legend.

Then again we encounter him as essentially the Irishman, with Irish manners and Irish turns of phrase, a little at odds with his English environment, and a little contemptuous, as he always remained, of English limitations. These English—they understand nothing of Ireland! "None of them cares for his home as much as an Irishman does." "Lovely Kingstown—no place like it—'breathes there the man with soul so dead!'" The art critic also began to appear—doesn't approve of the style of drawing enforced by the Rev. Samuel Cockin and his myrmidons and roundly declares that he won't learn it any more "lest his own style should become spoilt." Landscape is his line—no more of these "big heads" for him—Alexander and Bucephalus and such like, of which he has made "a regular mull!" He has "the greatest delight in reading about the lives of painters. I read a pretty story of Spagnoletto the other day and also another about the younger days of Murillo. We sometimes get a nice book to read here"—this is on his fifteenth birthday. In other things also he will go his own way: takes a long walk with "Colborne" and cuts across the fields, "it being my principle never to keep the road when we can get out of it." And here is a familiar touch of perversity. The cholera is raging (1848) and he has been warned not to eat fruit, whereupon he writes that he is "eating apples and pears without number." It would seem, moreover, that the embargo on novels has now been withdrawn—perhaps because it could no longer be enforced. He is reading Rienzi and Paul Clifford—the latter "utter trash." Meanwhile he is getting so big that "he hates to be laughed at;" and sends home his poem on "Boadicea," his first effort, with an entreaty that his brothers be not allowed "to make game of it."

THE MOTHER OF BROOKE IN YOUTH AND AGE.

[*To face page* 30

On the moral and religious side, indications of that double bent, which I have already noted, make their unmistakable appearance. Writing to his mother, after proclaiming his debauch among the apples and pears, he goes on, "I certainly would follow Epicurus if he was on earth now, for I am especially fond of pleasure. I often think of the day at Dalkey Island." What he thinks of "the day at Dalkey Island" we know not; it was some memory, no doubt, of scenes and voices in which nature had been speaking a message not easily reconciled with certain other matters in which he had been taught to believe. With this explosion of Epicurean candour, which must have startled the sweet soul to whom it was addressed, it is instructive to compare some verses written on his birthday about a year earlier, evidently in response to a direct request from his parents. In the accompanying letter he says of them: "I tried the verses you asked me, but I could not make any good ones. However they will serve to show that I think of you and am attentive to what you wish me to do." Here are the first two verses of the poem.

> "All hail, thou happy cheerful ray
> That lights thy morn, my natal day,
> Teach me, O Lord, to keep it right
> And holy in thy blessed sight.
>
> Wash in thy blood, thou Son of God,
> Whose steps this sinful world has trod
> My erring heart and make me see
> The weight of guilt that presses me."

The rest of the letter, it must be confessed, contains no indication of "the weight of guilt" referred to in the poem. He is looking forward to the holidays.

While at Kidderminster young Brooke received from time to time long and serious letters from his grandmother, the widow of Dr Joseph Stopford, who was deeply solicitous for his welfare. A characteristic specimen, full of a quaint old-world flavour, is before me. It suggests that Mrs Stopford's influence was of a kind distinct from that of other members of the family. Her point of emphasis was evidently "the moral good," and her whole manner of exhortation is strongly reminiscent of Maria Edgeworth. She warns her grandson to fight "indolence or the desire to repose always on the *thing you like*." He must attend to "that method and order which they have the knack of in the sister country," and she hopes that he will come home with a straight back and less of an Irish brogue. She defines the just proportions of body, intellect, and soul. Whenever the "dragon insubordination raises its head and hisses" within him he is to "cut it down." This may seem to be placing too much stress on "works" as against "faith;" nevertheless "it is not popery." She bids him write her a theme on "Order." She wants none of his verses and urges him to cultivate "the Judgment" instead of the Imagination. "You Brookes are always soaring; I would clip your wings." "You know your grandmother must always be a zealous supporter, so far as she is able, of the Moral Good." For example: "We all drank tea last night with the Bishop of Meath. . . . As we sat down to tea some of our party were declaring how much they had been entertained in the morning with an exhibition of *Punch and Judy*. You know that about six years ago I wrote a humble petition to Parliament for the suppression of *Punch and Judy* as detrimental to the morals of the mob; to which I find I have your name together with that of Lord de Vesci's son, Master Nugent. I have just rummaged it out and sent it to your uncle with a request that he would present it before the Lords Spiritual and Temporal."

"HONEST STEALING"

Brooke, in after life, told many stories of his Kidderminster schooldays of which the following, which contains a characteristic touch, may serve as a sample. A group of boys, instigated by him, got up a game which might be called "honest stealing." Each boy in the game was warned that his goods were in jeopardy, and on that understanding was to try how much he could steal from the rest. At the end of the week an audit of results was to be held, and a prize given to the boy with the biggest "bag." When the audit arrived Brooke had an enormous plunder while the others had next to nothing. "I waited," he said, "until the others had completed their 'bags,' and then, rising in the dead of night, I went round and stole the whole lot. And that," he would add, "is political economy in a nutshell."

Fifty years afterwards Brooke, accompanied by one of his daughters, revisited his old haunts at Kidderminster. In his diary for November 14, 1898, he writes thus :—

"I walked with Mr Evans [1] and Evelyn round the old places I still remember. The school-house I saw built looked exactly outside as it looked of old. I found inside of it two of the old desks at which I used to sit. I showed Evelyn where I sat. The dais where Cockin presided, a little, rounded, red-haired man, and tried to fulminate, was gone, and I could not remember anything more. It is fifty years ago, and the only thing left in me was a vague sense that I existed then. But that I recollected as I might recollect that I was Pygmalion or Endymion in a bygone world. I did remember the churchyard, the side of which slopes rapidly from the avenue of trees down to the Stour, a dark, discoloured stream. There was no sunshine here, but as I got up on the height where the school-house stood, beyond the 'Butts' which were quite changed, things were closer to me. I

[1] The Rev. E. D. Priestley Evans.

remembered the house; the garden gate was open and I walked in, and the trees came sailing into memory. I saw the playground where I had lived so much, and the boys were playing in it, but they played football, not hockey as we used to do. I walked down the lane and passed the gate in the wall through which we used to file into St John's Church. . . . Then we left for Birmingham. Through what a Hell we passed! There close together on the hill were the fiery tombs, and from the central one of three uprose Farinata and surveyed the land with great disdain.[1] Well he might. It is the vilest villainy."

To his mother. (From School.)
1849.

"Here it is already Friday and not a note from a soul since Monday, and then only a short little scrap from you and a note from Minnie. I wrote to both Nannie and Bessie Gibton at least a week ago, and never an answer have I got; it is most abominably provoking. Every morning with anxious face gazing up at the Governor and my name never mentioned, I am half distracted about it. What is the matter with everybody? My only hope is to get a letter to-morrow. If I do get a long one it will allay my woe a little. I cannot believe every one is so engaged as not to be able to write me a letter—it is too bad, and I am lonely at present, and my head is aching with disappointment. Truly said Solomon 'Hope deferred maketh the heart sick.' I think I shall stop away to-morrow, it is the most maddening thing possible. Why does not Falkiner write? ? ? Talk of his friendship and such stuff, deeds are worth a thousand such garbage. What has possessed him that he can't devote twenty minutes to me? But I am getting so angry with him that I think I had better wait till I go back and then he *will* get it. Tell the boys to tell him this, but pretty good it will have on him; 'tis like

[1] "Ed ei s'ergea col petto e con la fronte
Come avesse lo inferno in gran dispitto."
Dante, *Inferno*, x. 35, 36.

expecting water out of a rock. I got a miserable letter from him once, so heartless I could not believe it from him; however, I suppose he has got some new friend, such as Edgeworth. I wish him joy.

"I would give anything to be going home to-morrow, for I am *heartily* sick and weary of school. I must complain for I am in the vein for it, and getting no letters to alleviate my sorrow I am gradually getting ill, so I implore you make the boys and girls write if you have not time yourself, for I don't know what I won't do if I do not get a letter soon. I wish to hear from Papa when he thinks of my entering College, for I want to know something about my future prospects; it is high time to think of them. I want particularly to know something about Colleges, so tell me what you think? I can hardly do anything now, such an ardent longing for home has come over me, I trust in God it won't be long before I see you all again in health, though I am so cast down now I hardly think it possible to remain here much longer. Don't think me foolish or absurd on account of this, for it is only the overflowing of my heart. I think the days pass on leaden wings and Time sails by on such lazy, groaning pinions, that I think the *Holidays* will never come. Oh! how my heart leaps at that word, the *holidays*. It is bliss to be able even to think of them, and when they come all is one short scene of overweening, overflowing delight, home and all its domestic joys around you. How often I picture the happy fireside: the boys drawing or playing chess. Nannie laughing, reading, or working. Dote playing with Arthur, or Baby's little silvery voice ringing through the room, and you, my own Mammy, sitting looking at all with your sweet face, and darling Daddy asseverating that he likes to hear the children making a noise, for it shows him they love their home. Oh! if he only knew how you and he have made me love it. How I long for the walks on the Pier and for the mountain breezes of Killiney. This schoolroom is so close, noisy and hot, compared to the picture I have been drawing and looking at in my mind's eye. . . . I am doing nothing worthy of writing in the verse line, so send you none. I will transmit you some next time. Give my dearest love to Papa, Bill, and Ned, Nan and Dote, Arthur and Baby—what a train of loved ones. The cholera seems to have been swamped in the German Ocean, for I hear nothing of it here. How goes on the starving poor of afflicted Ireland? Are they as bad as ever from their own laziness, or bad landlords!"

To his mother.
"June, 1849 [?].

"On Easter Monday we had a whole holiday and the Governor gave Colborne and I (*sic*) our liberty to go where we liked through the day. So off we set immediately and walked towards Wolverley, passing a beautiful grove of elms on our way, placed upon a sloping bank, making such pretty vistas of long parklike glades. We went on then through the town and passed out through a road with high sandstone rocks on each hand, then we went down a lane through a field (it being *my* principle never to keep the road, when we can go out of it), thence through a beauteous wood of lofty elms with black palings above our heads, and then along a little path to such a lovely spot. I never saw anything like it in any place. There was a rushing, boiling stream roaring among the rocks with all the different things to render it beautiful, such as little jutting points with stunted oak growing at the edge dipping their fairy leaves in the water, and rotting branches knocked and pushed by the current, and over this cascade was placed the very beau ideal of a little bridge. Above it the water was glassy, passing over paved stone; then came the rush, the whirl of the stream, and beyond that all was calm and peaceful—the trees hanging over and laving their leaves and boughs in the placid stream. So English and quiet the whole scene was. By the side was an old, rejected manufactory of iron, that if anything added to the exquisite charm of the place, the old iron lying rusted and rotten about the place, and the chimneys crumbling to decay. It was an exquisite scene; one could lie and look and wonder all the day and never, never tire of gazing and listening at one time to the rush of the water above the rocks, and at another to the wind sighing in the trees, and to watch the calm gliding of the stream. We then returned home from that, along the banks of the canal. In the evening we went in a totally different direction to a place called Honeybrook (I suppose because the water flows so sweetly) —such a lovely place."

To his mother.
"June 4, 1849.

"We went to take a walk to a place called Arly yesterday. We just went through Habberley and there was the pine forest I told you of last half. We passed Trimpley Church and then passed on through a beautiful English lane, the trees joining a dense shade overhead. Such a pretty little thing. The only drawback was that it was a little wet underfoot. After passing this we went through a gate into a field and then a most lovely view burst upon us. To the north Malvern with its numberless hills. On one of them a black cloud rested with its dark fringe of rain falling on the earth, and we heard the distant thunder muttering away among the hills. An extensive wood lay beneath our feet formed by pines and elms. Between it and us stretched a little glen dotted with green ash and elm. I thought what a beautiful place for an army to bivouac in, and in the distance myriads of trees, meadows, farmhouses dotting the place. It was such a beautiful picture of the wealth and glory of England. As we went on we entered a wild little copse wood of oaks with winding paths (not cut by the hand of man) turning and meandering in every direction. Oh, it was a lovely spot. At the bottom ran a rippling stream laughing over the stones. We ascended this and emerged on a pretty country road such as you see in England skirting the edge of the wood we had just emerged from. And the same lovely view before you. When you stood you might have fancied yourself alone in the world, only for now and then the merry laugh and the sweet songsters around you. After going along this we entered the wood again and proceeded over hundreds of stiles along the banks of the beautiful Severn till we came to the town, a picturesque little place on the banks. Above was a castle belonging to Lady Valentia on the top of a wooded height. We went into an inn here, for the thunderstorm had come on that had been threatening. Colborne and I stood at the door watching the forked lightning and listening with delight to the peals of thunder. I do like a thunderstorm so much. It continued raining for an hour and a half, when we started for home, and lo and behold the rain came on with double force. I had no coat on and I was literally drenched through, my shirt every inch wet, my feet, legs, etc. I had to change everything when I got home. I never got such a drenching, and as is usual when we got home the rain ceased. Such was our walk."

CHAPTER III

TRINITY COLLEGE, DUBLIN

"Called on McGee, the bookseller. . . . I have not seen McGee since I was a young man at College. . . . I talked with him of the ancient days, and a faint incense from them seemed to creep into my nostrils. I saw myself walking into the shop, with a blue frock coat, white waistcoat, and light grey trousers, daintily gloved; and I remembered how pleased I was when my turn-out was pronounced to be better than that of W., who up to that time was considered the best-dressed man in College. This, I may say, annihilated W. He never got over it. And I won my victory, not by money, for I had none, but by infinite taking of trouble. It was worth doing. Everything is worth doing, if it be done victoriously, if it attains its end. Yet it was but an episode. I had many other things to do—and this was done for fun. Episodes relieve and enlighten the epic of life."—(*Diary*, October 2, 1899.)

BROOKE entered Trinity College, Dublin, in October, 1850, and took his degree of B.A., together with the Testimonium Divinitatis, in 1856. During this period he won at least two prizes for English Verse, but beyond this there is no record of exceptional distinctions. It was not in examinations that he found scope for the expression of his individuality.

He always possessed the artist's eye for essentials, and could quickly reach the centre of any subject he set himself to study. Accordingly we find that his work at Trinity College was not evenly pursued, but focussed into short periods of concentration between which were long intervals devoted to general culture. And especially to the culture of the imagination. It was thus he worked throughout his life. At all times he had an intense hatred of intellectual disorder, and though his mind was far removed from the academic type, he knew the worth of sound learning and accurate thought. So when the examinations came round they had their due. He excelled in the writing of Latin Prose, for which he had an "intuitive gift," and in general gave a good account of himself in the classics and in the associated philosophical studies.

The studies for the degree were classics, science, and philosophy. The last subject included the Aristotelian Logic, Locke's Essay, and Cousin's Criticisms. Then, as now, all the examinations, honours, and degrees (except D.D.) were open to all denominations. The Rev. Dr James Drummond, whose College years nearly coincided with those of Stopford Brooke, informs me that at this period the College gave a good all-round education, and a genuine insight into the several lines of study. No knowledge of modern history or modern languages was required, but Brooke certainly read modern history on his own account, and had acquired a good working knowledge both of French and German in 1856. The theological teaching was orthodox; but it was honest and thorough without being oppressive or minatory. I can find no evidence that Brooke was greatly influenced by the personality or the doctrine of any of his professors. References in his later letters show that he respected his teachers, and did his best to satisfy their requirements. On the whole, he cannot be reckoned among the men who have been formed at college, or by college. He received what his college had to teach him, industry and sound knowledge within the limits assigned, and vehemently went forward on his chosen way.

His participation in the social life of the College was doubtless diminished by the fact that for reasons of economy, which had to be strictly considered, he continued to live at home in Kingstown, except for brief periods when he stayed in Dublin with his grandmother Stopford, a lady of strong character and intellect, whose memory he cherished in after years, and whom he would often mention as a liberalizing influence in his early life. His college friendships were not numerous, partly owing to the circumstance just mentioned, and partly also to an indisposition, which accompanied him all through life, to cultivate extensive acquaintance with men. His closest friend was his brother William, who entered College a year later than himself. It was understood that William also would take Orders, but deciding later on that he had no call to the ministry, he took up the profession of law. The two young men differed widely in character, but were at one in the love of literature and the arts. They shared the same studies, read the same books, and discussed together all problems, literary, moral, and religious. In the diary which Brooke kept in his old age there is an interesting reminiscence of these things, under date March 22, 1908, when he was seventy-six years of age.

"I read a good deal, last night, after many years, of Emerson's Essays. As far as they are the natural gush of himself they are good. . . . Of order, of continuity, of careful arrangement of thought on the subject, there is almost nothing. Excellent and striking thoughts pop up like a Jack-in-the-box. . . . There is no real philosophy in the book, that is, no real system of philosophy. . . . But the book has an awakening, stimulating force from the character behind it. It is well fitted to impel and kindle youth. It did a great deal for me once. William and I, when we were at College, lived[1] at my grandmother's in Pembroke Street. It was our custom at night to read together, and, in order to smoke, we took refuge in a garret at the top of the house, completely bare of furniture, except three laundry baskets. We turned them up. One held our solitary candle. On the other two we sat, and in this silent, bare and lonely room, we read Emerson's Essays night after night till we had finished them in the midst of infinite discussions carried on till two or three in the morning. And great was the influence of that time."

This is of great importance. Amid a mass of vague and uncertain evidence it gives a distinct record of one of the earliest influences which, acting in harmony with Brooke's temperament, caused him to break away from the evangelicalism in which he had been brought up. As an undergraduate he was familiar with Emerson's Divinity School Address.

The contemporary diary of Mrs Richard Brooke contains a few references to College events during this period, but throws no light on the changes which were beginning in the mind of her son.

February, 1852. "Dear Stopford got 2nd Honours at his 1st exam. He has been reading all day and night for the last fortnight. We have great advantages in this place [Kingstown] in the way of society for our boys. Next to the gifts of grace there cannot be a greater [blessing] than having nice acquaintance for our boys."

December, 1853. "The boys busy studying. S. for a scholarship [which he missed by one mark], W. and E. for examinations. They are great blessings so far as steadiness and good sense go. It is a greater boon than hundreds of pounds."

January, 1854. "S. is increasing in gentleness and sense. His mind has advanced far beyond his years. He is most studious."

1855 (month not stated). "S. looks very handsome."

[1] He means, for a time.

There is evidence that while Brooke was at College he began to stray widely from the strict orthodoxy in which he had been brought up. Whence came the first impulse in this direction is not easy to state with precision. Perhaps a sufficient explanation lies in the well-known fact that strict orthodoxy, of whatsoever form, is very apt to provoke reaction in the opposite direction when it comes into contact with imaginative minds. Certainly there was nothing in the domestic surroundings of Brooke to encourage these tendencies. On the other hand, I am informed that Dublin in the 'fifties of the last century was remarkable for the large number of cultivated women active in social life, and it would seem that Brooke during his College years was at home in the circles where the influence of these women was felt. That liberal tendencies were at work among them is likely, though such tendencies were certainly exceptional, not to say dangerous, in the atmosphere of the Irish Church at this period.

An admirable account of this atmosphere, from which I shall quote a few passages, may be found in an article by Dr Mahaffy, the present Provost of Trinity College, in the *Hibbert Journal* for April, 1903. Dr Mahaffy's picture displays the kind of religious teaching to which Brooke was accustomed; whence we may estimate the extent of reaction which, as subsequent evidence will show, had already taken place in the young man's mind.

"The great Evangelical movement," says Dr Mahaffy, "had been working in Dublin ever since the opening of the nineteenth century. It was discountenanced by most of the bishops and fashionable clergy, and did not become dominant till the very tactless rule of Archbishop Whately threw a vast number of the rich laity into the movement, who built free chapels, not under the archbishop's control, and filled them with able popular preachers, who emptied the parish churches, and monopolized all the religious teaching of the Protestant population. . . . The popular preachers of Dublin in 1850 . . . differed from the early Puritans in that these thought an accurate knowledge of the original Bible essential, while their descendants were quite content with the Authorized Version. But so convinced were they of the vital importance of Scripture, that I have actually heard a clergyman on a platform assert the verbal inspiration of the English Bible, on the ground that the same influence which guided the pens of the original writers could not have failed to guide in the same manner the translators who were to make known to the English nation the message of the Gospel. Regarding, therefore, the Bible, as they understood it, as the absolute rule of faith, they nevertheless acquiesced in the formularies and ritual of the Church of England. . . . They never quarrelled with the Book of Common Prayer: they read through the service devoutly every Sunday—even the Athanasian creed received its due place—and always considered themselves a distinct Church from their brethren the Presbyterians, with whom they were nevertheless, then, on very good terms. But the service . . . was but a long prelude to the real work of the day—the sermon. For this purpose the minister retired, and reappeared in the lofty pulpit in a black (or Geneva) preaching gown and bands. If he gave an extempore prayer before the sermon, it was not from any desire to violate the rubric, but only because he regarded it as part of his sermon. In this discourse, which often occupied three-quarters of an hour, it was his absolute duty to set forth the whole Gospel (as he understood it), so that any stray person, or any member of the congregation in a contrite condition, might then and there attain conversion (which was always sudden) and find peace. . . . They were distinctly Calvinists,[1] as their forefathers had been; they

[1] The Rev. Richard Brooke was a Calvinist in his earlier ministry. He gave up Calvinism soon after he became pastor of the Mariners' Church.

were distinctly anti-ritualists. The doctrine of justification by faith was the cardinal point of their teaching. . . .

"They did not hesitate to preach that all those who had not embraced the dogma of justification by faith were doomed to eternal perdition. They believed as strongly as Massillon in "the small number of the elect." They were not afraid to insist upon the eternity of the very maximum of torture. They did not believe in the Epicurean doctrine of pain—*si gravis, brevis; si longus, levis*. On the contrary, the great majority of the human race would be "salted with fire." But, on the other hand, they had the firmest belief in the future bliss of those that were saved, and upon their deathbeds looked forward with confidence to an immediate reunion with the saints who had gone before. They even had strong hopes of seeing visions of glory on their deathbeds. . . . They lived saintly and charitable lives, though they inveighed against the value of good works. They controlled their congregations as spiritual autocrats, though they denied all efficacy in apostolical succession. They were excellent and able men, proclaiming a creed which has, over and over again, produced great and noble types of men, though most philosophers would denounce it as a cruel and even immoral parody of the teaching of the Founder. . . ."

While at College Brooke attracted the notice of the editor of the *Dublin University Magazine*. He wrote reviews of books, sometimes with considerable fierceness; and two long articles, one on "The Growth of the Novel" and the other on "The Genius of Charles Kingsley." "With this article Charles Kingsley was greatly pleased, and wrote to Mr Brady, the Editor, to express his thanks and the great gratification he felt that at least one person thoroughly understood him, his aims as an author, and the objects he desired to achieve. He apologized for the character of O'Blareaway [an Irish clergyman in "Yeast," severely criticized by Brooke as untrue to the character of the Irish Clergy] promising not to offend again." [1]

From the article on Kingsley we may learn from what quarter the wind was beginning to blow. It shows further that Brooke had already formed that conception of the relation of literature to religion which led in 1872 to his sermons on "Theology in the English Poets"—the beginning of a new movement in Mid-Victorian preaching. I append a few passages. It will be noted that he speaks of "the great drama and novel of existence"—a significant phrase from a young man of twenty-four.

"It may be asked why does a clergyman write novels—is it not derogatory to what is called, in unpleasant irony, 'the cloth'? For our part, we think not; for rob a minister of the Church of the living God of those peculiar qualities which fit him for writing a novel or a drama, and you take away from him precisely those which fit him especially to be the interpreter of God to man. You rob him of the delicate perception of shades of character, of the power of grasping the main point of the story of a life and seeing the remedy thro' it for the disease, of that sympathy which chimes in with, and comforts deep feeling—you rob him of all these, for these are precisely the qualities requisite for a good dramatist or novelist. . . .

"Let us be free from narrow sectarianism, and believe that he who takes part day by day in the great drama and novel of existence, may reverently, as heeding the danger, and bravely and truly, as knowing himself, come forth to teach others in whatever form he please, what he has seen and learnt therein. . . . Our whole heart and life is continually calling for some one to explain it, to put it into words, for we cannot express ourselves; we must be represented to ourselves; and

[1] From a MS of "Memorabilia," by William Brooke.

this the drama does, and in England now, the novel, for the latter, as we said, has taken the place of the former. . . .

"For this Mr Kingsley is a witness. His fictions are not to amuse, but to rebuke, to exhort, and to exalt. . . .

". . . The main element of his books is the application of the principles of Christianity, living principles as derived from a living God, to the social, political, commercial, and mental difficulties of this age. . . . Mr Kingsley in treating of the various sects displays a tolerance, and a clear-sightedness which all parties in the Church would do well to imitate. . . .

"This principle is the head and fount of Mr Kingsley's religious opinions. That each man has a Father in Heaven who is directing, calling, drawing him to Himself, taking a personal loving interest in him though he may be ignorant of it. That this same Fatherhood and Kinghood is exercised over nations, and in proportion as individual or nation rejects this loving government so they lose themselves.

"But this Fatherhood and Kinghood were lifeless, and comfortless were they not understood as belonging to a personal Father and King. A Person like ourselves with a will, a character, not subdivided into lifeless attributes, and unreal abstractions, but a living, loving Person. But we are flesh and blood, and we cannot altogether realize to ourselves a spiritual Personality, so it became necessary that once the Godhead should take on Him flesh and blood and become a human Son of God, the realization of the ideal of Humanity making man Godlike to God, and God human to man; the realization of all the noble dreams of all mythology; the divine in the human; the accomplishment of all the vague yearnings of all ages."

Both articles have intrinsic merit which still make them well worth reading. That on "The Growth of the Novel" reveals a wide knowledge of the subject. At the age of twenty-three Brooke appears to have read every English novel of note which had been written up to that time. The matter is collated with skill and judgment; the style, method, and moral tendency of the different writers are compared; and there are admirable observations on the significance of the novel as a form of literary art, and as a vehicle of ethical teaching. Some of the opinions expressed, especially those on Scott and Dickens, were modified considerably later on, but on matters of principle the article is true to the type of his later literary judgments. The essay on Kingsley is even more valuable as a foreshadowing of his future work both as writer and preacher. Clearly apparent on every page is an essential sympathy with the views of Kingsley—especially with the desire to make theology a vehicle for vigorous manliness, broad human sympathies and deep delight in the beauty and wonder of the natural world.

The family life in Kingstown which Brooke continued to share was, as we have seen, quick with the interaction of varied and gifted personalities, and was a centre of wide social intercourse for the young men. Many visits were paid to country houses in the neighbourhood. Moreover, they enjoyed an unusually large number of girl friendships, which their father always encouraged, taking a keen and humorous interest in their development. William's "memorabilia," from which I have already quoted, contain some reference to these affairs, and suggest that even in matters of the heart a certain confederacy existed between the three brothers.

1852. "The great Irish beauty was M. When the Queen in 1849 asked to see the most beautiful girl in Ireland, M. was presented to her. . . . Though Presbyterians they always came to our Church on Sunday evenings. We generally made a race of it to meet [the sisters] in the vestibule. . . . They were to be seen continually at the window, especially M. How often we traversed that road with the sole object of seeing her!'"

1853. "When S. was at college he was in love with C. It was an interlude to more serious affairs. At lunch one day we were going in with the ladies, and as C. took the arm, which S. was somewhat slow to proffer, I heard her say in a whisper, 'Shure, you won't forsake me, Stopford,' and he said, 'No, never!'"

1853. "The two daughters of Sir —— we saw a great deal of. G. was a beautiful girl. . . . We often spent whole afternoons at their house, losing our dinner, which was at 5.30. There was some conversation one day about wealth and dress, when G. turned and said, 'Stopford, if you were dressed in rags you would always look a gentleman.'"

1856. "There was a great friendship with A., who was very good and had a private sorrow of an incurable kind. . . . She knew a good deal of German literature and took from S. a promise that he would never read 'Wilhelm Meister.' Every Sunday, after Sunday School, we used to walk for one hour with these people. . . . An old woman who sat at the top of our street with a pipe in her mouth and a few apples in a basket before her, viewed these proceedings in silence for many a long day. At last she was heard to remark, 'Bedad, that's the longest courtship ever I see!'"

Kingstown at this period was both a seaport and a watering-place. There was a large traffic of ships passing to and fro across the waters of the bay; there were storms and wrecks: men-of-war rode at anchor, and in summer a fleet of Cornish fishing-boats was moored at the quay.

On Sundays these fishermen crowded into the Mariners' Church, where Stopford, in the corner of the minister's pew, watched their bronzed and weather-beaten faces and tried to imagine their life on the lonely sea. They were all Methodists and quite at home in the Mariners' Church, finding the marrow of the Gospel in the sermons of the minister. They sang well; so well indeed that the Rev. Richard Brooke "gave up the singing to them" during the season when they were in Church. "Shall we meet beyond the river" was one of their favourite hymns. On week-days the fishermen came to the prayer-meetings, which had now become an important feature in the religious exercises of the Mariners' Church. They attended the "class" which Stopford occasionally taught—a Bible class, no doubt, with "experiences" introduced as occasion offered. They "came to tea" at the hospitable house of the minister, who closed the proceedings with reading from the Bible and with prayer. There Stopford talked to these men of religion and of the sea.

Meanwhile he is all for the open air; out in the bay in calm and storm, a cunning boatman and master at the oar. At night he goes out to the end of the pier and throws stones into the deep water to see the phosphorescence which, he says, "touches his sense of mystery." He knows Captain McClintock (afterwards Sir Leopold), and hears from him of great adventures in the northern waters. "The sea and all that is therein had taken possession of his mind"—so says one who remembers him in these days.[1]

Among stray voices from this period one tells us that Stopford is now "a young man of great physical strength." "He throws the stone" (puts the weight) against all-comers, and one of them is James White,

[1] His close observation of natural phenomena at sea is apparent in his subsequent work on the sea-pieces of Turner in the notes on the "Liber Studiorum" (1885). See also his description of "the Drowned Sailor" on p. 186, and the account of his conversation with Woolner on p. 237.

brother of George White, afterwards Sir George White, the defender of Ladysmith. The stone is thrown in the backyard of his father's house, in default of other place of exercise, and thither James White often comes to try conclusions. "He (J. W.) went out to the Crimea, and when he came back the first thing he said to Stopford was, 'let us go out and throw the stone,' the idea being that he had been practising in the Crimea in order to beat S.—which he had never done yet. The two went out into the backyard forthwith. But S. again threw further than White did."

The Rev. Arthur Brooke assures me that in the home life there were "lots of fun," which we can well believe. There were also endless discussions, and both the fun and the discussions were of the kind which neither evangelical theology nor anything else in the heavens above or the earth beneath can long expel from an Irishman's preoccupations. "Stopford," says Mr Arthur Brooke, incidentally revealing an important historical fact, "was always on the liberal side. William would be better from the logical point of view. I remember a discussion which lasted for days on 'the ideal apple-dumpling.'" On the issue of the discussion—whether decided by Stopford's liberalism or William's logic—we have no information.

Among the visits paid to country-houses during this period I find mention of the Rothwells of Rothfield; of Glanmore Castle, Co. Wicklow, the house of the Synges, "where the Vartry ran through a lovely glen"; of Granston Manor, a seat of the Fitzpatricks; also of a house at Delgany "not far from the sea where we had a delightful time, our neighbours being the Featherstonhaughs." Every year "the boys" went down to Glanmore Castle to dig the Christmas tree for the great family party on Christmas Eve. In 1852 Stopford takes part in a puppet show at Sir Jocelyn Coghill's, Killiney Castle: "The Coghills were very clever and amusing people." In the list of diversions nearer home I find frequent mention of Kingstown Pier, which ran out for a mile into the sea, and had a high and low wall with ample space for promenaders. There at the hours appointed for such things might be seen a gay and fashionable crowd of comely ladies and gentlemen in faultless attire. Conspicuous among the latter was young Mr Stopford Brooke, of whom the irreverent would say when they saw him approaching, "Here comes his Majesty the Sultan." With him would sometimes appear, either arm in arm, or at a judicious distance, the Rev. Richard Brooke, by no means out of harmony with his surroundings, and fully conscious that he and his son, whether singly or together, were worth looking at. "Whenever the three boys had gained honours in College, the Governor always went on the pier with them and trotted out their distinctions to admiring friends," greatly to the embarrassment of whichever of the trio happened to be the object of the paternal praise.

The following letter is interesting for its reference to Robson, the great comedian, and still more for the glimpse it gives us into the mind of Stopford Brooke at the age of twenty-three.

"10, Upper Pembroke Street, Dublin.
"October 8, 1856.

". . . I have just come home from the theatre where I have heard Robson act. . . . He is very wonderful, a short man, with dark eyes, and a countenance not so much flexible as ever changing in expression. The strange incongruity is that though a comedian, and that of the low order, yet in the midst of broad farce, a perfectly tragic position, and expression, and tone will suddenly appear and startle you, even shock you with its power, while you are amazed by it. He has travestied the Medea as acted by Ristori, and I know not what to say of it. All through the play you are on the borders of laughter, yet always recalled the next instant by something so intense, so tragic, so real, that you are filled with the thought of the injured woman, with pity, with horror. It is like Cowper writing John Gilpin, with the melancholy of life gnawing at his heart, or like some of those Dantesque conceptions, which considered apart from the Poem would excite a smile from their grotesqueness, but which with the shade of the Inferno thrown round them are terrible with Imagination. Some of his attitudes are pure Greek, yet he compels the comic element to struggle through, till the mixture has something horribly real in it, for have I not seen men laugh in the midst of agony.

"This may be all overdrawn on my part, but recollect I seldom go to the theatre; I have seen Kean, and in my judgment he is not to be compared to this man. Once in the midst of a comedy, he assumed an attitude and expression which for the first time realized to me, what Hamlet's face must have been when he began the famous soliloquy. I heard since that Ristori went to see him act this Medea in London, and was delighted with it. I own he has given me much to think of. It is not often that we realize the closeness of extremes, though comedy to me is often the very deepest tragedy.

. . .

"My kindest remembrances to Miss Beaumont,[1] if she is still with you."

[1] Afterwards Mrs Stopford Brooke.

CHAPTER IV

VOCATION

"How many fine intellects, how many men who might have done original work in many paths have been buried in the grave of the Church of England! It is shocking to think of it. The miserable conventions tread them down. The strong escape the bonds and do what suits them well. There are others whom the atmosphere exactly suits, and *they* do good work. But there are hundreds who, not being strong enough to resist the pressure, never develop as they ought, and year by year they rot and rot—and thereby hangs a tale. Just imagine if William Morris and Burne Jones had gone into the Church, as they intended, what the world would have lost, and what they would have been. Fancy Morris a fighting Archdeacon like Denison, and Burne Jones a rose fancier like Dean Hole!"—(*Diary*, December 20, 1904.)

"There is a settled melancholy at the back of the greater number of [their][1] ministers. Most of them have never lived, some of them have not even tried to live. They know little or nothing of the world—excellent men, but profoundly ignorant of any human nature save what they find in themselves and in their wives. How *can* they preach? The one thing to preach about they do not know."—(*Diary*, October 27, 1902.)

THOUGH the action of Brooke's mind was vehement and rapid, both in acquisition and creation, his development was slow. Had he died, like Robertson and Sterling, before reaching the age of forty, an immense amount of activity would have to be recorded, and it may be that even if the story had been cut off at that point the

---

[1] He is speaking of one of the Nonconformist bodies. For what he means by "melancholy," see his sermon on Albert Dürer's "Melancolia" in the volume "Christ and Modern Life." With the remark about ignorance of human nature compare his reference to Jowett, on p. 506.

impression would remain of a finished life. The fact is, however, that at the age of forty Brooke was barely half way to the goal at which his character and his message became perfectly united, and, by union, assumed their final form. I do not say that the process of his development was arduous, but it was very long and gradual, and for that reason, perhaps, exceptionally secure in its last result.

Moreover it was, throughout, consistent. The line on which he was to move forward may be clearly discerned in the letters written at the close of his college career, to be quoted presently. And when we encounter him ten years later, in the first volume of his published sermons, there is indeed a greater affluence of expression and a firmer mastery of his theme, but very little change in the essential nature of the theme itself—the application of the Gospel to every human interest and to the entire field of social life. In the twenty years that followed (1870–1890) there was an immense expansion, due to causes we shall consider, in his knowledge of human nature and of the world; and this reacted to some extent on the main idea, but never caused him to repudiate his starting-point. There is no period in the life of Brooke at which he had to begin his development over again. This is the more remarkable inasmuch as there was in him a double tendency, or perhaps a double nature—a condition attended in most men by a familiar alternative; either the one nature must suppress the other, or the possessor of the two is doomed to a troubled, inconsistent and divided life. Brooke escaped this alternative altogether. To each side of his nature he gave its full rights, and yet his life, throughout all its periods, was singularly at one with itself.

One side of his nature belonged to religion; the

other to art; two realms intimately related in the world of pure ideas but often widely sundered, and even at variance, in the actual lives of men. He possessed a deep natural piety, fostered by such influence and example as we have seen; and in respect of that we may say of him—*anima naturaliter christiana*. But his feet were firmly planted on the earth; no pagan ever loved it better or received from contact with the things of sense a fuller current of the joy of life. All his senses were fine, eager and explorative; he had the power of self-detachment which frees the faculties for delightful exercise in observation, and leaves them at the disposal of the object to be observed; his, too, was the artist's vision which seizes the inner meaning of things along with their images; and there is little doubt that had he lived in some age or society to which Christian culture was unknown, he would have found satisfaction and won eminence. "In my sixty-seven years," he writes in 1899, "I have only had a whiff of the joy to be got out of natural beauty. But when I have seen this earth well I'll have a look at other planets and at new beauty. I should like to come back as a landscape painter and wander about the world with pencils, brushes, colours, and a knapsack—walking, not driving, as Turner did. And indeed it could be a Paradise if only one had a fiftieth part of his divine power."

Between these two tendencies, the Christian and the Greek—so often reconciled in metaphysics, so rarely reconciled in actual life—the mediating power in Brooke was an impassioned love of beauty in all its forms, both natural and spiritual. Through the love of beauty he carried his art, with all its passion and fine sense of proportion, into his religion, becoming thereby a prophet of the *beauty* of holiness. By the same means he carried his religion, with all its piety and tenderness, into his art, and made it a vehicle for things that are lovely and of good report, and for them alone. Thus the two tendencies, which in most men are rivals, became confederates, and the story of their growing confederacy through a long lapse of years is the story of the life of Stopford Brooke. His finest work, which ripened slowly and late, was the fruit of their union. Never indeed were the two so closely married or so happy in their offspring as to forbid an occasional quarrel; but always it was a lovers' quarrel, and ended as a lovers' quarrel should.

So much must be prefaced if we are to understand the spirit in which Brooke accepted the career of a clergyman. To such a man we can well believe that the Irish evangelicalism of the fifties must have presented many features which made the clerical profession far from attractive, and indeed there is a well-preserved legend that "Stopford desired to be an artist." Perhaps it may be thought he had no option—his father being a poor clergyman, with a large family, and so many influences of heredity and environment tending in one direction. But let it be remembered that in after years when the desire to devote himself to art had increased in strength, so that he could speak of its realization as "a Paradise," and when the opportunity to indulge the longing was again and again thrown open, he neither yielded to the desire nor took the opportunity, but chose to live and die a minister of Christ. The truer explanation of his becoming a clergyman is that quite early in life, with little aid from others and in the face of much opposition, he had formed for himself an ideal of the Christian ministry which was to reconcile the two currents of his being in a deep synthesis of Art and Religion, of Nature and Spirit. The letters to be given later bear out this explanation. And what better indication could we have of the measure of the man?

There is, then, no question of a mind divided against itself and condemned to the lifelong agony of a conflict between two contrary principles, each striving to assert itself at the expense of the other. Had this been his condition he would soon have outlived his youth, as most assuredly he never did; perhaps like Robertson he would have died early, consumed by the inward strife. His imagination indeed was too affluent and adventurous to submit at all points and without protest to any rule, even the most liberal; and his realism, which was deeply moved by elemental forces, would often fly away with his thoughts and carry them hither and thither, winged with the pure joy of life. In this way he took his "moral holidays," continually expanding the range of his intercourse with Nature, and spiritual riches came to him accordingly. No fetters could hold him fast bound to a limited view of the world, or of his work in the world. Certainly the Philistines could never bind him. Each point of arrival was used in turn as a point of departure. Thus the step which led him into the Church in 1857 was only the first of a series of steps which led him out of the Church in 1880.

When the three brothers were young men the position of affairs was as follows. Edward, the youngest of the three, who became a soldier, desired to be a clergyman; William, who became a lawyer, desired to be a sailor; Stopford, who became a clergyman, desired to be an artist. The situation may give food for reflection—otherwise abundantly forthcoming—to those who philosophize on "the choice of a vocation"—a phrase which misrepresents the conditions under which vocations come to ninety-nine out of every hundred men and perhaps contains a contradiction in terms. Certain it is that if the ministry were restricted to such only as can give proof, with date and place affixed, of a clear and unmistakable "call," some of the most powerful voices of religion would be put to silence, while, among those left in possession, there would be humbugs not a few.

Search as I may among the records of these years I can find no indication of any particular moment or crisis when Brooke formed *ad hoc* the decision to become a clergyman. With the best men, that is the most sincere, such "choices" are not compressed into a moment but extended over years; indeed it is to be doubted if they can properly be called "choices" at all. Nor is there any evidence that he received a "call" in the sense of a spiritual crisis to which exact place, date, and circumstance can be assigned. But if Providence has a hand in these appointments, it can surely operate through the "influence of the stars" and the slowly deepening responses of the soul, as well as by sudden explosions of spiritual force. There is no reason, pious or other, why we should labour to construct a picturesque psychology round these things. It is conceivable that Brooke might have entered another calling, and become a leader of men on other lines—but practically no! As to the question of loss or gain to the world let it not be asked; for it cannot be answered. That the light he followed was the light of his loadstar the event seems to have proved: so much is clear. And what more do we require?

" Se tu segui tua stella
Non puoi fallire a glorioso porto."

Nor can it be said of Brooke, as Carlyle said of Sterling, perhaps with some exaggeration, that his taking Orders was the result of drinking "bottled moonshine," or of listening to the droning "metaphysical sing-song of Coleridge" or of anybody else. While at college Brooke read Coleridge with eagerness, especially his poetry and his "Aids to Reflection," and as I find him reading Fichte in 1857 it is to be presumed that he had some acquaintance with "the vacant air-castles and dim-melting ghosts" of the Kantian philosophy. He also studied Berkeley—with enthusiasm. But it was not this reading that made him a clergyman, nor the width of it that made him a broad one. Breadth with him was in the first place an attribute of his humanity, and only in the second an attribute of his "views." As contributory causes, books of criticism, philosophy, and science played their part; but the range of his reading in these departments was itself determined by the demands of a mind which had already broken its fetters through the force of inner expansion. I greatly doubt if what he learnt from such sources did more for him at any time than confirm the liberality of spirit which belonged to his nature as artist, poet, and lover. To this nature unquestionably must we look for the impulse which led Brooke to humanize his theology from the outset, thereby departing so widely from the lines in which he had been brought up. Truth had to be brought into harmony with beauty, and whether we consider him at this or at any later period of his life we find him incapable, naturally incapable, of believing anything to be true which formed a blot on the essential loveliness of the world. How was it possible for a mind so formed to accept the evangelicalism of the fifties? The thing was not possible. The recoil began when he was a boy at school; it had become an established movement by the time he was twenty-one. Even then, as the voice already quoted reminds us, "Stopford was always on the liberal side."

Among the causes which contributed to this, the natural and inevitable movement of his mind, the following incidents have some significance.

In 1849, just before his entry at Trinity College, when Ireland was beginning to recover from the throes of famine, Kingstown was invaded by the cholera. Richard Brooke, whose heroism in these terrible times was long remembered, attended over fifty cases. Stopford accompanied his father on some of these visits, and a vision of human wretchedness was there and then revealed to him which left a lifelong impression on his mind. Misery and rumours of misery filled the land, and there, in the plague-stricken dwelling, the meaning of it all suddenly unveiled itself to the young man. And the thought that came into his mind was this: "These things are not the judgments of God on the sins of the sufferers, who are undeserving of such chastisement; they are due to the neglect, ignorance, selfishness, and injustice of men." This thought, so familiar now, needed a prophet's voice to enforce it in 1850. Kingsley was busy proclaiming it, and the young Brooke, who was reading Kingsley, may well have said to himself, "Here is a gospel for me also to preach." And for forty years he continued to preach it with varying applications, but with the vision of those days at Kingstown never wholly absent from his mind. His later conversations also lead me to believe that it was on one of these occasions, when standing by the bed of some poor wretch suddenly stricken by the plague, and haunted by religious terrors, that he conceived his first hatred of the doctrine of Eternal Punishment, the beginning of his recoil from the whole evangelical theology.

Mention has already been made of visits paid to the seat of the Fitzpatricks. I find that Brooke went there in '47, '49, '50, and '52. On one of these occasions he was in F. W. Robertson's company for three weeks, and there is evidence that from the first the personality of Robertson made a profound impression on the mind and imagination of the youth. Doubtless the common vehemence of their natures would bring the two, though differing widely in age, closely together. Brooke used to tell me that his views about religion were not due to the influence of Robertson's writings, but were formed independently. All the same, I am inclined to believe that he owed more than he knew to Robertson—if not to the writings certainly to the man. For no young man can make a hero of another, on what ground soever, without receiving an influence which must penetrate sooner or later to the form of his thinking. Who can doubt that these meetings with Robertson set the seal of assurance, and imparted a certain fire of enthusiasm, to the tendencies which were leading young Brooke into the Broad Church. "Do you know," he writes to Miss Campbell in 1860, "I feel towards that man as a woman does towards her lover, only with a feeling more pure from passion."

At the time of which I am writing the Crimean War was in progress, and shortly before peace was declared (1856) Edward Brooke, who had obtained a commission in the Engineers, went out to the front. Stopford followed the developments of the campaign with the keenest interest. Moreover, he was deeply moved, as all men then were, by the character and work of Florence Nightingale, the central figure in the "Woman's Question" as it was debated in those days. On the significance of the war as a moral portent, and the challenge it brought to the profession of Christianity, he reflected much, just as we are now doing under a far more terrible visitation. The war revealed to him the need of public ideals which, as it seemed to him, were little likely to arise from the doctrines of personal salvation then current in the Churches, and in the character of Florence Nightingale (who was not an orthodox Christian) he saw a living embodiment of wider Christianity which is not of the letter but of the spirit. How these things affected him will be seen in the following extract from the article on Kingsley. They utter truths which sixty years afterwards the world has still to learn.

"Whatever may be said on the *vexata quæstio* whether foreign war be beneficial or otherwise in its effects upon a nation, there can be no doubt that a long-continued peace has not altogether good results. So long as selfishness prevails in human nature, so long will aggressive wars arise; and so long as a true and vivid spirit of hatred to the evil strength of Wrong exists and a righteous sense of the mightiness of Right, so long will there always be found nations who will take arms to a man, and with one heart protest against the unholy Thing.

"And in doing this they are morally benefited. The boundaries of justice and injustice are more clearly defined. The nation is given something else but itself and its prosperity to think of, for as the very life of the individual is to help others lovingly, so the life of a kingdom is renewed by a manful defence of the Rights of others against oppression. And this seems to us the solution. If a war be just, and for noble objects, it will practically do good to the nation who wages it. For every man therein consciously, or unconsciously, is fighting with God against Apollyon, the liar and destroyer. Men feel that whatever may happen that they die not for themselves, but for others, and that is the sweetness in the cup of the bitterest death. The soldier can go to battle with the light of Heaven on his face, and feel no shame gazing on it; as of old on the field of Bannockburn, even nature herself seemed to show, before the fight had met, when the sunlight strake forth in long lines on the kneeling ranks of Scottish freedom, while the clouds still hung dark upon the masses of English oppression. But when a war is unjust—we may never remark it, the very men may not be conscious of it, but still it is there, the sense of injustice and wrong-doing pervading the whole host like a faint pestilential smell—then war is death and loss to the nation, for it is doing evil for the sake of evil, the most ignoble, the most wicked thing in this world of ours, the very demoralization of a people."

The following letters from this period help to confirm the view that the form of Brooke's religious life, which was never essentially changed, had its origin in inward rather than in outward causes. His evangelical training is apparent; but something else is clearly coming to the birth.

To Miss Campbell.
"Aug. 7, '56.

"I cannot tell you now what I think of 'justification' or the meaning of the Atonement as I believe it, but if I may write you a line now and then or a sermon I will try. I cannot *talk*, I never could express myself well, I can write with much more ease, but I will only give you what I think, and what has satisfied my own mind, on this condition that you do not read what I say without taking up the Bible and praying for the help of One, without whom nothing is strong, nothing is holy. I say this because the human mind . . . is liable, whenever it is wavering, to seize on what pleases its natural bent of character, and at once make it its own, and afterwards attenuate or extenuate Revelation to the preconceived opinion. To me the opinions which I adopted came home at once, I could hardly be said to have adopted them, it seemed as if I had held them all my life, and that they only had *then* been known to me. My very heart vibrated to them. I could not but pass on to what I feel was higher, nobler, purer air. God became God—man became *really* man—*i.e.* I began to feel that every one around me was some one who *could live* and would die.

"I cannot put down what I felt then, I might put down too much or too little. I first, I know, seized it with delight, then I thought that all must think the same. I talked of it, and when opposed, no doubt overstated it. My Father thought I was very wrong, and opposed me strongly (he did not understand what I meant, and fancied that what I believed was totally different to what he thought right—in reality it was not). The consequence was I was thrown back on myself, and lived in my own thought almost always. Do not think now I am talking the cant 'of not being understood or being alone.' It is only cant when it is not true, or trumpeted forth to the world. You are the second I ever told it to. Then in a year after, all I thought, chiefly through watching the humble Christian life of another, had softened itself down to a surface cooler, but more useful with God's help to myself—like the iron we saw to-night.

"Now, save in my own heart, I am content with God —I can trust him as a God of Love for the world, ah, . . . it is hard to make Him your own, to say *our* Father, my God. You will sometimes say something to God for me."

To Miss Campbell.
"September 29, '56.

"I am glad you are beginning to care for 'In Memoriam.' The depth and beauty of that book is wondrously infinite. If you like it I will send you a short analysis of a few stanzas at a time till we get through the whole book, that is, if you have got the book, if you have only read it adrift on a drawing-room table it would be no use, it is a book which *must be read* steadily and connectedly from beginning to end, and studied, for it requires as much thought as Shakespeare, Bacon, or Kant. . . .

"In all things see an infinite tendency; in nature the visible garment of God. In music not the mere enjoyment of the nerves (sensual), but let it type the beautiful harmony of the divine. Ever see the invisible in the visible, the eternal in the transient, the unchangeable in the changeable, and you will keep out of the world, for the very characteristics of the world will be inevitably dwarfed by the majesty and reality of the thoughts which possess your soul. But this would not be enough. A philosopher might do all this. Nature would have this effect on his mind in her united and law-obedient operations. No, there is something more required than this living above the world—nay, there is a very worldliness connected with the philosophic pursuits. We must have spiritual faith, not the faith merely which sacrifices present good, because it hopes to be rewarded hereafter, that is a lofty selfishness—but that faith which despises all that is earthly and sensual, in comparison with the happiness of knowing Goodness and Truth and Love, that is of knowing God. . . .

"Speaking of what men call Worldliness, I went to the morning concert in Dublin, given by the Italian Opera. I was very much charmed by some things, but you know that Italian music does not suit me. It has no inner voice. It smells of the finite. I scent the stage and the footlights, and conventionality, and tinsel through most of it. There are gems of great price. But in the German, I see the soul, I see Heaven opened, the mysteries of the world to come. My whole spirit is interpreted; the incomprehensibility of life and the intermittent thought all are voiced to my senses. Though I am not so much excited outwardly by it, yet my whole inward being is woke up, questioning, imagining, plunging to and fro in a fierce delight of conjecture, and then comes the floating calm of some of those airs to subdue the tumult into order."

To Miss Campbell.
"Oct. 7, '56.

"O golden silence, great repose, all hail! Verily, my friend, I am thoroughly wearied, not in body. I have been talked nearly to death. Two hours of a continuous stream, like the torture of the Inquisition descending on my head have robbed me of all sense of rest, particularly as all the time I was endeavouring to read 'Burnet on the Thirty Nine Articles,' so that the conversation and the reading mingling together made my brain like a pot of porridge with a mighty Scotch lassie vigorously stirring. I am obliged to have recourse to my pipe to calm the confusion. . . .

"At intervals I am reading 'Lewes' Life of Goethe'—a large book in two volumes. To me it seems well, carefully, clearly, impartially written, not to speak of a style, and a mode of expression and illustration which are fascinating, thoughtful, and suggestive without being diffuse. And what a man this Goethe was. His autobiography, the Dichtung und Wahrheit, gives me but a faint idea of the youth of the man. It is written with the circumspection and the thought of age colouring the memories of youth, but *now* I see something of that complex Life, so imaginative, yet so real, always requiring a fixed basis for imagination to work on—an ideal Realist. He lived every moment of his life. Whenever he lost himself in speculation, or in dissipation, in sentimentalism, or in sorrow, he flew to Nature, and in her *realities* found relief and impulse. He thought no thought, he felt no feeling *that he did not reduce to form*. All his Poems are histories of himself. His life has done me good. I will throw off my ideal wanderings, my cloud castles, my dreamings of possible good, and act more, be more real;—I admire the man too much in this first flush to clearly recognize his faults, when I have found out the good I shall get at the evil, but the good first. His was a life reduced to order, a perfect picture of a man sitting above all circumstance and passion, and bending them to obedience, yet with all this, feeling every passion deeply, and yielding to every circumstance for a time sufficient to realize each, yet stopping when he liked.

"He reproduced everything in a determined form, and that necessarily from his character. For instance crossing a mountain alone in a storm, the wind beating on his brow, he did not shout as some would do, nor feel a silent exultation as others, but he poured forth a stream of irregular and wild metre, stormy lines, at the top of his voice. The Wanderer's Sturm Lied. Fancy meeting him, sparkling eyed, with his Apollo face lit up, his green shooting jacket flying open, his top boots and spurs, and his magnificent hair falling about his shoulders, on the brow of a hill, shouting spontaneous song, such a sight would be worth ten years of dreaming. Try to reproduce one thought a day even, try to reduce to positive form one hour's experience, and I believe that you will do more towards advancing the intellectual order of your mind, than if you were to see a thousand thoughts passing before your mind like swallows on the wing without arresting one, or making it your own. Are you wearied with all this? I must write, my mind is overflowing with this man. If I were not to get rid of my thoughts and excitements sometimes on paper and to one who will sympathize with them, I should be overwhelmed with them. I used to practise them, but I have given up poetry. I did not write well enough to please myself, nor any one else, so I concluded one phase of my life. . . .

"It *is* a good thing to consider evil as something objective, not belonging to your inward being, something to be opposed with all our might, something which we should have nothing to do with, but the Devil supplying us with a motive which is sinful, and which we are unconscious of, is nonsense; as long as our conscience is unseared it will always give us a conscious feeling of wrong. Is the Principle on which we act right? If we deceive ourselves we do it, not Satan. I am not sure of the determinate outward reality of an evil spirit. You will think this very wrong, but your faith is untouched by it. Certainly I do believe that the whole doctrine of Satanic power is carried too far."

To Miss Campbell.
"September 22, '56.

"Is not God there and as much the Ever Near, when you are walking in Princes Street, or kneeling at your bedside? You say too you can commune with God. Is not this prayer, the truest prayer? 'I commune with my own heart on my bed and *am still.*' The voiceless prayer, silent yet vocal in God's ear. Communing with God is the highest form of Prayer, mere asking is not. 'In that day ye shall ask me nothing.' A time shall come, when the ascription of praise, and the interchange of Thought with God shall be the truest prayer, when our Will shall be so on the side of God's, so coincident that we shall need to ask nothing, for we shall have all things. All things, says St Paul, are ours, *for* we are Christ's, and Christ is God's. . . .

"I think the whole dogma of Assurance, in so far as it is laid down that to be a Christian you *must always* be sure and feel a sort of joyous fountain faith in your soul, is false to experience and moreover to the history of all minds in the Bible. There are some of David's Psalms which express the depths of religious misery. Even he who lived the sinless Life felt the last shadow of loneliness pass over him when he said 'My God, my God, why hast Thou forsaken me?' It is the law of God. Night before Light. The knowledge of evil before the knowledge of positive good. As we grow older we shall grow more sure of God. Experience will teach us that we have conquered through Him, but in the first growth of a Christian life the contests are too frequent, the battles are not always victorious; we have not yet become strong in the power of self-submission, and the depression and sorrow, and feeling that all is lost are more vivid, because our joy before was so fresh and like a youth; for let us feel as old as we like, we have not the placidity and calmness of temperament like that we arrive at in age; there may be outward and apparent calm, but down beneath there are floods enough for a deluge."

The extracts below are from a lecture given to young men in 1857. Though written two years later, they doubtless tell us of ideas thought out and habits formed during the period to which this chapter refers.

MENTAL CULTURE.

"The first law of *Mental Culture* then is *Order*. To be able to refer each thought to some first principle, and so to make it a living part of a living whole. That, and that alone, makes reading, thinking and existence useful.

"The second law of Mental Culture is Attention—attention literally means stretching or straining at a certain object. As a man strains every muscle to reach the summit of a rocky mountain undeterred by weariness, unconquered by obstacles—longing with his soul to see the wide magnificence of the landscape which the topmost peak commands; so must we stretch every mental energy if we would win the heights of knowledge. Hard work, severe exertion, dauntless energy—these alone will vanquish the fortress of knowledge.

"The third law of Mental Culture is *Faith*. As in religion, so in the discovery of truth. Faith is the conquering principle. Believe in yourself and believe in your object, and you must attain it. Columbus believed in a New World. He had faith in himself, and lo a continent was given to him. Napoleon believed in his men, and Europe lay at his feet. Robespierre believed what he said, and France took fire at his words.

"And the fourth law is *Love*. If you cultivate your mind—if you follow hard after knowledge from low motives alone—to get on in life—to win fame—to gain riches—to have power over others which you may use for selfish ends alone—all the joy and elevating strength of knowledge will rot within your grasp—you will die a disappointed, hopeless, dissatisfied man. But if you desire knowledge for its own sake, if you would win it because you love it, then your mistress will open to you all her pleasures, all her stores, and so far as earthly knowledge blesses, you will be blessed. These Four then, Order, Attention, Faith, and Love are the genii who guard the temple of Mental Power. Win them, make them your constant attendants, and the massive gates of the vast hall where Plato, Bacon and Newton sit side by side with Homer and Shakespeare and Dante, the thinkers and the poets, will unfold their values to you.

". . . Observe the connection of all things. To be able to do this—to see the links which bind all things in the Universe to one another, and those in turn to man—that constitutes more or less the foundation of the imaginative and poetic faculty, and the more you train yourself to watch for and grasp the several affinities of things, the more you will cultivate and strengthen that imaginative power which is the mother of all genius; and more than that, the more you know of the wondrous connection between all things in Nature—the firmer will be your belief in the Unity of God.

"Still more it strengthens the imaginative power, for it binds the world into one; so that the Poet looking on a tree or cloud sees it—not as it is only in itself—but as it is in connection with all Nature and all Life—it suggests to him a thousand things and images.

"And again it strengthens belief in the Unity of God —for it makes manifest one lawgiver in all things. I observe a waterfall flashing downwards, and the planets moving onwards shepherded by the sun, and a stone thrown by a boy fall to the ground. At first these ideas remain isolated, soon afterwards I hear of gravitation, and find that the water drops, the stone falls, and the planets circle by the power of one Law. Instead then of holding three thoughts, I hold *one*—and one which I can apply to all the world. Instead of seeing each separately, I see them now connected, related to each other because they are joined to and obedient to one Law. Thus my mind is not only impressed with the religious sense of the Unity of God—but I am also led to generalize my conceptions—to range a number of floating thoughts and faculties and facts under one head, and their power, to which we are led by observation of nature, is the mark of a well-cultured, full-grown and expanded mind.

". . . Finally, the second mark of a well-cultivated mind is *aspiration*. Aspire always to new knowledge, to higher beauty. Never be satisfied with what you have gained. Press onward always to where the sunny summit shines. Seek to know something of the divine current of the Mind, that high proof of our immortal nature; live like the eagle—ever soaring to the sun. We live in the foremost files of time, advance, advance.

"But while I urge you to aspiration after knowledge and feeling, remember over that this aspiration dies with you—is practically useless unless it be connected with the highest aim of man. What is your knowledge at death but dust—without the certainty of Immortal Life before you? Therefore aspire above all things to the knowledge of God in Christ, to that knowledge which is gained by love to Him who died to redeem body, soul and spirit."

CHAPTER V

TO LONDON

"H. stood a long time looking out from the pier-head alone to sea in the silence of prophesying youth. So sometimes I used to stand in ancient days, but usually at night when I could see the stars. By day, the present was too much with me to admit care for the future. But nothing that I prophesied then even faintly resembled what has been. There is that beyond which shapes our ends to a goal we do not see in youth."—(*Diary*, January 14, 1902.)

In July, 1856, "Stopford," according to Mrs Brooke's diary, "got in College a £20 prize for an essay on the Sabbath." With the money thus obtained he characteristically resolved to give himself a holiday among the mountains of Scotland, a kind of "Sabbath" to which he always attached importance, though I doubt if the £20 had been awarded him for saying so. No time was lost. A scrap of paper in his handwriting, dated July 26th, informs us that he is at the "top of the mountain in view of Loch Vennachar—Ben Ledi, Glenfinlas, a fresh breeze blowing, and the hill-side full of sheep." Of this tour he wrote fifty years afterwards, "the first expedition I made after I was twenty-one was made with my brother (William) to Loch Katrine and the Trossachs, to Glenfinlas and Stirling, and it was one long ravishment, nor did I enjoy Wordsworth, who was then my companion, the less, but the more because I was living every step of the way with Scott."[1] It was then, too,

[1] "Studies in Poetry," p. 58.

that he renewed his acquaintance with Miss Campbell, a lady with whom he found, both then and for many years to come, a peculiar facility in opening his mind on religious questions; his letters to her being, in fact, one of our chief sources of information for the movement of his thought at this period.

Returned to Kingstown we find him hard at work on the Kingsley article, and on other literary efforts, by which cash, much needed at the time, was to be earned. He is also preparing for ordination, studying Burnet on the Thirty Nine Articles and *id omne genus*—with no great enthusiasm. But above all, he is now in contact with Goethe—reading G. H. Lewes' "Life" and then launching into the works of the poet himself. "My mind is overflowing with this man," he writes in one of his letters. "I cannot get him out of my thoughts "— with what result to his studies of Burnet we may imagine.

From a small diary of this period I gather that he was then in the habit of making "vows" to himself, the nature of which is not indicated. A story which reaches me from another source, however, throws some light on one of them. The incident already related of the discussion about the "ideal apple dumpling" reveals what we might expect, that these lively young Irishmen spent a good deal of their time in light and airy conversation. A "vow" therefore had to be registered with a view to checking this waste of time, regarded as flagitious in view of coming responsibilities. This was accordingly done. The "ideal apple dumpling" is now laid aside and Tennyson's "In Memoriam" takes its place. Stopford and William resolve that they will study that poem to its innermost depths and talk of nothing else till they have mastered everything it contains! "What those two brothers knew," writes one who has a claim to speak, "I can tell you they knew *well*." Behold them as they are sketched by my informant. The scene is the kitchen of their father's house in Adelaide Street, Kingstown—the kitchen, because smoking was forbidden in the more exalted apartments. The time is the small hours of the morning. The fire has gone out in the grate and the cockroaches are swarming over the floor. But a certain canto has to be finished that night, for the "vow" has so determined; and it happens that this particular canto is provocative of argument—and of theological argument too, in which William's "logic" and Stopford's "liberalism" are at war. In this manner the vow is kept, and the foundations laid for the work of the coming years.

Among the stray anecdotes from these times, all authentically written down by a careful hand, is one which shows him in the attitude of theological recoil. His father had a curate, a redoubtable Calvinist, who held a weekly class for the exposition of the Scriptures, attended by the two brothers. On a certain occasion this gentleman, expounding his text, declared it clearly proved that God "made free choice of who should be heirs of salvation, irrespective of personal merit or demerit." So he went on for some time when suddenly "Stopford standing up in wrath called out 'Mr. —— if your views are true, I'd rather be a dog or a cow, than a man!'" So impressed was the instructor by the flaming countenance of his pupil that he never alluded to the subject again.

By the summer of '56, the question of his future career, never very doubtful, had got itself finally settled, and the only point still to be debated was—where to begin? From many indications it is evident that he was eager for a wider field than that afforded by the

Irish Church as it was in those days; nor were there wanting influential friends to help in these designs. In the autumn of that year he paid another visit to the Fitzpatricks, a family of wide interests, extensive social connections in London, and many friendships with artists and men of letters. It is reasonable to suppose that on the occasion of this visit prospects were discussed and a line of action decided on which would launch him in London society, give him contact with the great world and place him where a talented man with a love of freedom would have a chance of making his mark. This visit to the Fitzpatricks was the occasion, already mentioned, on which he first saw his future wife, Emma Beaumont, whose home was in London; and perhaps we shall not greatly err in assuming that this had something to do in sealing the decision to make London the scene of his labours. Visiting Abbeyleix twelve years later he thus records his memory of their first meeting in a letter to his wife.

"All along my drive in from Roscrea Junction yesterday I thought of our first meeting here and went over the vision on the platform, my journey on the box-seat, little dreaming then that my fate was within, the evening talk over the tea in the little boudoir, Lady —— displaying her grace upon the sofa, your appearance as dressed for dinner in a quaint dress, with lappets on the skirt; my trial talk with you at dinner (I used then to pose every woman I met with a set of carefully prepared questions); and then the after days—my regret when you left and my wonder as to why you left; for you gave yourself out as ill, and you looked remarkably well; our parting at the station. . . . Dear me! how short a time it seems. Happiness makes life brief, sorrow long. You have been very good to me. . . ."

Yes, he would seek ordination in London and take a

preparations for that event more Burnet and less Goethe. On February 27, 1867, Mrs. Brooke records "Dear B. left for London preparatory to a final leave. How we shall miss him!"

Some interesting glimpses of the man as he was at this turning point of life are afforded by the notes in a diary which he kept during the weeks preceding his departure for London.

January 1. "Went up to my sisters' room. Read them In Memoriam, XV. and XVI. of St. John, and prayed. Went into kitchen, smoked and read. . . . Bed 3.30. . . . I can do all things through Christ who strengtheneth me. Brady gave me books to review . . . "O God, I could be bounded in a nutshell, and count myself king of infinite space but that I have had dreams."

Jan. 3 "Left for Rockheld a cold impressive drive. Read 'Vicarious Suffering,' and (word illegible) on Job. Read 'Memories of a Detective.' . . . Wrote to Adelaide."

Jan. 4. "At Church heard V. preach. These sermons on the wickedness of our nature make us very *hard*. Is it fighting against truth, or only the natural rejection of a half truth and the uneasy feeling consequent on not hearing the *whole* of anything? Read on the Loneliness of Christ The tact of love is to *think*, in order that you may say nothing that may *offend*. . . ."

Jan. 6. "Read Tennyson (Love and Duty), Grimm, Robertson. Wrote at review ('Memories of a Detective')."

Jan. 11. "A little tiff with O. Books to read, McClure's N.W. Passage; Anderson's Lake Ngami; Harry Coverdale's Courtship. Looked at Lavater. Greatly charmed with Goethe's Essays on Art, yet there is something frigidly intellectual and real in his writings. They are devoid of *warmth*"

Jan. 14. "Wrote to [half a dozen lady friends,]

Read the Administration of Alva. Began Shakespeare's Sonnets."

Jan. 15. "On Pier. Reading Fichte's Characteristics of the Present Age. Borrowed Herder's Werke."

Jan. 17. "Read Fichte. Lee on Inspiration. Essays on Art. Neander. Martineau."

Jan. 18. "Drove down in the night, raining and very dark, to Bray. Mrs. O. had died suddenly: sat up all night with O. O. calm: read him the Psalms. All this time greatly struck with the thorough truth to Nature of In Memoriam."

Jan. 22. "Our Society [a literary Society founded by the brothers Brooke] in evening: Chatterton. Get Niebuhr's Letters."

Feb. 3. "Dined with the Fitzpatricks. Read Phaethon: MacIvor's Pamphlet of National Board: Darnley: Martineau; Alford. Wrote 'Beauty and the Beast' (a moral story, founded on the legend)."

Feb. 9. "[List of debts amounting to £5 19s. 3d.] I make a vow to pay all this with money for my review. Am reading Schiller's Aesthetic Education; Humboldt's Travels. Glanced at Margaret Catchpole. Berkeley's Hylas. Iphigenia. Alford. Robertson. Bougéaut."

Feb. 15. "Reading H. on Justification. Kingsley's Two Years Ago—judgment and impulse-giving."

Feb. 21. "To Uncle William's—smoked in bedroom—which fatally ended."

Feb. 22. "Spoken to about smoking: very shocking! Reading the Prelude. 'The Angel in the House.' Livingstone's Travels."

Feb. 27. "Started by 2 o'clock boat to London. Very wearisome journey all night."

The first visit to London, primarily undertaken to see the Bishop, appears to have had some connexion with one of the most interesting events in Brooke's career—his writing the Life of F. W. Robertson. We learn from the diary that while in London he twice went to see Mr Henry King,[1] who subsequently published the

[1] Afterwards a member of the firm of Smith, Elder & Co.

Life, and that he spent a night at Mr King's private residence in the country.

There appears to have been some difficulty in finding a biographer for Robertson. In the interests of the Broad Church party, then in the throes of its early struggles, it was important that the Life should be written by a highly competent, trusted and judicious hand. Robertson had died in '53, and the pressing question was still undecided in '57. The Robertson letters, without which the biography could not be written, were mostly in the hands of a few persons who would naturally claim a voice, perhaps a directing voice, in the selection of the biographer. These persons, as it happened, had formed a high opinion of the literary and other gifts of the young Stopford Brooke.

On August 8, 1857, he writes in one of his letters:

"I will write Mr Robertson's Life some time. But it will not be for some years—perhaps in two. In the meantime, if you can pick up any anecdotes of him—even of the slightest character—they will be most useful to me—what was thought and said of him, what he did, how he walked and dressed and looked, where he walked most—anything—how he spoke, how he looked in the pulpit."

Viewed from the inside the selection of Brooke as Robertson's biographer is deeply interesting for the measure it gives of the man as he was at this period. It proves that his abilities were known to an inner circle long before they were known to the world. It suggests, moreover, that this inner circle was of sufficient weight and influence to carry their wishes with men of the world like Mr Henry King, and with a judge on higher matters like A. P. Stanley. As I have said, great interests were known to be at stake in the Life of Robertson; the whole status of the Broad Church party was in question. Is it not, therefore, astounding that a task on which all this depended should be entrusted to an Irishman fresh from College, only twenty-four years of age, who as yet had made for himself no literary mark, and was entirely unknown either to the world in general or the Broad Church party in particular—a man, moreover, who had never once heard Robertson preach. Thirty years later there was no name in the religious world of London better known than that of Stopford Brooke. In 1857 he was unheard of. The decision which made him Robertson's biographer would therefore be unintelligible but for the circumstances to which I have alluded. It was a venture of faith in those who so determined, and a greater venture in him, which the result amply justified. It bears witness to his courage, to his power of facing a great responsibility. It enforces the cry which was constantly on his lips throughout life—"attempt the impossible if you would succeed."

Arrived in London he went sightseeing as any countryman would do. Among other things he came across the Duke of Wellington's funeral car, which gave him occasion for a characteristic outburst against Mid-Victorian vulgarity and English vulgarity in general: " a fine concern for the undertakers: how much better to bury the old veteran with his martial cloak around him. But these English! tied to the chariot of solid wealth. They do not pride themselves on gorgeous parade, as the French, but are more hopelessly the victims of outward things. Not theirs to 'wear beauty lightly, like a flower!'" Then he goes to hear Lord Palmerston—not greatly impressed! Also he hears the Bishop (Tait) preach in St. James', Piccadilly: "a tall,

BROOKE IN 1857.

large man, with strong Scotch features; a fine deeply curved mouth; a forehead rather wide than high. A strong very simple sermon, remarkable for no ideality, with a style which was good but not finished flowingly. He did not seem to have a correct ear for rhythm." Then to the National Gallery. "Saw the Turners! This man Turner"—he is writing to his brother William —"*haunts me.* What cloud effects! What seas! What rocks and trees! It is the very core of Nature's heart. . . . But it is two o'clock and I must go to bed." Next day "Henry King gave me Ruskin's Notes on Turner."

Between times he flies about with letters of introduction in his pocket—to the Bishop—that the episcopal eye may survey him, for he is not yet ordained—to King, as we have seen, to various persons of importance on an errand of which the sum and substance seems to be this: "Can you help me to get a curacy in London?" One crowded day ends in a jolly dinner in the Euston Hotel with a Kingstown friend accidentally encountered—"one of the bhoys," that same O. in fact to whom he read the Psalms at Bray, now wonderfully recovered from the late decease of his wife. "O. kept us in roars of laughter with a multitude of stories. You know the way he opens the first parallel of an acquaintance—with a set of anecdotes which like pick-axes break open the ground of reserve. A good plan after all. For if you have had a hearty laugh with a man you generally are friends with him." This was on Sunday evening, after the Bishop in the morning, and the Irvingite Church in the afternoon. Another dash to see pictures—the Vernon Gallery—that solitary Tintoret in the National Gallery —those two Turners, "Dido building Carthage, Sun rising in a fog—oh!" and then back to Kingstown, the curate business well afoot, the Bishop favourably disposed, Mr King duly interested and impressed, Turner still haunting him, a string of O.'s stories for the receptive ear of brother William, and pockets well stuffed with his favourite remedy for sea-sickness—cigars. To all of which the diary bears witness in detail, not omitting the pounds, shillings and pence, so that a meticulous biographer might even calculate the amount of tobacco purchased before embarking. And to this there is added a note "that he must read forthwith Butler's Sermons, the Espousals, and Stanley's Sinai and Palestine." Whence we may infer that a ship of many cargoes is already under way.

"London," he writes to a friend on his return, "made a great impression on me. The masses of humanity which surge there so unceasingly both weigh with an awful burden on the heart and excite the spirits. I can scarcely fancy any one in London being *ennuyé*. And if ennui does come on it is only of that self-imposed kind which the Frenchman spoke of as 'm'ennuyant pour me désennuyer'"—an opinion greatly altered later on.

The two months which followed were spent in Kingstown. They were crowded with work, excitement, life; various reviews for the University Magazine, essays on "The True Greatness" and on "Prayer": multifarious and apparently furious reading, Ruskin's "Modern Painters," Olshausen's "St John," "Maud" ("*accuraté*"), Fougé, Kane's "Arctic Explorations," Alford's "Greek Testament"—and what not; anxieties about the London negotiations and sudden development of the same; meetings of the Student Society, and speeches on Buonamico Buffelmacco, on Music, on the Difference between Sexes in Nature; visits, dinner parties, excursions; meetings with O. and other genial souls; experiments in mesmerism with disastrous results and forswearings of such things for ever and ever—a "vow" never broken; and in addition to all this an ever-increasing number of fair friends eager to place their souls under his direction and to guide their lives by any word he has said or written, whether on Prayer, the Sabbath, True Greatness, Buonamico Buffelmacco—or anything else. A current of high seriousness carries the stream along; there are also ripples of laughter, jests, high spirits, energy, joy, and a sound of the rushing waters of life.

As one reads the diary of this period a sense of confusion arises, and we begin to ask what will he make of it all and where will he come out. But looking nearer and reading between the lines we see him following his star, though cross-currents are undoubtedly at work, and there are embarrassments—of various kinds. But neither then nor afterwards did he ever dance attendance on his difficulties, or wait for embarrassments to overwhelm him. While the net is being spread that might entangle him he is off and away, outpacing the laggard feet of "captor circumstance." He has begun his life, and at no snail's pace. Presently the pace will increase, and for a few months become so swift that the eye can hardly follow its course.

"May 6th is 'a splendid day. There are nineteen of us at the Dargle, a picnic, with lots of Wordsworth and a political row about Lord Palmerston.'"

Next day two curacies in London are offered him simultaneously. So off he goes to Monkstown, not to select the curacy but "to collect sea-anemones with Minchin." The sea-anemones disposed of, he writes an acceptance of Dr Spencer's curacy at St Matthew's, Marylebone, at a salary of £60 a year. A vow is promptly registered, this time against vanity—on £60 a year!—with a Latin prayer appended. A mass of correspondence is then polished off, and the soul problems of various correspondents dismissed with hasty solutions. Finishing touches are given to the article on Kingsley, farewells distributed, his Bible class finally admonished, "ten pounds borrowed from the Governor"—and he is off to London for good and all.

Mrs Brooke writes in her diary: "May 24. Oh! how sad I felt at the Sunday School, looking at my dear, dear first-born, standing in his accustomed place, one of his scholars weeping behind him, and thinking how soon that spot may know him no more."

A large number of letters written immediately before, and after, his ordination in June, 1857, have been preserved. Brief extracts will be enough to illustrate the lines on which his mind was moving.

"January 17, 1857.

... "You 'must move on.' There is a terrible meaning in that common term—no place, no room in this wide world for the loiterer or the sleeper, or him who stops to rest. How often have we wished for a moment's respite. Not to *feel*, or *be*, or do for a day or so, that we may not be so overwhelmed. Now I say there is but one remedy for this Life Weariness and that is Love. Be loving, and the mystery of Life is solved. . . .

"The dogmas laid down about Assurance are true, only in a one-sided manner; these men wrapt up in their own experience argue from their own to the experience of all. Many a Christian of a joyous temperament feels assured of God's love all his life; there are others by whom the Love of God which embraced them all their lives is not felt till the very heart of Heaven opens to receive them. Like Hezekiah, they walked softly all their days in the bitterness of their soul.

Prayer is the act of communion with God, not so much petition. In it God reveals his Love and Peace to us. As I once told you Prayer is not to change the Will of God, but to change our will into His. It is at our peril we change the prayer 'not as I will, but as Thou wilt' into ' not as *Thou* wilt, but as *I* will.' The answer is not removal but strength, not changing of God's will, but changing of ours. . . .

"It is not in 'main points' that character lies. Many have the same, but it is the *peculiar* way each one develops these. It is in the multifarious details which all bear the stamp of the inward spirit, and not only that but of the individual physical constitution, that the distinctive features of a character lie, and it is in the acquaintance with these, and in seeing how they unite with the main principles of the character, *i.e.* in understanding the person as *a whole*, that the charm of sympathy lies. So that to the friend you are not one thing to-day, another to-morrow, but always the same, though differently worked out, as in the varied views of the Kaleidoscope the glass bits are still the same, yet never the same apparently. . . .

"Why cannot men write like 'Hohenlinden,' or 'Scots wha hae'? A good war song should stir the blood like music. The L. C. Charge is Tennyson all over, so thoroughly plain are the marks of labour; such a specimen of the careful careless I do not think I have ever read. You see how he has elaborated every line like a Dutch painter, and yet the effect is swiftness. It gives you the idea of the speed of the charge, the rapid onset and slaughter, and the quick retreat, you feel yourself dashing along with the six hundred, and yet when you have finished you cannot help thinking of Tennyson sitting in his room, correcting and abridging with the birds singing in at his windows. It is wonderful the labour that man spends on his poetry, when we think him most careless he is often most laborious. There are numberless instances of this in 'In Memoriam.'"

BOOK II

CURATE: CHAPLAIN: BIOGRAPHER

CHAPTER VI

FIRST CURACY: MARRIAGE

"I went up Baker Street to Regent's Park, crossing the bridge near Hanover Gate, over which forty years ago, when I was curate at St Matthew's, I used to walk so often when the autumn sun was setting, after a stormy season, when I was out every night. How many seas have I sailed on since, and how many islands have I visited, nor do I care now to look back. Yet the little wooden bridge and the iron network, and the sluggish stream spoke like music on the waters."
—(*Diary*, October 27, 1898.)

BROOKE is now entering upon his career in London, where, for fifty years, his part is to be that of the poet-prophet. At one step he passes from restricted opportunities into contact with the main currents of the world. It is a great and sudden change; but he is not unprepared. Let us glance at the lights that are guiding him.

James Martineau once said of him that "he never grew up," on which Brooke remarked, when the saying was repeated to him, "that is the finest compliment I have ever received." The saying of Martineau is true in the sense that Brooke's intellect never developed the kind of activity which stifles the spirit of youth. In another sense he was "grown up" at twenty-five, as few men are at that age. From the letters and extracts already given it is clear that he had found the angle of vision from which he was to interpret the nature of Christ, and had formed his ideal of the Kingdom of God as founded on social justice and kindness between man and man. He had also committed himself to the way of the poets in the search for truth, his will to follow it was resolute, his emotions were high and impassioned, and his imagination enriched by a wide knowledge of literature. In short, to use an expression of which he was fond, he had "gravitated to his centre." From that point indeed he grew up as few men have done; but not by outliving the insights of his youth. Of Brooke it may be said, with a literal truth that is seldom applicable, that he was "rooted and grounded in love"—a condition full of promise, and admitting of confident prediction on certain lines; but fraught also with unknown possibilities.

At the age of twenty-four it had been revealed to him that Nature is one Being, the expression of a single mind, and the intimate companion of the awakened soul. With Nature thus conceived and loved he had begun to hold the communion which is the life of poetry and of all the arts. He was one of those who make this discovery early and with ease, and enjoy its fruits with abiding happiness. He could have made it for himself, but the poets had aided him—Wordsworth, Coleridge, Shelley, Tennyson, Goethe—and he had already learnt to give expression to his insight in verse. This fellowship with Nature was destined to furnish his life with a master impulse, to give form to his thought, to quicken him into constant self-expression and to be a light of his seeing to the end. With this, as the main factor in his spiritual equipment, he entered upon the work of a London curate.

He brought with him also a theology which had a different basis—a theology firm as to its centre, for it was founded on the love of Christ, but fluid towards the circumference. In essence it was the theology of Kingsley, but kindled with an evangelical fervour, which he owed to his early training and to his father. It had yet to be brought into harmony with his master insight, and in the process of accomplishing this it was destined to be greatly transformed. The process lasted many years.

Both of these guiding lights shall be described in his own words. What nature meant to him, what she had meant to him all his life, he wrote down more than forty years afterwards in his diary. What his theology was when he began his work shall be indicated by a passage from his first sermon, preached in St Matthew's Church on June 10, 1857, three days after his ordination by the Bishop of London.

The two passages are widely sundered in the dates at which they were written, and, as we might expect, there is a striking contrast between them. Both sides of the contrast were present and active in the mind of Brooke when he began the work of the Christian ministry.

The passage from the diary (January 31 and February 2, 1899) runs as follows:—

"I never humanize Nature; I don't care to illustrate my own woes and joys by her, or to get her to sympathize with me. I've no selfish fancies about her. On the contrary, I lose myself in her beauty, when it is really fine beauty. But she varies just as much as humanity, though she has nothing to do with humanity; and she is often ugly and disagreeable and ill-conditioned, and always without any love for me or anyone.

Separate from us altogether, and with no pre-established harmony between her and us, as Wordsworth tried to assert. When I use in describing her the 'pathetic fallacy' as Ruskin called it, and say that the wave runs lazily up the strand or that the trees are whispering, I know that I am only explaining my own mood, not explaining her. She obeys law and does what she *must* do. I do not.

"But I do see in her Order and Splendour and Beauty—the Order, Splendour, Beauty of a part, a hundred-million-millionth part, of the Infinite Thought of God, expressing himself in a musical joy, which elsewhere or in the end resolves all that seems to me ugly and ill-conditioned—even criminal in her—into Absolute Loveliness. Therefore, though all my life I have loved Nature, even more than Humanity, were it not for duty, and though I have mingled her with every vein of my life, I am never in danger of being content with her, but hungry for more, for the infinite infinitude of which she supplies me with but a film, a scrap, a grain—enough to wake but not to satisfy the thirst for her kind of beauty.

"I'm not sure, after all I have written about Nature and the Poets whether what Mr Squeers says, speaking of human nature, may not be the best and wisest thing to be said about Nature outside of us. 'She's a rum 'un, is Nature!' Face to face with that undesirable truth, so universal in its application, all my fine spun theories seem wind and froth. But then the theories I put forth [in my lectures] are not mine, but those of the poets. My own is very simple, clear, workable, and it enables me to get every grain of joy out of Nature that she is capable of affording me. And, by Zeus, I do get joy out of her!"

A Passage from his First Sermon

"It is the strange truth of Christian life, that by helping others to bear their burdens we not only lighten them, but also our own. Sympathise and assist truly one human brother, and you will find your own sorrow inexpressibly relieved, for we forget ourselves and our tears, in the wish to give comfort to another—but if you hug yourself in your grief, and shut yourself out from this living human world, gnawing your own heart, every hour the torture and the weight increases, and you end in becoming either hardened, or despairing. But the true way is to go forth and pour what sunshine you can on the lives of others.

"To make the Christian life easy then we require two things. A love for Christ, and a love for others.

"Secondly remark—That we must, if we wish to live the Christian life get hold of principles, true motives to act from, not mere feeling which by itself is worth little or not. For he is not necessarily a Christian who acts on impulse. To do good to another, only because our feelings are excited, and our sensibility is aroused is not necessarily a Christian act. For the feeling perishes as quickly as it is excited.

"We are Christians when we act from an abiding and eternal Principle. We do good to our fellow men, not from excitement of feeling, but from a deep-seated belief that because He laid down His life for us, we ought also to lay down our life for the brethren.

"And what was St John's principle? It is shown us in the last word of my text—'Brethren.'

"He believed that all men were his brothers. Christ came to reveal the Fatherhood of God, and the Sonship of all men; and if we are all sons in him, we are all brothers one to another. There is no difference for we are all *one* in Christ Jesus.

"That was St John's principle. God has loved us all as sons, we should love one another as brothers.

"To do that is to know God, and to know God is to know Love, for God is Love."

Such was his essential equipment. The scene of Brooke's first labours as a clergyman was better adapted to the theological part of it than to the poetic. St Matthew's, Marylebone, was in the midst of a congested population living in sordid streets, which might well suggest the need of a Saviour for mankind and of a social redemption to continue the Saviour's work. But it was a hard place for a poet. It was here that he received the impression, never effaced, of the horror which broods over the life of great cities. Later on he described them as "festering sores, eating into the body of humanity." "Especially for the poor," he wrote in 1899, "there is no torture of all the past history so terrible as life in great towns, and in London the greatest of them all." That, in part, was a reminiscence of '57.

Dismal and depressing indeed was the parish into which there entered, in the early summer of that year, the apparition of this ardent young Irishman, with the love of Nature stirring his soul, exuberant in spirit, affluent in imagery, brilliant in conversation, impatient of control, announcing by his presence that no conventions could hold him, a radiant, athletic, powerful figure of a man, very comely to look on. In a letter to his brother William he has incidentally recorded an impression, the naïveté of which is worth many laboured descriptions of his person. One day, soon after his arrival in London, a poor woman from the congregation paused in front of him, and, after looking him up and down for some time, said in a tone of amazement, "My word! You *are* a strapper!"

To him fall the duties, and the reward, of a poor curate in the London slums; prayer-meetings, mothers' meetings, Bible classes, visitations, distribution of soup and blankets, and an occasional sermon to a congregation mainly composed of old women in quest of charity—and £60 a year. All which is seriously undertaken and with the ardour he was incapable of withholding from anything he undertook. A life ill-matched indeed with the man who is living it, and within which it is clearly impossible that his energies should be confined. Hard work enough in the courts and alleys of Lisson Grove. There is many a day when he is "dog tired" with that alone, and "oh, for the blue hills, and the rushing waters, and the sunlight of Killiney"—so lately left, so fondly remembered.

But that is not all. He has other friends who have soup and blankets enough and to spare; and other haunts where the door is opened to him, not by "the woman with cancer" but by a tall gentleman in livery. Of the Irish gentry not a few have great houses in London, where the walls are hung with Giorgiones and "magnificent Sir Joshuas," and where bright eyes grow brighter when the doors are flung back, and "Mr Stopford Brooke" announced. Among these is the house of Mrs Fitzpatrick, his intimate friend and counsellor. Along with the entries in the diary about Lisson Grove and the mothers' meetings mention is made, almost daily, of Piccadilly, of Grosvenor Place, of Portman Square, of meetings with Ministers of State, Ambassadors, artists, men of letters—and of other meetings too, "on a balcony, overlooking the Green Park," when "Maud" is quoted under the moon. I perceive very clearly, from this diary, that Brooke has become a welcome presence in a brilliant coterie. And among the many bright eyes that await him there I can watch one pair growing brighter and brighter. Clearly great matters are afoot, and things are hastening to a crisis.

It was the *annus mirabilis* of his life. The months, from June to December, were a maelstrom—impossible to any man not possessed of enormous vitality. Things and forces not naturally assimilable were clashing together and driving him onwards, and calling for reconciliation. By day he was working among the poor; at night he was entertained among the rich.

"Bible class in afternoon. In evening met Ristori, Blumenthal." "Called on widows . . . went to Lord Bute's Gallery. Called on . . ., sat two hours. Asked definitely to write Robertson's Life and edit his letters." "Met Stanley, Kinglake, Owen Meredith, Lady Palmerston—also a stream of geese . . . writing my sermon till past four in the morning. . . . Clean done up." "Went to the Crystal Palace with . . . What a dream of beauty that place is! Shall I ever forget it!" "Went down to Woolwich and studied the new plan of sewage for London—the pipes laid down by the side of the river." "Went to Grosvenor Place and saw the Rosa Bonheurs. Preached (Wednesday evening) on Miraculous Draught of Fishes. Read on the Hindu Drama and Theology in Germany." "At the Trovatore. Heard Mario. *Voce divina!*" "Finished Charlotte Brontë's Life and Jane Eyre." "Went to the Crystal Palace and read Wordsworth to E." "Life seems so fresh to me! strange, when I thought all dead." "To Lord Lansdowne's to see Ristori's portrait by Watts. Heard Gabriel play. She is the Devil!" "Again to the Crystal Palace with E. B. We sat among the Preadamites—lost!" "Read Childe Harold at Grosvenor Place. Lectured on Pharisee and Publican. Gave E. B. 'Maud' to read." "S. talked to me of all things new and old, confidentially—like Wise Annie—a pretty puzzle it was." "Went to Folkestone—asked to France. What a bore I can't go!"

A strangely perplexing environment for a young man of twenty-four just launched on the career of a clergyman. The wonder is that throughout it all he kept a firm hold on the thread of his life and never lost sight of his aim. He reads hard—"reads as much in one hour as most men get through in five"; studies the Broad Church movement in being and whatever of

Broad Church theology was then accessible; plans out the Robertson biography; gives increasing care to his sermons, and sends them for William to criticize; takes a lectureship of English in Queen's College, Harley Street; writes incessantly to his mother, sisters and brothers; keeps up correspondence with the troubled souls of the Kingstown period; visits the sick, reproaching himself bitterly when by chance he came too late to comfort a dying man. He was seldom in bed before four in the morning, and sometimes never went to bed at all. "I wish I could dispense with sleep altogether," he wrote. It was a time of fire, movement, passion, work and adventure, all intense; and the strain, physical, mental, emotional, moral, must have been very great.

I have spoken before of the double nature in Stopford Brooke. At a time of life when both natures were quick with the idealisms of youth he was suddenly plunged into London society at its two extremes—Lisson Grove and Piccadilly. At the one extreme he was in daily contact with the misery, filth and vice of the great city, fighting them with such weapons as came to his hand, himself living in mean lodgings and on hard fare. At the other extreme he was "a portent of the drawing-room" of a type unknown to the most experienced, provoking wonder, prophecy, emotion; a "sculptor's model," with an "attitude" that was remarked and remembered; but vehement and explosive as no "model" should be, whose voice might be heard above the babble — "we must have more joy in life — I say, more joy!"—to the amazement of dowagers and the delight of more impressionable souls. Meanwhile he is interested in another "society," of which there is little prefigurement either at Lisson Grove or Piccadilly —the Kingdom of Heaven! Of this he preaches once or twice a week, preaches with fervour, "not choosing any existing ideas of the Kingdom, but on the contrary proclaiming his own ideas of it"—coldly watched meanwhile by an unsympathetic vicar who is afraid of him. And often his thoughts fly back to Ireland, and to his brother William; would rather talk to William "than to any of these people"; recalls familiar scenes and faces; and a great home-sickness comes over him.

Thus Brooke was living two lives—or was it three—related to one another by contrast, or not related at all; and he was living intensely in each. He was making experiments in many directions, or perhaps was being led into making them by some directing genius which teaches men wisdom in that way. It is idle to speak of unity at such a moment. Unity there was none, but division, and the sundered elements were such that no "logic of the inner life" nor any other "logic" could combine them. An *event* was needed to cut the knot of these bewilderments. It came swiftly, and came in time.

Woven in with the perplexity of his circumstances there was the peculiarity of his temperament—eager in action but with a reserve of its own. He was at this time (and always) subject to violent affinities and repulsions, and wherever affinity existed he had the gift of reading the mind of another in a flash. This was the root of his power as a physician of souls. It opened the way for his sympathies, which were instantly given at the first sign of an appeal. Those who won his friendship won it all at once, and seemed to know him after an hour's interview as if they had known him all their lives. And yet sympathy with him was not spontaneous; it waited for the first approach to come from the other side. Now men do not make such approaches, at least not easily, fearing repulse. But women are more discerning; the temperament I am describing being one which they understand and, by understanding, inspire. Of such inspirations a man needs but one. The nature of Brooke exposed him to many. It is indeed the woman's own nature, of which all men partake in some measure—for are they not the sons of their mothers?—but of which he had a larger share than most.

He abhorred hesitation. To linger in the midst of confusion, to wait while opposing currents struck their own balance, to sit still in the vain hope that problems would resolve themselves—this was never his way. These conditions, which reduce weak natures to paralysis, were those in which his individuality asserted itself most promptly, dividing the darkness before him by the light of his intuitions and the swift impetus of his will. He would never court defeat by delaying a crisis, when once he was convinced that the crisis was inevitable. Hence his rapidity in love, as in all else. He was out of confusion in a flash; and a great calm, essential for his ripening powers, sank down on the tumult of his life. Many wondered, and some wept, but he himself wrote joyously in his diary "I have cut the knot!" It was a knot of many strands in which Lisson Grove, Piccadilly, and the Kingdom of Heaven were all entangled—and by cutting through it he came to himself and to the work of his life.

A few days after "the knot had been cut" he wrote to a friend :—

"Why should we 'stagnate in the weeds of sloth'? That is the fate in the end of all who fix themselves in the present enjoyment, and will not seek for something beyond their own circle, socially or religiously. Stagnation! So ended the Greek. All that beautiful life

EMMA BEAUMONT

gnawed into its own heart and died of atrophy. I know one of the cliques in Dublin, five families who are all clever. Content with themselves they revolve year after year within themselves, and the consequence is that they are now badly dressed, degenerating into vulgarity, with all their ideas contracted, home-spun, and intolerant of every subject which does not chime in with their peculiar craze. So it is too in religious sects and in religion itself. Give me 'the voluntary exile' and the pang, and let me open my leaves and develop the flower. True, it is sometimes painful, but we enter on all life with Pain. There is a water flower which is bound by a root to the bottom of the pool, and no doubt is very contented with its glassy existence there, but the time comes and the tendril snaps with a crack, the plant shudders, but the bud rises rapidly to the surface and in an hour opens its white chalice to the sun and wind and light. Think you it regrets the still existence of the depth, or remembers the pain of the parting tendril?" (September 22, 1857.)

The "E" to whom the poems had been read on the balcony was Emma Diana Beaumont, daughter of Thomas Wentworth Beaumont. The Beaumonts were friends of the Fitzpatricks. On September 13, he writes in his diary "alea jacta est." Six months later Emma Beaumont became his wife. She was his *donum Dei*. "Had I not felt," he writes to William in 1860, "that God had given me Emma I should not have married so young."

The following was written to Lady Castletown (then the Hon. Mrs Fitzpatrick) while he was awaiting the reply to the letter in which he had proposed marriage to Miss Beaumont. The reply, which came a few days later, was favourable, but the actual engagement did not take place till December.

"[London] September 15, 1857.

"... I wrote you a hurried note last night to tell you that the die was cast. What will it be? An ace—I feel almost sure. I know not why, except it be the conviction that nothing will turn out really well for me. And yet that is unjust to God, for He has blest me very abundantly. I have friends such as have been granted to few, I have had my lot cast in very pleasant places, I have had much and great happiness, and if this should come, it might be too much for my good. I pray for nothing more than patience and resignation to His will. I cannot, I fear, have an answer till Friday. These leaden footed hours—how I chafe at them. I feel so angry with the cool nonchalance, and unbroken regularity of that very old fellow Time, that if I could catch him I should, I fear, knock the hour glass out of his hand, or commit some rudeness or other on his scythe. This is of a piece with what you aver is my dislike to the virtue of Order. Do you remember the description of the Car of the Hour in the 'Prometheus Unbound' of Shelley, and of the Spirit of the Hour 'leaning forward and drinking the wind of his own speed,' while his long hair streams backward, as he 'sweeps onward.' That description has been tormenting me with its contrast all the morning. I think the Spirit has gone to sleep in his chariot, and the horses are no longer 'fed with the lightning nor bathed in the fresh sunbeam,' but have been put into such good condition by mundane oats and hay that they are fit for the slow pace of the drive in Hyde Park on a full day. This suspense is the very mother of twins—Inaction and Discontent. I never felt discontented before, never at least unpleasantly so. I suppose it is Love, or something very like it, which is the reason of all this, and yet I should not have felt it had not the volition been embodied; but once I have made a feeling into an action, then the feeling becomes no longer a dream, but a reality. ... It was a strange experience—putting that letter into the post; an emotion so utterly new, and vague, accompanied with dread and joy that I cannot analyse it, would not if I could.

"How can I ever thank you for all you have been to me through this. I wonder at your interest, and scarcely can conceive it. It seems so strange in me to find in you one who so beautifully and graciously combined towards me the Mother and the Friend. Believe me, there is nothing which as Son and Friend I would not do for you, not to repay you for your kindness, but because I feel for you the affection of a Son. Whatever may happen in this matter, I *will* never forget what you have been to me, I will never forget all your interest in one who is so unworthy as I am of it, and who can never repay you otherwise than by true affection. . . . 'Words are weak and most to seek, when wanted fiftyfold.' So I felt bidding you all farewell that last night—how can I speak when feeling chokes the throat—I can scarcely tell you how much I sorrow at your going, a year or more seems so long, and so much may happen in this waving uncertainty of life that I shrink from parting with those I love, as I should from the cutting of a nerve. May our Father keep you all, till I see each of you again. I am so glad I saw the last of you with no confusion to disturb, and no incongruous people to jar upon the impression. I am glad Miss G. went to bed, and her voice no longer cut the air like a knife ; I am glad we were all so happy and so calm ; I am glad it was late at night, I am glad we had an impromptu supper, for that was thoroughly in character. I am glad I staid to the last, and went away with a quiet scene laid up in my heart,

> ' To flash upon that inward eye
> Which is the bliss of solitude.'

I am glad I had that peaceful happy walk with you by the shore of the white cliffs, I am glad I had that week of quiet joy, and unrestrained intercourse with you. . . . I enjoyed it so deeply and fully. I enjoy the thought of it now more than all thing else. It is a blessing to have met such friends in life, and such a perfect intercourse as mine has been with you all has an exquisite charm about it which can never be surpassed in life; it was all so free, so trustful, so pure, so true, so open, and so affectionate that I thank God for it with my whole heart. I know not what I have done to deserve it, but its being a gracious gift from you and them gives it a higher beauty to my heart."

It is not surprising that these events were followed by violent reaction, almost collapse. "Dizziness in Church: blind; all but fainted in reading-desk" is the entry for September 23. "I have not been well all this week," he writes to his sister Cecilia. "I knew that the reaction after all that stirring life would come, and would affect me much. Last night in Church there was quite a scene and I fancy there is an interesting halo thrown round me which will be very touching! . . . Shall I not have much to tell you in every way! Things seen, things lived, things done. I seem to have been here twenty years."

Long afterwards he told me all about this and would often refer to it as a warning to young men in danger of breakdown from overwork. He said that as he stood at the reading-desk a dark terror suddenly overwhelmed him, and that for months afterwards he was haunted by the fear of its return.

It is remarkable testimony to his power of resilience that the very next day he wrote a long letter to his sister Cecilia containing an admirable exposition of the principles to be followed in the study of painting, from which I will give two passages.

"It is a grand office, that of the artist, to be the orator of Nature, the exponent in form of the loveliness of colour. Two ways of studying Art: the first and the highest is by seeing and lovingly putting your heart to school before the works of the great artists. The second is by reading what the best art critics have said on these works. And you will find that the best criticisms have been written by those who were not great artists themselves. But previous to this you ought to gain some knowledge, and this I believe indispensable, of the principles of Drawing, some knowledge of the truths of colour, and of hues, some knowledge of chiaroscuro."

"Approach a painting, not to criticize it, not to find out its faults, but to understand its beauty. Believe that he would not have painted it at all, had not the inspiration within him longed to express something. It is that something which you are to discover. He had something to tell, and he told it as he could. Be sure if you come to his work, in the spirit of charity, that it will disclose itself to you, perhaps not in the form it presented itself to him, but in a new form, for it will be modified by your cultivation, by your feelings, and by the mode of your education. But the truth which he laboured to announce is not less than truth, because you have gained it in a new form. Truth or rather Spirit is eternal and unchangeable, while form is perishable, and variable. One truth may be expressed in a thousand forms, yet nevertheless the same. So you may receive his truth modified by your own cultivation in a different form, and yet it will be the same."

In the autumn he paid a visit to his home in Kingstown—the Beaumonts being then in Scotland. He had promised to preach for his father in the Mariners' Church. How he looked forward to that event may be gathered from the following letter to Miss Campbell on September 22, the day before the breakdown mentioned above.

"Next Sunday week I shall have something to face— my Father's Congregation. The danger is so great that I feel that half-fear, half-excitement, which I should think a tiger-hunt is calculated to give you. It is not that I am afraid of speaking to a large number; but I know that many of my relations will come, excellent, most good women, but of a very stern evangelical type, who will expect to hear from me (God knows I do not say it mocking) 'the scheme of Salvation' drawn out in all its parts. Well, I cannot do that, and yet I do not like them to be horrified. I will say what I believe to be the Truth, my tongue would burn were I not to do so, but I must try and not offend. It is this which I find so difficult. I fall back on my fatalism. So let the day bring forth its own child. I will be a father to it whatever it may be."

On October 4 he preaches accordingly: "the whole family, uncles, aunts, cousins, as well as the family circle are present—a host in themselves." "Dear Richard sits in the minister's pew, his eyes suffused with tears, so pleased, so proud of his noble son." "Stopford is eloquent and his manner very impressive and quiet."

He is back in London on the 22nd, and there is another breakdown—for the Beaumonts are still in Scotland, and there has been a silence, an interference, an uncertainty, a hitch—and on the whole the course of true love is not very smooth. So the record for these days is—"ill, ill, ill," and nothing more. With November come signs of returning life—the Beaumonts will soon be back—and I find him lecturing on Spenser's Poetry, on Milton, on Alaric, Genseric and Attila. Then comes a page covered with writing—"The Beaumonts are at Tunbridge Wells, am going down to-morrow!" "Went"—and it was all right. After that not a word in the diary to the end of the year.

At the time of his marriage Brooke was twenty-five years of age; he had been in the ministry for ten months, experiencing in the meanwhile much of its hardship, its limitations, its incessant demands on mind and body, and the seeming pettiness of many of its

AT THE PARTING OF THE WAYS 103

preoccupations. His worldly prospects on that side were poor. What private encouragement he may have received I know not; certainly his vicar had not encouraged him; and the Broad Church party to which he belonged was then so small, shunned and suspected, as to give him at best but a narrow range of opportunity. So far as the outward life is concerned, nothing had occurred to enamour him of his profession, while much had occurred to have the contrary effect; and had he chosen then and there to abandon it for ever, there is not a doubt that in a few years those months would have become a half forgotten episode of his career. No man could know more clearly than he that the position of a London curate—and no other position was in view for some years to come—would afford him little leisure to indulge his tastes and develop his genius on other lines. "The position of a curate in London," he writes to his brother "is Nil." And why should he hesitate? His marriage brought affluence and powerful friends—powerful in the world of literature, art and politics. He was meeting artists and men of letters every day; and one of the leading publishers in London was his personal friend—a valuable start in life for a man with literary ambitions and gifts. He was marrying into a family with no clerical associations. The Beaumonts could introduce him to ministers, ambassadors, to men of influence in many spheres; moreover, they controlled more than one large constituency in the north of England. Thus the door of secular opportunity was flung open; there were voices without that bade him enter, and voices within that echoed the call. Here was a chance for the poet whose place of inspiration "is by the side of running water"; or for the social reformer aflame with the ideals of Kingsley, Ruskin, and Carlyle; or for the artist "haunted by Turner"; and, be it added, for the descendant of Fergus Graeme with the spirit of adventure hot in his blood.

But his natural piety willed otherwise—and it found a consenting partner in the will of his future wife. He neither resigned his curacy nor thought of resigning it. We need no further proof that his consecration to the work of the ministry was irrevocable. A few days after his marriage he wrote to William Brooke, "I do so long to be in that little box (the pulpit) again. It is the only place and time in which I feel that I am thoroughly alive. There only—*je sens fortement l'existence*, Emma's favourite phrase."

They were married on March 23, 1858, in St James', Piccadilly, and went off, by Dover, to France and Switzerland. Needless to say, he paid due homage to "his other mistress"—Nature: insomuch that Mrs Brooke writes herself down as a little jealous of his passion for the high mountains, "whenever it is a question of the mountains or me, the mountains seem to have it!"

On returning to London they lived for some time in apartments at 16, Westbourne Terrace, removing after three months to Mrs Beaumont's house, 24, St James' Place, Piccadilly, where a son, Stopford Wentworth William Brooke, was born to them in January, 1859. After that they lived six months in the Alexandra Hotel —the reason for this unsettlement apparently being that Brooke was now looking for another curacy and would not take a house till the scene of his work had been determined. When this question was settled, as I shall presently relate, they removed to Fern Lodge, Campden Hill, next door to Holman Hunt, where they resided till 1863.

LETTERS BEFORE AND AFTER MARRIAGE, 1857–1859.

To William Brooke.
"June 1, '57.

"Yesterday a sermon to write on 'Put ye on the Lord Jesus Christ'—a *viva voce* exam. from Stanley,[1] in which I was cantered over Ecc. Hist., the Bible, critical points, such as the usage of ὑπόστασις in the New Testament and in Ecc. Hist., the biography of the Fathers and the Prayer Book. As far as I hear I had the most difficult exam. of all. I suppose I owe this to A.'s talk of me, however it was a sort of compliment, and I answered, I think, well. . . . To-day, an exam. from the Bishop, chiefly on points of practice.

"1. How I would act and speak, if a man were to say that going to Church was useless, or would not go to Church?

"2. Suppose a Baptist or Presbyterian rebuked Liturgy what I would say?"

To William Brooke.
"June, 1857.

". . . Both of us [himself and William] got into a bad style from reducing whole sentences of books to a few words, in the analysis we used to make. Too many short sentences do not read well. I remember Stanley remarking to me, that Macaulay always relieved the ear by interspersing a long sentence now and then in the middle of short ones. I thought it an excellent hint. In all this I am speaking to myself—or rather writing to myself as much as to you, for I feel that I err in the same way. . . ."

To William Brooke.
"July 3, '57.

". . . The evening congregation—in fact all our congregations are of the middle classes, I do not see a single gentleman or lady. One or two of course there are.

[1] Stanley was then Regius Professor of Ecclesiastical History in Oxford and Examining Chaplain to the Bishop of London.

Spencer only allows me now to preach in the afternoon. He has an appetite for preaching, and has taken the Wednesday evening too. I generally lecture extempore on Friday, and preach as I told you on Sunday afternoon. The poor like my sermons, say they are beautiful, etc., all of which resolves itself into this—that they are short, and however they may be sometimes difficult to understand, there is three-quarters of them very comprehensible. They say at least that they understand. I visit almost every day, only among the poor. I get on much better now. . . .

"I read something on the Nemesis of Faith the other day, which I extract for you. Poor Froude! . . . People often mistake a contortion of anguish for a diabolical grin. Often the cry of despair is taken for a shout of savage triumph. . . . No one can understand the horrid laugh of hopelessness which delights to scatter its scorn on what has, he thinks, deluded him, but he who has felt the ice of doubt cracking beneath his feet, and seen himself alone on a single iceblock severed from mankind. We do not excuse, but we can understand the want of reverence, and the immoral life which result from such despair."

To William Brooke.

"August 5, '57.

". . . I have been very dissipated this week, last night I was at Savile Row, the Vernon Smiths, I did not get there till eleven as I dined at the Sitwells. It was interesting and very pleasant, as I saw people I wished to see. Lord Lansdowne, a small compact old man, really very small, with a square head and a worn face, and his diamond star ribbon. I was talking to Mrs Fitzpatrick when he came up. Lady Palmerston was there. They say she is one of the cleverest women in the world. I watched her for a long time. A large woman, dressed all in black, with one diamond brooch in her hair. A large courteous face, with command therein, and I could not help thinking a quiet, feminine reflection of her husband in it—just his look as he gets up to silence an objector. It was quite a picture to see her reception of the Prussian Minister—a tall, large florid man, starred and ribboned, with a small imperial and no whiskers or other hair. She took his hand as she was sitting, and bowed thrice slightly over it, with a sort of condescending grace which said, "It is not the man but the representative I welcome." Very quiet and dignified she was. Every one rose when she went away. The Turkish Minister was there too, wearing his scarlet fez in the drawing-room, and with a blazing star. The Bishop of London came across the room to shake hands with me, as I was talking to some lady. The Beaumonts also were there, and a quantity of men whiskered, black and dandified, and thoughtful. How beautifully the women do dress! There was an American girl there, a very beautiful woman, she is one of the régnantes of the season. I had such a charming evening, just two hours of most pleasant conversation, as I left at one.

"I have nearly finished C. Brontë's Life. I do not dislike Mrs Gaskell so much as you do; I think she has done it *rather* well. But C. B., what a noble suffering woman she was! I am seldom affected by a book, but her picture of herself wandering up and down that bare parlour alone where her lost sisters used to talk, and muse, was too pitiable, too desolate. What a constant, loving, deep nature she had, and that undertone of saddest sound which flows beneath all those letters, so repressed, and so nobly borne is very touching and beautiful. How true is all you said about her unostentatious religion."

To Miss Campbell.
"November 27, '57.

". . . I trust you are not reading morbid religious works, in which death is represented as a true Christian aspiration. We should not wish to die as long as we live, for while we live, we live in His sight; and for Him. "Whether we live, we live unto the Lord, whether we die, we die unto the Lord, so that living or dying we are the Lord's." Believe me, we are here to live and not to die, we have no right to die, every right to live."

To William Brooke.
"February 27, '58.

". . . Last night I was at the Royal Institution, and heard Baden Powell on the stability of rotating objects, *i.e.* of objects rotating with enormous swiftness, very clear, interesting, and conclusive. He is a fresh coloured grey haired man, rather stout, with a benevolent forehead, cool eye, and pleasant mouth which ever seemed to be amusing itself with the difficulties of his subject.

"If possible I will give you an analysis of the subject. It has been found that if a circular plate be perfectly balanced, and then impressed with immense swiftness of rotation, it will resist all efforts to put it out of its place of rotation, *e.g.* this circular plane 'A' when rotating with great swiftness on its axis 'B' will resist all forces up or downwards."

[Here follows a drawing of the figure and a minute description of the mechanism.]

To William Brooke.
"Ouchy, sur Lac de Genève.
"Sunday, April 5, '58.
(On his honeymoon.)

". . . I am sitting on the shores of the lake, with a pocket ink bottle and a pen, smoking my morning cigar. I am only allowed two a day, which is very short commons to me, who used to smoke so much, but with E. it can be borne. The mountains are all unclouded this morning, but are sleeping in a sunny haze which lessens their height, and softens their ruggedness. . . . As far as I have gone into Switzerland, I have seen nothing to equal Snowdon. But we intend to go on to Chamonix and see the Mont Blanc range and the glacier. Then, I suppose, I shall feel satisfied, if such a thing is possible. The eye is never satisfied with seeing. Byron wrote The Prisoner of Chillon in the Inn we are staying at, Hôtel de l'Ancre; and it is a fit place for a poet. The scenery is not too grand to strip a writer of his self-consciousness, and is noble and tender enough to wake up all poetic power and delicacy. . . . I have either not settled down into realized married life, or I have settled down too completely—I cannot tell which. Time will show. Sometimes I am immensely happy—at other times I am as downcast and ennuyé as ever I have been, but with my character I shall be for ever subject to these continued alterations of feeling. . . .

"Yesterday we attended the English Church here, a hideous edifice, where I heard the service very badly read, and a sermon by a friend of the rector's, which had the peculiarity of shaving close to good points, and yet never touching them. Emma and I stayed for the Sacrament which we liked, and afterwards took a most lovely walk by the shores of this blue, blue water. I have so often wished for you, even with my wife and in the honeymoon I want a man to talk to now and then. . . . I felt so thoroughly inclined to rush out of my seat yesterday and mount the pulpit. . . . To-morrow I think we leave this place for Bex in the valley of the Rhône, from thence to Martigny or Chamonix, certainly to Chamonix in the end, and then homewards by the Belgian towns."

To William Brooke.

"16, Upper Westbourne Terrace,
"June 7, '58.

". . . I am almost too sleepy to write, but I must begin a letter to you, and I shall be certain to finish it in the morning. My exposition was not spoken so of by Stanley before all the examined, but I heard from Wilkinson[1] that Stanley had stated to them in another room his practical points of view in almost the same words. . . . Your congratulation and the way you wrote it touched me much, my dear brother. It is pleasant to meet in life delicate and true sympathy from a man, and when that man is a brother it is something more than pleasant: it strikes home. As to your confidence in me and mine in you, I trust that shall never fail. Some way or other the tie of Brotherhood does not

[1] Afterwards Bishop of St Andrews.

seem to me *now* to be felt as it should be in the world. In this constant flux and reflux of social life, more especially in London, the sure faithfulness and inner circle of the Home affections appear to be losing their ancient meaning. It is a cruel loss, for domestic, social, above all true national life depend on the sacredness of Home. Let us keep it up all through life. It is so dear a delight to feel that you can talk to a brother as you would to a woman; and to be able to say that, is to speak of a real brotherhood indeed."

To William Brooke.

"London, December 15, '58.

". . . You cannot tell how much I want you here or some one like you. I know no men in London, except the Sitwells and a few clergymen, and they are on the whole such lifeless, unantagonistic creatures, that were it not for reading and writing I should fall into an atrophy of life intellectual. I talk much to E., but I want a man.

"Have you read Carlyle's History of Frederick the Great? It is well worth it, though at first there is much to get over, both from the scattered nature of his subject, and from the marvellous Carlylisms which multiply around you. Reading his book is like walking in one of those old German Forests described in legends, where the trees and rocks are rapidly and feverishly changing into grotesque faces, and leering eyes, and moving lines which are not frightful altogether, but rather humorous, Troll-like, a wild devilment altogether about them, with marvellous insight and sense. But as you go on it is dramatic, and ambiguous, and above all he never gives you too much of the same subject.

"I go a-drawing at the Turner Gallery two days in the week, in order to get up my sketching. Good-bye, old boy."

To Miss Campbell.

"24, St. James' Place, Piccadilly.
"April 13, '59.

". . . I have just come in from visiting a poor woman who is dying in all the agonies of cancer; she describes the pain as if some one with claws were scraping all her bones against the grain; and yet she is as peaceful, and as calm as a summer sea, only reproaching herself a little for want of patience.[1] It is these things that make a clergyman feel that there is reality in Christianity, and give him confidence in the power of what he preaches. It is these things too that dash all pulpit pride, all ministerial self-sufficiency to the ground. I teach and read and speak and pray at dying men's ears, and all appears to fall short of moving them, till something which you have said unconsciously almost, something which fell from your lips you cannot tell why, falls on them with the Power of God unto salvation. The more I visit, the more I am convinced that it is not the man, not intellect, not even zeal or sympathy which does the work on human hearts, but the Spirit of God. . . . I often cannot realize my life, or myself as a personal, responsible being. I feel myself at times floating as it were a monad in an ether, where other men and women are monads too, towards some of whom I am as blindly attracted, as I am repelled from others, and that is all. The very awfulness of life in this vast city makes it phantasmal to me, and I often can realize the old seas of the Devonian Period with their cuirassed and helmeted fishes, far better than I can this oceanic roar of human passion and crime, of humble martyrdom and sorrow which swells and falls in the ear of God from the largest city of the world. . . . Visiting the dying should awake the heart to a knowledge of reality, but it is strange that as yet I have seen nothing, which I do not feel as if I had seen before, and known from my

---

[1] This woman made a deep impression on him. Fifty years afterwards he would often speak of her.

very youth. My experience, so far as it has gone, has never outrun my knowledge."

To William Brooke.

"November 25, '59.

". . . One other piece of literary gossip. Have you heard the end of Comte? I think it quite glorious; and his followers who thought that here was the man at last, and that in the positive philosophy they had at last got rest are immensely confounded. He is dead, three months ago, but before he died, and shortly after his Positive Philosophy he fell in love, and immediately reversing all his thoughts wrote a book declaring that intuitive feeling was *all*, that positive truths apprehended by the intellect were as nothing to the truths gained by feeling.

"His followers were utterly confounded. I think this quite glorious—well done womanhood, say I! Funny, isn't it, how positive phenomena vanish before Love!"

CHAPTER VII

KENSINGTON

"A poet ought to marry—if he marries—a gentle, steady, good woman, who will confess him to be a poet, admire him, but keep him in order, and in harmony with the Earth and Man. Flighty things don't count, or ideal creatures. . . . They over-stimulate, and the man having soared beyond himself, his wings are melted, and he drops down like Icarus. Just think of Alfred de Musset. Mrs Browning who was ideal was also full of the common-sense of home."—(*Diary*, September 30, 1899.)

THE years which followed Brooke's marriage were years of inward calm, of steady work, and of domestic happiness. Between him and his wife the bond was all the stronger because it was in many respects a union of opposites. She shared his natural piety, his love of beautiful things, his moral preferences, and she was prepared both by temperament and by training to follow his steps into the broader world of religious thought. But she had none of his impetuosity. A nature exquisitely refined, calm, reflective, much turned inward, in feeling as in thought, and with a tendency to consume itself in silence. Her charm was great, and it was deepened by reserve which was perpetually struggling against itself. Self-expression, which came so easily to him, was difficult to her, so that her finer qualities were revealed only to those who could discern them, of whom her husband was the chief. With her the sense of duty was an instinct, and showed itself not merely in the loving performance of the thing which lay to her hand, but in the discovery of hidden opportunities and fine implications, and in a gracious invention of the deeds of love. "She dwelt in the doing of right and *made it*," were the pregnant words which Brooke in after years wrote upon her tombstone. It was good for him that early in life his nature, which was subject to rapid changes of mood, should be wedded to another so calm and deep. It was good for him that he found in his wife an independent character, not blinded by his genius, not dominated by his powerful personality, who idealized her husband, it is true, but wisely, and had the courage to speak the truth whenever performance fell short of the ideal. He would often read his sermons to her before preaching them. She would sometimes remark, "That is not the best of which you are capable: write that again."

Having resolved to give up his curacy at Marylebone, Brooke now began the quest for a sphere of larger opportunity. This was not easy to find. Then, more even than now perhaps, it was better for a man's prospects in the Church that he should be "safe" than "promising." Brooke was known to be promising, but there was a large question as to his being safe. Indeed, from the point of view of bishops and vicars in 1860 he was distinctly "unsafe," and his Broad Church views, extremely moderate as they now seem, were a barrier which not even the influence of powerful friends could always overcome. "Did he not know much more than a young clergyman need know, or ought to know, of Geology and other subversive lore? Was he not lecturing on English Literature and exalting the 'Prelude' and 'In Memoriam' into dangerous rivalry with Holy

Writ? Had he not been heard in drawing-rooms and elsewhere proclaiming 'we must have more joy in life'? Nay, was he not authentically reported to have said, *sans phrase*, that 'a man might learn something from Martineau,' and actually written the same in letters to his friends? A dangerous man, and for all his eloquence, his fine presence and the rest, it were better to have nothing to do with him." So the London vicars of '58 looked askance on his applications, and shook their heads when powerful friends suggested him as "the very man for the place."

A letter to Mrs Fitzpatrick in 1861 sufficiently indicates his attitude towards the Church of England during the early years of his married life. "I look forward," he writes, "to a complete revolution in thought before I die. Men do not expect it, but there are signs of the earthquake to those who see. I feel that unless the Church of England expands itself and widens its dogmatic boundaries it is all over with the Church. When any institution refuses to be as free as its age, the age—so to speak—walks it down and makes macadam of it. It is useful for *walking over* to something better." Curates who compared the Church of England to macadam and proposed to "walk over it to something better" were not encouraged in those days.

However, he was able to bide his time, which was well employed in wide reading, in laying the foundations of his home, and in studying the marvellous ways of his infant son. At last, after some months of unemployment, he was appointed in the autumn of '59 to the curacy of St Mary Abbots, Kensington, of which Archdeacon Sinclair was then vicar. Like his previous vicar the archdeacon was watchful, as his duty was, and began after a time to attend the afternoon services which the curate conducted. Yes, he was keeping an eye on the young man. This state of affairs made not the least difference to Brooke, who continued as before to preach "the Kingdom of God not according to any existing ideas of it, but on the contrary according to his own idea of it." His "own idea of it" at the time called more distinctly than before for an open welcome to the truths of science, and for close identification with social and political reform. His letters to William Brooke, which, in spite of wide differences of opinion between the brothers, accurately reflect the movements of his mind, now suggest that if Turner is not haunting him less, Darwin, Lyell, Huxley, and Tyndall are haunting him more. He is also reading Robert Owen critically, but with so much enthusiasm that he cannot refrain from opening his mind to William—who gives him no encouragement on that line. He has adopted Mill's views on the political status of women, and writes an article on "Womanhood" for the *Dublin University Magazine* which he sends to William for criticism, "Emma taking no interest in the practical part;" which article Mr Editor Brady finds too radical, cutting it down, and that in such a way as "to sacrifice the branches with leaves on them and keep only those that are withered and dry." Then there is Mill on "Representative Government," a "masterly work," which is studied line by line and page by page, for the rule still holds "that what those brothers knew, they knew well." All this finds its way, by indirection, into the idea of the Kingdom of God, and into the sermons thereupon, now attended by a larger and more thoughtful congregation. "I am delighted," he writes, "with the work at Kensington."

Meanwhile old friends are remembered. Intelligence

reaches him from Ireland of certain young gentlemen who are contemplating matrimony. To these, in virtue of experience gained, he gives some trenchant advice, in which, after probing the matter to the bottom, he bids the young gentlemen trim their sails to other courses. There is much in these letters about his "ancient" O.— him of the many anecdotes, who stormed your friendship with a joke. O., it appears, is about to emerge from the shades of his widowerhood, but writes not one word of this "to *me*," sending the news in an offhand manner by a third party. "What does he mean by it? Does he call that friendship? Inform him that I wish him joy of his second wife—of whom he has told me absolutely nothing!" After which we hear no more of O. with his gush, his emotions, his punch and his jolly rhodomontades—who once, we learn, had fallen into Stopford's arms in an extremity of grief, and vowed that he would be his friend for ever and ever, and declared that the sight of his face was more reviving to men in sorrow than all the whisky in Ireland. This windy traitor disposed of, the letters go on to other matters. There is a young man about to enter college—"tell him I will send him a cheque;" and "let him spend some months with me; I will work him up in Latin and Greek, and pay his fare both ways."

In all these letters there is much about religion, which centres in a very simple thought—that God has appointed him his work, given him his wife and children, and set him where he is. In 1881 we find him preaching on this idea in a series of sermons on the Call of Abraham, and there is little doubt that these sermons, like so many others that he preached in later life, have their roots in the experience of his early manhood. The call of Brooke came *with* his work and in a manner as convincing as it was natural—in the consciousness that the life of the preacher would give full scope to his powers, leaving nothing unused, neither the love of nature nor the love of man, neither his personal loyalty to Christ nor his reverence for scientific truth. On no other conditions would it have been possible for Brooke to write the sentence, "I am delighted with my work in Kensington." For he was so made that to be unable to throw himself entirely into what he was doing would provoke in him at any time profound unhappiness. He could not tolerate reservations, least of all that kind of reservation which forces a man to confess "there is some part of me which I cannot put into my work." The movement of his thought subsequently brought him to that very condition, from which he promptly escaped by leaving the Church of England.

Yet, even at this early period, there are mutterings of unrest, prophetic of things to come. From the notes in a diary, kept at intervals between 1860 and 1863, it is clear that already he felt himself hampered and had begun to chafe under enforced limitations. He sharply criticizes the education of the Anglican clergy, compares them unfavourably at certain points with Nonconformist ministers, shows his dislike of the clerical habit of mind, and points out some objectionable features in the Book of Common Prayer. In one important passage, to be quoted presently, he outlines a theory of the basis of Christian truth, which, if pursued, must inevitably bring him into conflict with the doctrinal standards of his Church; and in a note added eight months later he states his solemn intention to pursue it, and his foresight of the conflict which it will involve. "This I cannot do," he says, "*until I am free.*" What precisely he means by the words I have italicized is not clear;

possibly they refer only to his position as a *curate;* but they show that "freedom" was in his mind and that he was contemplating some step that would give him more of it. Moreover, he is again studying Martineau's sermons—no doubt the " Endeavours after the Christian Life." "Read him," he writes to a friend in '59, "and see if a Unitarian cannot teach and comfort somewhat." Dining at the Archdeacon's one night he meets "a Dr Wayland from Boston," who tells him that "after reading Channing he felt as if he had never known Christ before"—with much else to the same effect, all of which is noted down in the diary as a thing to be remembered. Interspersed with these notes are several of his early poems—experiments, all of them, in regions of thought and feeling not covered by the Thirty-Nine Articles.

Extracts from Diary 1860—1863.

October 5, '60. "Visiting a poor woman to-day, she said of Christ: 'Dear Soul, how He suffered, and all for me.' Nothing has so brought home to me the blessedness of His utter humanity and His brotherhood as that expression—'Dear Soul'—said as it was in a kind of half soliloquy."

October 21, '60. "I am more and more impressed with the thought that Christianity is the ultimate and only religion for man. And that, for this reason, that its principles are *human,* and all the precepts resting on these principles are commanded because they are necessary for human nature, *e.g.* every side of the law of love, forbearance, forgiveness, veiling a brother's faults. These are not necessary for us to observe, because they are commanded, but they are commanded because they are necessary. The necessity for this observance arises not out of God's command, but out of the necessities of the Race. In this Christianity differs from all other systems. It accepts the facts of Humanity.

"Again it is *the* Religion of the Race because its principles are at one with the principles of Science or rather with the principles God has given to the world of man and nature, *e.g.* the laws of Political Economy rest on the same principles on which Christianity rests. The principles of Science are identical with the principles of Christianity. The principles by which God rules the life of nations and of the history of the world are the same as those by which He rules the individual.

"I would I could make this an object of my life—to preach to the world the reasonableness of Christianity, as shown by the identity of its principles with the principles of human life and human knowledge, so far as they are true ; *i.e.* simply to show that Revelation and Science and the laws of Human Polity, not those which are made by men, but those which are—are all the product of the same mind and that there is a point at which they all meet.

"I cannot do this till I am free. But I can mature it. Let it be my struggle." [June 8, '61.]

June 10, '61. "It is curious and sad to think how much of dirty human passion underlies the Prayer Book ; *e.g.* the word 'Schism' in the Litany was inserted in 1661, and in the prayer for the Parliament—our most *religious* King was said of Charles II.!

"There is a lull and the hurricane of wind which blew from one quarter against the Essays and Reviews is sinking. The calm is like that which interposes itself in the midst of a tornado, before the wind begins to blow directly from the other side of the heavens. We shall have a great reaction, and I who thought that progress in wide views of Christianity and in scientific and yet religious criticism was put back for fifty years, have hopes now that it will be more rapid than it could have been before this book was published. Its opponents have overshot the mark. They have vaulted too high and are falling on the other side instead of on the back of the horse."

July 14, '61. "The veil between, though very dark, is very thin.

"The question is—do we ever meet a fissure in it through which we can for a moment look? I believe that *that* is possible to us, under certain physical and mental conditions. St Paul's ecstasy is a case in point. There comes at times an inexplicable sensation when all the outward world seems to become only projected thought, and our own body only a form of thought. It is attended sometimes by ghastly fear, and sometimes by a strange exhilaration. That is I believe a glimpse into the unseen world. It is as if we were swept past a rent in the veil with lightning speed, and saw through, yet too quickly for the sight we see to become a definite object of thought. There *is* something at the root of the insane imagination of Swedenborg and the cheats of the Spiritualists."

July 16, '61. "I began Mr Robertson's life to-day. I cannot feel that I shall be able to accomplish it. Indeed, so strong is this feeling that it is with a kind of despair that I write the first few sentences. Yet I will try against hope, and if I fail—I fail. This despondency increases tenfold the difficulty of writing, so much so that I seem to have forgotten how to frame one single sentence in correct English.

"Book English and sermon English are as distinct as possible. The latter must partake of a colloquial character and have more of passion and abruptness than can be permitted in composition for the public and it is only in this style that I have written anything of late years."

March '62. "Why have dissenting clergymen succeeded so well in drawing congregations?

"Our clergy are too highly educated for the poorer classes, or rather let me say, they are the slaves of their education, they cannot shake off its forms of thought and forms of speech. These forms are too rigid, too confined, and the clergy will not or cannot travel out of them and take up the forms of thought and speech which will suit a less educated mode of thinking and speaking.

"They, the Dissenters, are on the whole more in

earnest than the generality of our clergy. They are men who have almost always worked out their conclusions for themselves; they have had personally a train of religious experiences which they have won their way through by their own unaided strength. Seven-tenths of our clergy have modified their religious experiences in conformity with rules, or borrowed them from their theological reading. They preach not their own experiences, but the set of doctrines which they have gained from their college books, and the skeleton of which they have at home hung up on a peg in their study. They lecture on Christianity as a Comparative Anatomist lectures on a Squelette. If this bone of the Christian religion be here, this other bone must be there, and so on till they build up the whole fleshless array of bones, and then they clasp their hands—inwardly it is true, and cry, 'There, there it is, my Scheme.' There is nothing personal in it; no life, no nerves.

"The Dissenter preaches doctrine, but it is doctrine which means to him experience which he has felt. It may be all very foolish or very vulgar experience, but it has life, because himself is in it. Now the smallest spark of life communicates life, and earnestness bought by personal struggle gives a rude eloquence which suits rude minds.

"The fairies, the sylphs, the gnomes, the Undines are all forms under which men endeavoured to represent the nameless and graspless Beauty of Nature to themselves. They have perished because in the search after material interests, men lose the sensitiveness of spirit which can feel the inexplicable thrill of Nature. They have perished also, because science has explained so much of the inexplicable.

"Man looks on Nature as a mirror and sees himself reflected there. His image is not inherent in a mirror; no more are his conceptions and feelings inherent in Nature, but as without the mirror we could not see our forms, so without outward nature there are many feelings which we could not realize. The feelings exist in us, but only in germ, they must be developed by the outward world. Nature is to our minds what rain and sunshine are to the plant."

Letters 1859–1861.

To William Brooke.
"Jan. 3, '59.

"I am half-way through volume 2 of Carlyle ('Frederick the Great'). . . . Never throw by a book because the style displeases you at first. . . . Submit yourself to the author and strive hard to listen to him patiently. . . . Nothing I dislike so much as hearing sentence passed on a book without study of it, without a temporary submission to it. . . . Only by self-submission will you ever get good in anything. Bacon's principle—we conquer nature by obeying her. We gain the *power* of judging a book by sinking our own prejudices and theories *for a time* and reading submissively. . . . I think the meeting of father and son at Custrin one of the most touching things I ever read. . . . Of Buckle I have only read the celebrated and controverted chapter which is so plausible and so false. I believe I could overthrow the argument. . . ."

To a Young Man in Love.
"Jan. '59.

". . . The first question to be answered is—do you love her well enough to marry her and live with her all your life? And the way to answer to yourself is this. Is her character such as will suit mine? Is her nature not discordant with mine? Does she draw out what is best in me? Do I feel myself more myself when I am with her? If you can feel so, why then *I* can tell you that though you may not feel that romantic love which we read of in novels, you may safely marry, and every day when the first strangeness is gone will make you love her more, till life culminates in a union of soul with soul. Such has been my experience. I cannot say that I married for love, that is for *passion*. Passion had long died in me. But I married because I felt I could answer those questions I have written, and now I love my wife with all my nature. It is not passion, but something far more enduring."

To William Brooke.
"Feb. 21, '59.

". . . I have just finished Arnold's 'Lectures of Modern History.' Do read them if you can. Seldom have I read a book so practical, so general yet so particular, so full of condensed thought and strong truthful English—or rather, Arnold-thinking. Wonderful it is how the simple style of that man grows on a reader, and impresses him far more than the Macaulean—healthful, open to the air, like the Parthenon. . . .

"I was at H.'s wedding. One of those strange religious affairs which partake to me of most painful cant. All the speeches at the Breakfast were religious speeches. The health of the bridesmaids was given by H., who declared that he would not shock their delicacy by any of the common—here he stammered—worldly jokes and follies (I felt condemned!), and then after introducing Christ . . . we drank the toast in champagne! R. spoke of Cana in Galilee and the marriage supper of the Lamb. . . . But, my dear boy, is all that right? N. is not pretty . . . looks passée, sharpened features, no style. H. looked ineffable and gave one the idea that he thought the whole thing wrong and that he ought to beg pardon of everybody. I think he made a muff of himself."

To William Brooke.
"April 4, 1859.

". . . One would think that O. imagined himself some deity who has always to communicate his wishes, almost his commands, through a Mediator. . . . I cannot pump up an ounce of interest in the lovely [bride] or the enamoured swain. It has not been made a personal question to me. You say his friendship for me is undiminished. But I say, the tree is known by its fruits.

"The Ministry won't go out. If Pam were Minister war would ensue in 24 hours. The Queen, acting on the advice of Lord Lansdowne, refused point-blank to accept Lord Derby's resignation. . . . The Queen says the ministry shall not go out on a 'dodge.' That word of Cairns has stuck fast. Lord Derby's allusion in his speech to the deep gravity of the occasion was prompted by fear for the stability of the monarchy if Bright and Russell got into power. The Conservatives are getting more and more afraid of the firmness of the Throne, and it seems to me—Liberal as I am—with some reason. This is some of the gossip of the Clubs for you. Now to tell you of the speeches. . . . Osborne was cheered as schoolboys cheer an acrobat. A gentleman told me that in asking a member what was thought of Gladstone's speech, he said, 'By George—it was the most astonishing speech—there was not a point on which he did not touch, and that with the most splendid eloquence, but he so confused them all, so wrapt them in a maze of words, so distributed them under various lights, that not a single member in the House knew what he had said when he sat down! . . . The whole House despised Lord Palmerston when he sat down. . . .' Bright's speech was thought an insult. He had talked so large in the provinces and sang so small in the House that people said he was untrue. Major S. asked me what I thought of Disraeli's speech. I said it was the calmest, sublimest, and noblest piece of statesmanlike oratory I had ever read. Major S. replied that I had not said more than D.'s bitterest enemies were saying, . . . that he astonished every one; that in '52 D. had died like a cat, scratching all round, and now—when he rose he could not speak for ten minutes, the cheering was so great, and that when he sat down there was 'solemn applause'—they were silent almost in presence of such a torrent of genius and strength. . . ."

To William Brooke.
"April 18, '59.

"As to connecting myself with this movement [the Woman's Movement] I see no opening, but it is a great wish of mine, and if I should ever be placed in a position where such a course were possible, I should enter on it gladly and I hope earnestly. But a curate's position in London is Nil. . . . How glad I am you like the article [his own, on Womanhood]. . . . I do not know anything of the morals of French Vivandières, but those of the English soldiers' wives in the Crimea were most degraded. The fact is, if women are to have anything to do with the Army abroad or even at home, in hospitals or in domestic work, so to speak, they must either be of higher rank than the soldiers, ladies, or they must be religious women, or trained and constituted nurses. With regard to female clergy, I do not know that they would not be useful, but as our Church is at present constituted I think it would be an impossible anomaly. In an abstract light I see no reason why women should not exercise all a clergyman's duties. Elizabeth Fry preached and was listened to reverently by crowned heads and by multitudes of men. I believe that female preaching, based as it would necessarily be on the nature of women, on a deep intuition of truth, and not on doctrinal argument, is a great want in our Church. . . .

"I still hold my view that all noble work is accomplished slowly, silently, self-sacrificingly. . . . Geology proves the slowness of God's work. . . . However, we should remember that God works in Eternity and we see results in time. . . . With regard to the elevation of the working classes, I said it must arise from their own native strength. . . . Your account of the Hospital interested me deeply. What do I care whether the noble woman you mention be evangelical, tractarian, or Roman Catholic . . . likeness to Christ will be God's test, though I would not be thought for a moment to disparage the importance of doctrinal views of Christian truth. . . . Again I thank you for your letter: you have struck the exact chord of my thought. . . . I deprecate all outward and forcible change and believe that true reform is to be wrought by the infusion of a spirit . . . silently spreading till the whole mass is leavened. By 'silently' I mean without ostentation.

"I met Poerio [Italian exile] the other day. . . . He complained of my Chianti, and as he had a very bad cold, I pardoned him. He said the sun here is like the moon in Italy. Goethe in his 'Römische Elegien' says the same thing. . . . People here are charmed at the absence of all self-martyrdom the exiles show, and by the sparing use they make of the money so freely subscribed.

"I heard Maurice preach the other evening. The main idea he impressed upon me was that of forcible energy and by a quiet belief in what he said. Before I heard him five minutes—with shut eyes—I could have sworn to the man—for his root doctrine crept out immediately: selfishness the root of all sin, Christ the root of all righteousness in man."

To William Brooke.
"May 27, '59.

"At last this wearisome farce of an examination [for Priests' Orders] is over. . . . I had not much more than a week to read. . . . Two papers—one on Galatians, the other on Hooker and Luther. . . . We had a practical exposition of Dives and Lazarus and an analysis of our last sermon. Then we played bowls all afternoon. . . . Stanley told me my sermon was good and said aloud to all . . . 'there is scarcely one of you who has not mistaken the drift of the question "a practical exposition of the doctrine of the corruption of human nature and of the Trinity." You have all stated the Doctrine. I wished it shown in its influence on life and feeling,' and then turning to me, '*you* have given a practical exposition, I think,' a compliment at which I blushed."

To William Brooke.

[Month omitted] '59.

[In answer to a criticism that his sermons were not "simple."] "Men are too lazy to think in Church, they want something which gives them no trouble. Now I want if I can to give them trouble, to make them think, to make them say, what does this man mean—does God say as he says—is he telling me right or wrong, and so to awaken personal investigation of the Bible, personal prayer for light. With this object I try to make my sermons novel with as much clearness of expression as I can use.

"After all, what is simple to one is dark to another. I, for my part, cannot understand the Evangelical scheme of doctrines. I cannot find them in the Bible. They are to me a mélange of impossibilities *as they are stated*. It is true that to raise men you must speak to them as an equal—as a man to men, but I do not talk a language unknown to them. I use Saxon words. I tell men that God is their Father. Surely that is comprehensible, that they must be like Christ—surely that is clear, that they must labour to enter into His rest, that is not dark—and then I try to apply these and all the great principles of Christianity to the various modes of mind and modes of action in different periods of life—and in this, which ought to be done more than it is, I daresay I often have been hard to be understood by many. That must be expected. If I were to preach a sermon on Desertion by God, those who never felt what it was to lose God's light in their hearts would not comprehend a word. But others would. Am I not to preach on it because I know that many in my congregation will listen to it as idle tales? I believe I must. On other Sundays these will hear. Your illustration of Robertson is unlucky. The shop boys of Brighton and the working men were his devoted and comprehending followers, and yet you infer that it was only the educated people who understood him. But with all this defence, I am trying and do try daily to render my preaching plainer and plainer. I am sure that my sermons at Kingstown were not so marvellously incomprehensible. It is paying a wretched compliment to the intelligence of the Mariners' Church. It is a mistake to suppose that the doctrines of Christianity are easy of comprehension. There is not one of them which has not been obstinately controverted by learned and unlearned, and scarcely a sect which does not interpret one and all of them in a sense different from and opposite to that of another. I half fancy that your meaning of the word 'simple' is 'evangelically orthodox.'

"Nevertheless I promise you to try and become more plain and easy, to study the simple in its truest sense, and believe ever that I receive your criticisms with a most thankful heart and a mind ready to give in and own myself wrong."

"Sept. 12, '59.

"Coleridge's Notes of Shakespeare . . . I have [at last] met. They are quite invaluable for thought and suggestiveness. . . . I cannot call them metaphysical, for that seems to partake of the obscure, but they are accurate psychological studies clear and true."

To Miss Campbell.

"July 6, 1860.

"I cannot say that Brighton air did either of us any good. To me it is an intolerable place; glare and glitter, fashion and fuss, restlessness and roaring of sea, chalkiness and conceit, popular preachers and other mountebanks—a most deafening, maddening place. I was worried to death by noise, and blown to pieces by the wind. To leave it was a resurrection. I went there only to see Mr Robertson's tomb. I found it and could not but think on all I might have been, had he but lived. Yet perhaps he never would have influenced me so much, had he not died. God has wonderfully justified Himself for Mr Robertson's death, for no man in our Church has ever had the same influence on men generally quite unreached by the clergy. I liked the tomb, and liked its place. Usually I hate tombs; stone lies looking shamelessly to the sky and shamelessly misrepresenting the dead, ascribing to them virtues which they never had, and vices which they abhorred: erected because the family must be honoured, or the opinion of the world respected. But here I felt that all was genuine, inscription and flowers making its strong base delicate with fairy shadows: like the man himself where intense forceful strength rose from a soil of heart, where the most womanly, delicate, sensitive feelings grew like flowers and the fairest imaginations wandered like the million coloured tribes of insects. And above the tomb the fresh upland slopes of the Downs whence the free wind came to stir the grass around him, and beneath him the broad sea whose waves for ever in my ear were singing his requiem. Do you know I feel towards that man as a woman does to her lover; only with a feeling more pure from passion."

To William Brooke.
"July 24, '60.

"I have only read two volumes of Froude. He has come down heavily on poor Anne Bullen. . . . I have read lately Essays and Reviews. And 'Robert Owen and his Social Philosophy,' by Sargant, a very interesting, impartial, and politically scientific book. Read it. Have read, too, a French novel by George Sand, 'L'Homme de Neige,' a wonderful book and very free from her impurity, and from the usual sentimental immorality of French literature. I am going to read Tyndall's 'Glaciers.' I have nearly finished the fifth volume of 'Modern Painters.' I do not think it equal to some of the former. The style is more broken and the thoughts rather confused. But the chapters on leaf vegetation and on Venetian Art are very valuable. I am reading Jowett's Thessalonians, Galatians and Romans. In many ways I quite disagree with him, but I think him penetrated with the desire of arriving at the spiritual truth of things, and a thoroughly honest and Christian investigator. . . . Huxley I have heard of as a man of great power and greater promise. I think he opposed Forbes' viscous theory of glacier action."

To his Mother.
"July 31, '60.

"You say that life is becoming to you more a thing of intensity than of enjoyment. Such it must needs be now with you. But the question is—is the change really a source of regret? In proportion as life becomes a thing of intensity it becomes a thing of depth and of added truth of view. Feeling and thought are deepened in power, and these when rightly directed are exalted in aim. Eternal realities take the place of earth. We cannot help regretting the old freshness, the vanishing of the glory and the gleam, but which is noblest, which is the highest and truest—the life of enjoyment or the life of intensity? Surely the latter. And then in turn the life of intensity gives place to the life of calm. There is a second youth in Christian old age, which is the most beautiful thing on earth, when to the experience and the sorrow and the memory of the woman is added the child-heart without its worldliness. Be sure, dear Mother, that is before you. The evening of life sets calm on the Christian's life. . . .

"I wish you would promise me to read every Sunday with care the 'Christian Year.' I know no book so exalting, so true, and so comforting. Here and there a little Tractarianism appears, but what does that matter to you? You are far beyond its reach. It is now just three o'clock, and I shall get such a blowing up from Emma, so I shall go to bed and finish this to-morrow. . . .

"Did my Father see Lord Enniskillen's collection of fossil fishes? That and Sir Philip Egerton's, whom I met last year in London, are the finest in the world. They collected them together, Sir P. told me."

To William Brooke.
"Aug. 8, 1860.

"The good that came of [Robert Owen's work] was this—that for the first time the attention of men was drawn to the social improvement which attending to the dwellings and all the *entourage* of working men [would bring about]. He took to spirit rapping at the close of his life, and I know no history which so clearly points out that atheism and credulity are brother and sister. He is the man mentioned in 'Aurora Leigh.' . . . Ruskin's book is not such *beautiful* reading as you suppose. It is even tiresome in parts and too minute. . . . Jowett's book is not all metaphysical, and to revolt from true philosophic theology is simply to revolt from St Paul. Mind I do not say that Jowett is true philosophic theology. . . .

"I have made acquaintance with Mr Senior, the political economist. He is a very acute, agreeable man. Said to me the other day that the two cleverest men he ever met were the vainest—Lord . . . and the Archbishop of . . . He gave me his Resolution and Report on the Privy Council of Education. . . . I have a glut of sick people in the district, and am kept busy with preaching. . . ."

To William Brooke.

" Jan. 21, '61.

"I am attending Huxley's lectures on Physiology, which are given on Saturday nights at 7 o'clock in the Jermyn Street Museum. It is a long way to go, but I find nothing helps me more, in writing sermons and in thinking than some study of Natural Science. It adds tone to the necessarily speculative character of Theological writing.

"I have been reading a very pleasant light book on 'The Sea and its Living Wonders' by Professor Hartwig. It is fresh, lively, and full. . . .

"I wish you would get for me Greene's 'Manual of the Sub-Kingdom Cælenterata,' which I suppose has now come out. . . .

"A. gives a most dispiriting account of the missionaries, says the native Christians are the most immoral men in the place, Hindoos and Mahometans without the restraints of their old religion. His account of the missionaries tallies with Kavanagh's.[1] He excepts the Baptist missionaries, who, he says, wear the dress of the natives, and mix with them at home, and do not confine their teaching to Christianity, but instruct the men in mechanics, etc. I have long believed that till the missionaries learn to act thus, assume the dress of the people and their customs, so far as consistent, and go to their homes as Christ did to the outcast publican, there is no hope of any real advance in the proselytizing of India. He says these Baptists succeed, and are looked on by the natives as friends, and consulted by them in difficulty."

To William Brooke.
"Feb. 3, '61.

"I am glad you have begun to take some interest in Robertson. His mind is worth taking some pains to comprehend. I scarcely know one wider or truer; or rather, I should say, one more singly devoted to truth; for he would be the last man himself to assume that what he says is ultimate truth in matters of opinion. My judgment is not now what it was some years ago—the once delight of a mind charmed with the originality and freshness of the thought without experience enough to judge of its bearings, or of its reality.

"*Now* I have some right to judge. I have read and studied his thoughts for five years, and that for two years at least with, I trust, impartial calmness. I have applied his method to life and thought, and my steady judgment is that in method he is right and in principle. His opinions are but rarely crude, and in many cases, so startlingly true that they seem to me like a revelation, and I read them each time with new wonder. I have tested them by applying them to circumstances

[1] This was T. H. Kavanagh, the hero of a famous exploit during the siege of Lucknow. Disguised as a native he made his way through the Sepoy lines, bearing despatches from the beleaguered garrison to Sir Colin Campbell. He made the acquaintance of Brooke, who gave him much literary help in writing his book, "How I won the Victoria Cross."

and to things, and the clue they have given has solved many a riddle. . . .

"You come severely down on the Essays and Reviews and then say you have not read them. That, you know, is a mode of procedure I cannot like. How can you tell whether they be chaff or wheat? You have accepted much which you used to refuse. Do you remember how you used to abuse In Memoriam? I have done the same, and have learnt never to be too hasty in judging the spirit of a book,—till I have understood it. . . .

"For my own part I do not approve of the spirit in which some of these Essays are written. Powell's is full of that *esprit moqueur*, which I hate, and is flippant, and in its desire to extinguish the supernatural has a tendency to degrade everything to the level of the merely natural. Rowland Williams, too, on Bunsen's theories, is also flippant, and seems to attack existing opinions for the mere pleasure of attacking them.

"But the great question which underlies them all, what is the Inspiration of the Bible? is one which must be settled. It underlies nearly every question of the day, and till it is settled, and that wisely and critically, we have no real ground as a body of ministers on which to stand against the spread of infidel opinions.

"I am glad of the publication, and glad that the battle is to be fought out. I sniff the contest like an old war horse, and rejoice that I live to see it fairly begun.

"You are wrong in calling the Essays speculative. Particularly, and in portions, they are so, collectively they are practical. You ought to read them, not in order to discover their mistakes—or to be horrified by their downright blows, as in Rowland Williams, at what we have received so long as sanctities of belief—but to find out what they all mean at root. But I will write more on the subject when I have time."

To William Brooke.

"March 19, '61.

"... Of course, if you think to read the Essays and Reviews would be 'detrimental to your peace of mind,' I say at once, do not read them; but I say also—without reading them you have no right to call the writers sophistical, dishonest, untruthful, dishonourable, and tricksters—nor even illogical. What on earth can you know about the book from extracts, torn from their context? What do you know of *any* book from extracts, simply nothing—for every reviewer can select what he pleases, and hush up the rest.

"It is a disgraceful thing to call them infidels. The way that word is bandied about, and tied like a tin kettle to a mastiff's tail, is a blot upon any Church, especially on a Protestant Church, the very principle of whose teaching is free thought—in opposition to the Popish spirit of intolerance which cries mad dog after every one who differs from the dogmatic rules of the Church. What are all these names in your letter, but a page out of the bulls of the Popes?

"These men are no more infidels than you or I. I do agree with much tha they say. I do not agree with much also—and whether I agree or not, I am glad that members of our Church have come forward to put into a concrete form the difficulties which have been floating about in men's minds for the last ten years. I see in it a healthy sign. Our Church has too long put its head in the sand like the ostrich and said, 'I see no difficulties but those which have been answered before; I ignore the new phase under which the old difficulties have arisen, demanding new answers.' No, it will not do. We must face the difficulties and see what answer can be given. They are of a different sort to those brought forward in the Eclipse of Faith, except Powell's Essay, which I disagree with almost altogether. The only real answer is contained in the answer to the question, What is Inspiration, a question which has not been answered yet.

"You made me smile by talking of Wilson becoming

a Papist. The main spirit of the Essay is to advocate greater freedom from restrictions of thought, and the whole spirit of the Papacy is directly the opposite. . . .

"And now, dear old boy, I have liberated my soul, and pitched into you sufficiently to make you laugh at me, and cry, What a fire-eater he is! It is a great comfort to be sure enough of the affection of one another to know that hard hitting on both sides does not touch for an instant the current of true love beneath."

"July 8, '61.

"I had not heard of the death of Mrs Browning. With you I fully sympathise, and it is sad to see one by one the great spirits of English Poetry die away. Who is left now but Tennyson? It seems to me that the era of intellectual activity in poetry is fast drawing to a close, and that we are about to be doomed to some years of stagnation, such as has followed the time of Schiller and Goethe in Germany. For the poets of Germany now are all below par."

"October 2, '61.

"I am really delighted to find that you have taken up geology with interest. . . . It would be a splendid thing to see Lord Enniskillen's collection. Sir P. Egerton told me that they used to travel together on the Continent in a huge carriage of three compartments— one where they sat, the other two full of duplicates of their collection of English fossil fish, which they used to exchange for foreign, and so come back with the two compartments full of strangers. . . .

"There is an article in the July number of the *National Review* on the Spectrum Analysis, which is the best *résumé* of all that is popularly known on the subject I have seen. Do get it; it is most romantic in its interest. As I read of things like this, there seems a possibility of science becoming the ground and subject of a new school of Poetry. Certainly apart from human feeling nothing can be more suggestive to the imagination than their analysis. To be able to tell the metals and elements of Sirius—at our distance, and to read them off, as one reads a book, in colour!"

CHAPTER VIII

THE QUEST FOR KNOWLEDGE

" You should always try to *complete* your knowledge of a subject, and to see it in at least two different points of view. Above all, if you are reading a 'book of thinking' on any subject—not a history,—do not go on to another chapter till you have mastered the last. Or rather let me say: read two chapters and then go back to the former and examine yourself in it till you feel sure that you have grasped what the Author means, and so on throughout. Read a book at first passively—in order to receive fully the ideas of the writer: if your mind is always fighting with him, or if you read in order to find out where he is wrong, or if you do not, by an act of self-surrender, divest yourself of all prejudice, it is simply waste of time to read, and more —it is a positive injury to your mind. But do not stop there. When you have received, then go back and sift his principles. If you are in doubt as to his being right, find out where he is wrong; do not be content with vague feelings against him—or vague denunciation; discover his error moral or intellectual, and do not relax till you have either proved him or your own feeling mistaken and that on *clear grounds*. By doing this you will get real good from everything you read: you will have taken in all that the Author could give *you*, and you will have exercised your own intellect."—(From a letter to his sister Honor, December 11, 1863.)

In a letter (1856) already given Brooke writes: " To me the opinions I adopted came home at once. I could hardly be said to have adopted them, it seemed as if I had held them all my life." And in another letter (1859) to the same correspondent he says : " It is strange that as yet I have seen nothing which I do not feel as if I had seen before, and known from my very youth. My experience, as far as it has gone, has never outrun my knowledge."

These are not, as they might seem at first sight, the words of a man who feels that he has nothing more to learn. To the end of his life Brooke remained the most eager and, I must add, the most childlike of learners: in early years his eagerness amounted to rapacity. In the presence of a new scientific discovery, or indeed of new information about anything, he was like a boy listening to a traveller's story of distant lands. The knowledge which "his experience never outran" was knowledge of another kind. It was what philosophers call "intuition."

The development of Brooke was rooted in the intuition of love, as the ground of existence and the rule of life. To watch his development, therefore, is simply to watch the growing ascendancy of this intuition throughout the entire domain of his thought, experience, and expression. As a personal characteristic it was dominant from the first, being born in the blood, and so it remained throughout, the moving spring of his intercourse with nature and with men. At first it was little more than a temperament, or a passion, which he was feeding unconsciously on nature, art, and poetry, especially the poetry of Tennyson, Wordsworth, and Shelley. But very soon reflection was turned upon it, and from that time onward love became the loadstar of his life, a guiding principle consciously recognized as such, and followed with all the vehement ardour of which his nature was capable. This reflective grasp of his principle came to him quite early in his career. Enough has already been quoted from his letters and writings to show that the master-intuition was formed and active when he crossed the threshold of responsible manhood. To the end of his life he remained unshaken on that foundation.

The course of his subsequent thought is a history of

the gradual sloughing off of everything which the main principle could not assimilate, with a growing intensity in the principle itself. This began with his recoil against Evangelicalism in general, and his indignant repudiation of Eternal Punishment in particular. Those were forms, he thought, in which love could not express itself, and for that reason they were abandoned. Other forms suffered the same fate later on, and as they departed one by one the main effect was to leave Brooke standing more firmly on his original ground, more radiant in his defence of it, more deeply in love with nature, humanity and art, and more eager for every kind of social and political reform which promised to restore men to nature or to give them fellowship with one another.

Proof of his main principle he hardly attempted, though he would welcome proof wherever he could find it, for example, in the philosophy of Fichte, ardently studied during the years of which I am now writing.

There was a deep vein of mysticism in his nature, the evidence of which is not to be found in recorded "visions"—to which he was certainly susceptible—but in his attitude towards the world of knowledge. He found that every kind of knowledge as it came his way fell like fuel on the inward fire and gave a new ardour to its flame. Living in an age of profound intellectual disturbance, he was so made as to find confirmation and support in the very truths that were shaking the faith of other men. To him widening knowledge seemed only to extend the range for the application of his main principle, and to deepen the conviction that he was *known* even as he knew. Hence he pushed forward as far and as rapidly as he could into every realm of knowledge, even into those where danger was thought to lie in wait; and the dangers when he met them increased his security.

"And so, whether in life or death, in this world or any other, we will pursue, we will divide, we will overtake the spoil!". These were the last words I heard him speak in public, and they characterize his spirit at every stage of his development. Love with him was not only a guiding but a conquering principle, and all knowledge was its spoil.

His mind demanded a constant sustenance of new ideas, and in the pursuit of them, whether in men or books, had a swiftness and sure instinct like that of a wild creature in quest of its food. He loved intellectual order, and whatever he learnt was soon correlated with what he knew already and given its place in a unitary scheme. Moreover, his memory was good, and to this cause we may partly set it down that his life contains no revolutionary changes of thought, for these are oftener due to the forgetfulness of old truths than to the acquisition of new ones.

I have before me a collection of his note-books, belonging, or partly belonging, to the time when he was a curate in Kensington. They reveal the extraordinary variety of his intellectual occupations, and might at first sight suggest the conclusion that he was dabbling in too many waters. On closer examination one is astonished at the thoroughness with which everything noted is worked out. Many of the pages are covered with writing so fine and small that it can only be deciphered by aid of a glass. On one of them I find a full analysis of the *Kenosis* doctrine of the person of Christ (which he adopted for a time), with the arguments for and against set out in detail, and his own conclusions carefully deduced. On another is a detailed study of a geological period, with specimens of the characteristic fossils beautifully drawn. Near to this is a long account, running into many pages, of the dip and variation of the mariner's compass, with remarks appended which show that he was deep in the study of magnetic phenomena. Scattered about among these things are notes of which the following are specimens.

"Our Liturgy needs a new clause: 'from all manner of fools good Lord deliver us.'"

"The cry of dismay with which Darwin, Geology, Criticism are hailed in England is pitiable. The shifts of argument, the endeavours to get round the truth, are miserable in men who ought to feel that God's truth must become clearer and clearer as time goes on. Our sermons want that joy of faith which belongs to men who are sure of conquest. . . . I look upon all these exciting differences, discussions, oppositions with pleasure and hope. It is the state of stagnation and conservatism that I should fear."

He is evidently hard at work on the Life of Robertson. There are first sketches of Robertson's character, and the progressive developments of these into fuller details. There are important passages written and erased and then rewritten, three or four times. There are plans for treating the particular aspects of Robertson's work.

His work as a preacher is evident throughout. He writes out for his own reflection various theories of preaching, and lays it down that "all knowledge" is the preacher's province. He discusses the various kinds of sermons—written and extempore—and prefers the written. He constructs innumerable sermon plans.

In another place I find him deep in the prose works of Milton: cannot get on with them till he knows more philology; and signs of philology soon make their appearance. Presently he is analysing Milton's diction and tracing the history of Miltonic words.

Other portions were evidently written during his holidays at home or abroad. There are geological sections drawn to scale and described in detail. There are architectural drawings of windows, doorways, towers. There are sketches in crayon of scenery in Switzerland or Italy, some of them, I think, of great merit. Many pages are filled with closely-written notes on the art galleries of Italy. Every notable picture is carefully described and studied, and some are reproduced in rough sketches, and the peculiar manner of each artist defined and distinguished. Mingled with these are experiments in verse, translations of Heine, aphorisms in many languages, the striking sayings of friends, witty stories, and illustrations grave and gay.

In one of these note-books I find a list of books to be read forthwith. There are sixty-two of them. In theology and philosophy there are Ewald's "Leben Jesu," Strauss' "Leben Jesu," Irving's "Works," Maurice's "Conflict of Good and Evil," Pigou's "Sermons," Grote's "Plato," Ferrier's "Lectures on Metaphysics," "The Reign of Law," Mill's "Comte and Positivism." In science Hoffmann's "Chemistry," Buchan's "Text Book of Meteorology," Percy's "Metallurgy," Bevan's "Modern Geography," Herschel's "Lectures on Scientific Subjects," Darwin's "Domesticated Animals," Agnes' "Kestrels and Falcons." There are four English Histories by various authors, Trollope's "History of the Commonwealth of Florence," "Early and Mediæval Antiquities of Rome," and two county histories. There are various biographies—Raphael, Brunel, Whately—and a large number of books in general literature, including Balzac's novels. On social subjects there are the works of Mill, Fawcett, F. D. Maurice and Stanley Jevons.

Did he read them all? is the question that naturally occurs. I have no means of answering, but I do know that all these books relate to subjects with which he showed himself familiar in later life. One detail may be taken in proof so far as it goes. "Jevons on the Coal Supply" is mentioned in the list of books. A few pages further on I find a full analysis of this work with various comments and criticisms by S. A. B.

Are we to infer from all this that Brooke was intent on "self-improvement" after the manner of mid-Victorian young men and according to the precepts of the excellent Samuel Smiles? I think not. The "self-improver" represents a well-known type which in its worst examples degenerates into the prig. In better examples he remains self-centred, cannot lose himself in the object of his study, and has neither enthusiasm, élan nor joy. We shall be nearer the truth if we think of Brooke as urged onwards partly by a passion of intellectual hunger, partly by the spirit of the explorer, partly by an imagination which found enchantment in the tales of science; all these confederate in a single aim—"to pursue, to divide, to overtake the spoil."

For four years he remained at his post in Kensington, increasingly beloved by the parishioners, but regarded with much disquiet by those set in authority over him. His power as a preacher was growing, and his love of preaching was great. But as time wore on signs of restlessness appeared. With the Church of England as an institution he had as yet no quarrel, but the sense that he was *not free* became oppressive. Watchful eyes were upon him, and it was a state of things he did not like. He had served his apprenticeship as a servant, but nature intended him to be his own master, and it was plain as daylight that whatever is to be gained in this world by subservience to others would never be gained by him. He began to look out for a position of greater independence. The desire to travel grew upon him, and he took long holidays in Switzerland and in Italy. Moreover, the Life of Robertson was unfinished, nor could he finish it amid the pressing duties of his curacy and the intellectual temptations to which his London life was exposed.

In January, 1858, the Princess Royal had been married to the Crown Prince of Prussia, and an English Court had been formed in Berlin. An English Chaplain was already established there, but without official connexion with the Court. It was understood, however, that this gentleman would presently receive a living in England, and it was accordingly proposed to form a chaplaincy at the Embassy, the intention being to unite the existing congregation with the new one whose centre would be on official ground. These proposals were in accordance with the wishes of Queen Victoria and of the Crown Princess, who desired to have a chaplain of her own. The arrangements were left to the Foreign Office, the Liberals being then in power and Earl Russell Foreign Minister. Brooke was a candidate for the post, and in April, 1862, received a letter informing him that Earl Russell had accepted his application. It had been ascertained that he would be *persona grata* to the Crown Princess.

On receiving the appointment he wrote to William, " I always feel that my proper centre is London, and I will always keep before me the *duty* of returning to it. It would not do to die out of the *Lebensturm;* and parish work is necessary to keep me alive and humble, and out of too wide and dangerous speculation. The Archdeacon

[Sinclair] was struck dumb when I told him [of my appointment]. He imagined that I had not a chance."

Brooke went out to Berlin in the autumn of 1863. Just before his departure he received the offer of a valuable curacy at Hammersmith. He would have accepted it gladly had this been possible, for he shrank greatly from the idea of "going into exile" and taking his family so far away.

LETTERS.

To William Brooke.

"Jan. 19, '62.

"I rejoice that you are pursuing geology actively. I hope to go over to Kingstown for the Shrove Tuesday Commencements. Could we have a day or two then into the country on a geological trip? Even two days would be charming. What are the fees for a Master's degree? Are these 'syllogisms' to be written? Can you get them and the 'Compositions' done for me? Do not forget to answer these questions."

"March 19, '62.

"I have already projected several expeditions: one to Bognor to study the Lower Eocene; another to Swindon, where we have splendid sections of the Oolites, and the chalk and quarries full of fossils; another to Charleton (Eocene); another to Lyme Regis, if possible. There is Oxford close at hand. I have a proposition too for our holidays: Cheltenham—a week; Bristol coal-fields—a week; and perhaps a race from that to the South Coast of Devon. . . . [Then] go over the Cotswolds and all the Oolite and Lias. I have identified all the Carboniferous Limestone fossils. . . . I have been arranging my fossils and have a lot for you; . . . all our Ludlow specimens and my Wenlock series."

"Feb. 22, '63.

"Get from the Library and read 'The Camp in the Highlands, or Thoughts about Art,' by P. G. Hamerton. It is a little conceited in tone, or rather it seems so, but it is really well worth reading. It certainly chimes in with my views as to what landscape art should be and should attempt, except in one point, that it entirely shuts out true idealism. Read also Stanley's 'Lectures on the Jewish Church.' It is in substance though not in detail the best answer to the whole drift of Colenso's book. I have begun Lyell's 'Antiquity of Man.' He seems fair and anxious to state facts without prejudice. He has not the irreligious animus which belongs to Huxley's dissertations on the same subject. Tell me what you are reading and doing, and I promise—though my promises are light as gossamer—to write almost immediately in reply. By the by read 'Biographical Sketches' by Mr Senior. . . . How I wish you would come with me to North Wales in August and study the old glaciers! Ever, dear old fellow, your most loving S. A. B."

"April 17, '63.

"I copy the letter received to-night. [Here follows the official appointment as Chaplain to the British Embassy at Berlin.] So, dear Bill, the die is cast. Whether it will turn out a Venus throw remains to be seen. I am glad and sorry."

"June 7, '63.

"The whole business of Monarchy, settled government, and all else looks very stormy at Berlin. It is almost amusing, were it not so sad, to watch that poor old fool playing such fantastic tricks with his power and his people. How vainly for some persons has the drama of history been played out! Taxes, army, breach of privilege, repression of the press—here it is all being acted over again—all except the scaffold or the flight, and one of these is coming. It will be interesting to be at Berlin, but our relations with Prussia, owing to her close alliance with Russia, are so shaky that it is quite on the cards that the Embassy should be recalled. . . . Do read Mrs Norton's 'Lost and Saved,' a novel, but also a sermon to our present social state. Another book I can recommend is [Bates'] 'The Naturalist on the Amazons.' Are not Senior's 'Sketches' well done?"

"June 21, '63.

"I am going, please God, to Derbyshire on the 30th to hunt for fossils. It is the richest carboniferous limestone in England. It is a lovely country into the bargain. . . . There is a jolly little town called Longnor where we can lodge for a week and explore the county. . . . Then we might go slowly home through Dudley, and I should like to turn aside and see Kidderminster and my old school haunts. . . . But Derbyshire is the place. I have got a geological map of it and shall come primed."

"Aug. 17, '63.

"Berlin still continues in an unsatisfactory condition. I have written to Sir A. Buchanan [the Ambassador] to ask whether he thinks I should go at once or not. . . . It is like appointing a man to hold the chair and then making the iron bottom of the chair red hot as an additional mark of favour. I should not have accepted it unless I had understood, as I did from the Bishop, that [the chaplain on the spot] was to be pensioned off with a living."

To his Mother.
"Sept. 21, '63.

"When I left you all at Wyton [his father had now the living of Wyton in Huntingdonshire] I had then a real sense of sorrow: I had enjoyed my time so much and felt so much once more as if at home in the old life at Kingstown. But after all I [shall be] only 36 hours away from you. I can come back in a whizz."

The letters from which extracts follow were written to a lady in profound sorrow for the death of her husband.

"Fern Lodge, Kensington.
"May 8, 1860.

"I am glad that your husband had been with you at Tenby; connected with him the quiet stillness of the place will transfer itself to him in your mind, and you will, I trust, lose some of that passionate regret. I do not say lose regret, but I hope for you that regret will become calm, not passionate. The more you think of him among the great realities of Heaven, at home with God, at peace for evermore, the more there will come upon the useful quietude of sorrow, a quietude which will give you time to think upon your life, and all you have given you by God to do therein. I have said to you often that God would not have left you behind if He had not work for you to do for Him and for others. It should be your aim to find out what that is, and with all your heart to do it. We lead useless lives, many of us, just because we do not give ourselves the trouble to discover what God means us to do, and because we do not half believe that we have a Father in Heaven who has sent us into the world to finish a certain amount of work for Him. The one thing clear before you at present is the education and training of your children. That is God's mission to you now, to teach them how to live as children of God. That too is what your husband in that other world is watching now, trusting too in you. I doubt not, with the large trust of love that you will prove worthy of the task. It is a difficult thing for you to escape from the benumbing touch of sorrow and take up your life with chastened and sad hope, alone. But its very difficulty is your impulse, for the Christian is not nurtured on a bed of down, but trained among the rocks to spiritual strength. Like the air of the Alpine peaks, the air of the heavenly life is difficult, and we need severe training before we can breathe it freely. Your training has begun: do not disappoint God your Father by shirking the trial because it is severe. Rather begin nobly, and at every step the journey will be easier and the mountain climb fresher. He will be with you. He never leaves one of us; but we shut our eyes to Him.

Do but realize that saying of Christ's—'I am not alone, for the Father is with Me.' And then an unknown power will awaken in your spirit, and your own strength—the strength He will give you—will astonish you.

"Do not despair of life. Despair is the worst kind of unbelief, and is simply the utter ruin of the soul. God calls you His child, and while that is true hope should never fail or faith be lost. He lives, your Father, and endeavour and prayer will soon bring to you the conviction that you live in him for evermore, living a more vital life than ever he lived on earth, keeping still untouched all the old living human feelings, only refined and purified from human weakness He loves you now better than ever. He loves you well enough now not to grudge you your sorrow if God through it lead you to perfection. He watches over you with the large tender care of a perfect spirit, and I believe, marks every one of your struggles, and rejoices over every one of your self-conquests. This thought is yours with all its comfort, but do not remain in it too long, lest you should forget that all this is only possible because Christ has died and risen. Connect both together and then the former will not destroy the latter. Your husband is in Heaven now only because Christ has died and lived for him. He is living an active, conscious, loving life now only because Christ has risen, and so without Him all is dark and impossible; mist and uncertainty; but with him the sad mystery of life and death and human pain is solved. 'Because I live ye shall live also.' To believe that is calm.

"Will you pardon this didactic lecturelike letter? I am tired and unfit to write, but if you will write to me I shall then have something to answer, and all questions put to me are as I told you a kindness. To feel that I can help one human soul is a pleasure than which life has nothing better to offer."

"Fern Lodge.
"June 7, '60.

"Remember the great danger of grief is lest it should become selfish. To think of nothing else but your own sorrow, to wrap yourself so up in it as to be unable to lose something of yourself in others—to say, I cannot give any time to my children, or to helping them, will end in the worst, because it is the most insidious form of selfishness. I do not say for a moment that this is your case now, but I do say that this is what you might become, and that comfort, and loss of all that agony of regret will never really come to you till you begin to do something for others, in fact—to follow Christ in His self-sacrifice. To follow Christ simply means the sacrifice of self, the giving up of what we like that we may give to and bless others.

"You say in one place—that 'try as much as I may, all my labours may fail.' That is impossible. No true work ever fails. It may *seem* to fail to us—but it never, never does. It is *the* only lasting thing; for it is done by God in us, and done on immortal spirits. Nothing done in love ever perishes. A cup of cold water given in Christ's name, that is for the sake of Christ—or as Christ would have done it, in true-hearted love, can in no wise lose its reward. You *cannot* fail if you work in love."

"Milford Haven.
"July 4, '60.

"It is well for you to feel that you 'must act alone.' Keep the thought before your mind. Remember that to be noble, to be a brave follower of Christ, to ennoble yourself to meet him and your husband hereafter—you must act alone. In all true human life there come these times of loneliness. We are all driven up at some time or other into the wilderness to be tempted of the Devil. But we meet our foe as a conquered one. He was vanquished by Christ and the virtue of His victory is consciously ours, if we believe that it *is* ours. You cannot know at once what to do—or how to act in this loneliness, but continue *to do what you can*, and trust in Him always. Do not mind your difficulties when you are left to your own resources. Think and think again, act and act again, do what you have thought as fully as you can, put your feelings into some action and ask and ask again and again of God your Father for help and guidance and things will slowly become clear, and by thought, action and prayer will grow into assurance and possession. You will know what to do in time—only do not give in for an instant, do not despair for a moment. Whether you feel it or no—for feeling it or not feeling it does not alter the truth a whit—God is your Father and is directing, guiding and inspiring your life. We cannot cease fighting this sad battle as long as we believe that He is on our side. Believe it though you cannot feel it, for though your fears should give your faith the lie, each hour—yet it remains immutably the Truth. God has loved, does love you. Christ has saved, does save you now."

CHAPTER IX

BERLIN

"Coming back from [the] Ludwig [Brunnen at Homburg] I met Sir F. Lascelles and walked part of the way home with him. I asked him if there were many changes in Berlin, and he described those he had seen. I have not been there since '65, and, as he talked, I felt again the ancient days, and all their events and oddities. One good thing I did there. It was there I wrote Robertson's Life. There I also made a friend of [Sir Robert] Morier, and there I met Gifford Palgrave for the first time. And few men have I more liked, I may say loved. I was curious to feel it all over again as Lascelles mentioned streets whose names I had forgotten. I must go someday and see Berlin again. Most of the men I knew there are dead. G. Bunsen, Ranke, Gneist, Morier, and many others. And the Emperor Frederick and his wife, then Crown Prince and Princess, whom also I liked well. And once I had a long talk with Augusta, who was then only Queen of Prussia, and who aired her little theory about a union between the Church of England and the Church in Prussia; and every word she said was ignorance."—(*Diary*, August 20, 1907.)

When Brooke went to Berlin in '63 four children had been born to him: two sons, Stopford and Graham; and two daughters, Honor and Maud, destined to be his close companions in later life. The removal of his household to a distant foreign city was a difficult and unpleasant undertaking, and for that reason among others he went reluctantly. But the need of leisure for completing Robertson's Life was imperative.

So far as the main purpose was concerned he attained his object and came back eighteen months later with the finished MS of the book. In other respects the experience was dreary enough. He disliked Berlin and its climate, was not attracted by the Berlinese, and was continually longing for his old work, his old friends, his old pursuits. His actual duties as Chaplain to the Embassy were limited and uninspiring, and had to be performed in makeshift and ugly surroundings. In some measure they were rendered unpleasant by friction with the English Church already established in Berlin, the minister of which retained his post in spite of the understanding under which Brooke had accepted the Foreign Office appointment. Moreover, he greatly missed his daily contact with the poor, and when he attempted to reach the English workmen living in Berlin he found himself confronted with a variety of annoying obstacles due to the cause just mentioned. While away for a holiday in 1864 he writes to Edward Brooke, "How keenly I felt that my whole spiritual life was deteriorating in Berlin."

A mistake which has obtained some currency is that Brooke, during his Berlin period, devoted himself to the study of German theology, and fell under the influence of the more destructive school of German critics. Of this I can find not one particle of evidence either in the letters written by him from Berlin, some of which go deep into theological questions, nor in my memory of any conversation I ever had with him on the subject. He was too much preoccupied with Robertson, who gave him all the liberalism he wanted, and too little in sympathy with his Prussian environment, to lend a ready hearing to ideas that were then current in Berlin. Indeed, his letters show little respect for the native savants with whom he came in contact. Moreover, so far as theology is concerned, I can discover no definable difference between the opinions he held when he went to Berlin in '63 and those he brought back with him in '65. He went "a liberal conservative," and as such he returned. At no time of his life was he enamoured of German criticism, and so far as Berlin influenced him at all in these matters, it was rather in the contrary direction. Both then and afterwards he looked in vain for a contemporary German thinker whom he could accept as a competent exponent of the essence of Christianity. Goethe he loved; Fichte he honoured; but these great men were long dead, and other voices were calling the tune in the Berlin of '64. Of things distinctively German, or rather Prussian, the fullest account that we find in his letters is a description of the needle-gun, with careful drawings of the mechanism and cartridge—matters which were then State secrets, but which, by some means unknown, he had managed to find out. This weapon was being used in the Danish war of 1864, and as the relations of Great Britain and Prussia were then ambiguous, Brooke took occasion to ask himself what, in the event of a conflict, would happen to a British force with an inferior armament, and worked out for William's benefit some interesting and rather alarming tactical problems. He was, in fact, much more concerned about the needle-gun than he was interested in current German criticism of the Bible. He stood aloof from the life around him.

His position naturally brought him on several occasions into contact with great personages, notably with the Crown Princess and Princess Alice, for both of whom he conceived a great admiration—a connection which was destined to bear fruit later on in his appointment as Chaplain to Queen Victoria. But in general the Court did not interest him. It "bored" him, and on one occasion when he was invited to a ball, he had the temerity—a characteristic temerity—to refuse; "he would not make himself ridiculous by appearing at a ball in clergyman's robes!" It appears also that through ignorance of the social customs of Berlin he neglected to call on the great families, expecting that they would first call on him, according to the English rule. He discovered this when it was too late, but though he truly attributes the mistake to his ignorance, I do not believe that knowledge of the rule would have made much difference, his mood being what it then was.

Brooke's position in Berlin was not what he expected, not what he had been led to believe it would be. He was uncomfortable and restless. He felt that the course of his life had been arrested, and it is quite clear that he was, from the first, resolved to leave as soon as the literary work he had on hand was done. Except for a long holiday in Switzerland in the summer of '64 he was in Berlin from October, '63, to April, '65, when he left it for good, bringing back with him only one memory on which he cared to dwell in after life—the completion of the work he had set himself to do.

The suggestion has been made that the appointment was an attempt on the part of the authorities to "side-track" a man whose theological tendencies were thought to be dangerous. Of this also I can find no evidence; moreover, it is inherently improbable. Such a design, had it existed, would not have escaped the keen observation of Brooke, nor would he have suffered himself to become its victim. He was not the kind of person who is easily "side-tracked" either by guile or by force. It is, however, a significant circumstance, which throws some light on the state of the Church in '63, that at a time when good preachers were scarce in London, no attempt seems to have been made to dissuade a man who, as he mentions in one of his letters, could draw 900 people to hear him, from burying himself in Berlin. The following letter written to the Bishop in answer to the request that he should withdraw his resignation of the Chaplaincy shows pretty clearly that Brooke would not let himself be long buried. The date of the letter shows further that he had resigned before the end of '64, though he did not actually leave till some months later.

To the Bishop of London.

"Berlin, Dec. 28, '64.

"My Lord—I have as you desired taken into consideration the possibility of remaining here as Chaplain to the Embassy. I have resolved *not* to withdraw my resignation. I have nothing to do here, and I wish to be at work again. Moreover, my position has been so anomalous in this place, and my own feeling with regard to its circumstances—the unfitness of the service, the want of a proper place to worship in, the enforced opposition to Mr ——, the enforced isolation from any professional work—so strong that on no conditions would I remain. The post is untenable, and I cannot now wait till it becomes tenable. I have been waiting for more than a year for the fulfilment of the promise of providing for Mr —— elsewhere, a promise which I understood was made by the Foreign Office, and without having received which I should never have accepted this post.

"I have therefore once more the honour of placing my resignation in your Lordship's hands, and I shall consider that my term of service ends—unless it is inconvenient to you—on the last Sunday in January.—I am your Lordship's very faithful servant,

"Stopford A. Brooke."

The following extracts from letters afford us glimpses into his preoccupations, his mode of life, and his contact with the Prussian Court.

AT THE EMBASSY CHAPEL

To William Brooke.

"Hôtel d'Angleterre, Berlin, Oct. 24, '63.

"I am here at last. We arrived after 13 hours of a night journey from Cologne, the children sleeping most of the way and behaving under novel bed-circumstances very well. [He then describes his vain attempts to get definite instructions from the Foreign Office as to how he was to proceed at Berlin in view of complications with the existing Chapel.] I commence service on Sunday in the large reception room of the Embassy. Sir A. Buchanan [the Ambassador] is agreeable, cordial, full of bonhomie and open-heartedness. . . . One of the attachés told me that from two years' experience he could pronounce Berlin to be the dullest place in the universe. . . . He looked overwhelmed with ennui. If one could only rouse those young fellows to a higher life, it would be really an advantage. I foresee that this must be part of my work here. . . . The children are very well and proportionately noisy. They must be the agony of the Hotel."

To William Brooke.

"Nov., '63.

"I read service at the Embassy to-day. At one end of the room a full-length picture of the Queen rises from a dais to the ceiling. Three huge glass lustres holding about fifty wax candles each hang from the roof. There are five windows with yellow curtains very ugly. At the end opposite to Her Majesty we have rigged up an old desk, covered with a scarlet cloth for a pulpit—very shabby; and a table covered with the same scarlet cloth —which I shrewdly suspect from its trimming did duty formerly as a curtain—serves as a communion table. [Here follow drawings of these objects and a general plan of the room.] I felt nervous beforehand . . . the thing was new, and the pettiness of it after a London church was unpleasant. But I was not nervous when I began to read. Had I not been habituated not to see or think of my congregation as critics—indeed to be conscious of nothing except that there are persons before me whom I have to teach—I should have been discouraged by the smallness of the numbers. . . . They seemed to make it a point to stay away. Sir A. B. and the Household were there, of course, and Lord and Lady Blantyre, who are staying with them, but only two young men; on the whole, including servants, there were about 20 people. I fancy the English who have to do with the Embassy are rather displeased with my arrival. . . . I have no doubt they all think my arrival a bore, and feel inclined to impute to me as a fault the fault of the F. O. in not providing B. with a living.

"You have no idea how difficult it is to find a place to live in. . . . We saw to-day a suite of rooms with a look out over the Thiergarten, but the price is enormous, £270 a year. [Here follows an account of the insanitary conditions of the Berlin houses.] So far as work goes I am doing nothing but reading. I have just finished Tyndall on Heat. I wanted a history, to make me uneasy, so I bought Lord Mahon's. I like the book. He has his partialities, but they are moderately held, and he avows them. There is here and there a pleasant vein of very courtly humour. . . . I was charmed with those lines of Claudian's which Mahon calls well known—but which I did not know—

> O nimium dilecte Deo, cui fundit ab antris
> Æolus armatas hiemes, cui militat æther
> Et conjurati veniunt ad classica venti.

In almost every century of her history England has cause to apply these lines to herself. [Further criticisms of Mahon's History.] Tocqueville's L'Ancien Régime still interests me. If you can get the book, read it carefully: it is an exhaustless mine of knowledge. . . . I do not know if I agree with Goldwin Smith about [the surrender of] the Colonies. [Reasons then given which show plainly that he does not agree.] . . . Thank you for your details about the Archbishop [Whateley]. . . . Should Stanley be made Archbishop [of Dublin] I will certainly send you a letter for him. But I should not wish him to be exposed to the blind baying of all the ignorant bigotry among the lower classes of the Irish Clergy."

MRS. STOPFORD BROOKE.
From a drawing by E. R. Hughes.

e page 158.

To William Brooke.

"Hôtel de Russie, Dec. 6, '63.

"... Jukes' theory of the Irish rivers interested me much. I have just got my maps, and have followed as far as possible your explanation of them. ... Scrope's Volcanoes I have just finished. Mallet's books, and the very loose way he illustrates phenomena, according to your account, gives me no desire to read it. As to Renan's Life of Christ (*sic*), it is only just arrived here ... before the week is out I will tell you as rapidly as I can what I think of it.

"It seems almost a settled thing that I should stay here as a carpet minister and preach in a room like an ancient Hussite in fear of persecution. I do not like it, but now having made my bed, I must lie in it. ... We dine about once a fortnight at the Embassy—very stupid. ... My congregation consists of the Buchanans (2), the Lowthers (2), the Moriers (3), the wife of the Danish Minister, Dr Mayer (a German), some young men, Emma and servants—about 20 people. The young attachés do not come to Church. They either lie in bed, or go to the [other] Chapel.

"We have found no house as yet. I shrink from accomplishing my exile from England by the act of taking a house. I feel it more and more each day, and I hope, and hope as yet in vain, that I may reconcile myself to my banishment. It is wonderfully dull, and the only thing that supports me is reading, reading always ... I find it hard to regain [here] the habit of severe study. I recall with wonder how we used to sit in old days for seven and eight hours without moving— you, Edward and I in the little study at Kingstown. I find my spiritual life failing for want of external work, and a sense of uselessness creeping over me which gives me a gnawing twinge of remorse. ... No religious feeling seems stirring among the English I meet: no interest even in the religious movements of the world. I would I were again in London ... Ces choses-ci s'arrangeront."

To his Father.

"Dec. 27, '63.

"How I hate this ceremonial visiting, yet I suppose it is very good for me to feel my social duties as duties and to be conscious that I am of sufficient importance to give offence. I assure you that is a new experience. I feel still so much of a boy that I cannot conceive that I stand on the same ground as other men.

"We went last night to a reception at Count Karolyi's —the Austrian Minister. I was introduced to Countess Brühl. I had some conversation with Professor Ranke— the Pope man. He is a miserable wizened-looking monkey of a man: one has to stoop to talk to him. He had two orders on, tied or rather cast loose about a dirty cravat. He shakes about his little head when he speaks with an air of wonderful self-conceit. He smiled contempt on all our English writers: seemed to think they had no stamina, etc., etc.: on the whole bright and intelligent. I felt I should like to hold him up between my finger and thumb and shake him like a mouse. I saw Bismarck—a tall, fine-looking man, slightly bald, with grey hair thinly laid upon his head. A good head of the obstinate military type, shrewd rather than cunning, and with the look of a man whose shrewdness would fail him when he was emporté with passion.

"I was so rejoiced to read that portion of your letter in which you say that you do not now judge men but opinions. If a man loves Christ and does all he can to serve Him, what matter his opinion on points of doctrine? ... So far as C. Wordsworth's letter is a protest against Stanley's views—so far fair and just, but when he descends to hint that S. is dishonest in making his subscriptions ... so far unfair and unjust. It is the curse of nearly all schools of theology that they will go on imputing motives which are base, and making innuendoes which are infamous. ... As to his remark on the Prayer Book, I wonder how many clergymen could remain in the Church if they were to adopt his view of signature ... the Absolution in the Visitation of the

Sick—how many clergymen can say that in its full meaning? . . .

"Miss Senior writes me in the saddest way . . . her father is very dangerously ill. I ought to have been in Kensington."

To his Mother.
"Dec. 28, '63.

"A thousand thanks for your accustomed cadeau [a note-book]. . . . I remember the time I used to jot down in them sonnets to my mistress' eyebrow in Kingstown. I have one or two at home full of snatches of poetry written to half a dozen young ladies—and now I am a father, four bouncing children! . . . The baby has the voice of a Stentor—nothing of Cordelia about her. . . . I am going to be presented to the King: it is a dire necessity. . . . Tell them all at home I think of them all lovingly. Give my love to my Grandmother."

To William Brooke.
"Jan. 11, '64.

[The first part of this letter is a long discussion of Inspiration.]

"Whatever Colenso's book be worth—very little I think—it at least proves not only inaccuracies but contradictions in history . . . it is allowed on all sides that the Bible is inaccurate with regard to scientific fact. Kings and Chronicles are long contradictions of one another. . . . The rationalist says—all human; I say, historically, scientifically human, but spiritually Divine. How do I distinguish the two? The New Testament lays down the rule—the particular is human, the universal is spiritual. The universal is spiritually discerned. As God's work the Bible can be understood only by one who has the consciousness of God. Herein I differ from Jowett and others. Study the Bible like any other book —yes. But if you want to get to the core of the Bible there is only one way—to be like God as far as possible —to walk in His spirit. This inward pervasive inspiration of the Bible is what the liberal school have neglected to assert and prove. Stanley's work is the only one which has it on a foundation. Colenso's book will perish, Stanley's will last. The former forces us to lose all principles taught in the history of God's Government: the latter retains those principles. . . . I agree with Stanley that the Pentateuch was not written by Moses. You say you cannot believe it because our Lord says he was the author. Here I must have recourse to the accommodation theory. Our Lord had willingly limited His Godhead by His Humanity. He *increased* in wisdom—He *marvelled* at the faith of the centurion. I believe that He really did share the opinions of the Jews on the authorship of the Pentateuch. His knowledge on purely critical points was limited. His want of omniscience was self-chosen. He *emptied himself* of certain powers belonging to His Godhead. . . .

"The cold here is intense. . . . The countrymen are clothed in sheepskins—the wool within, the drest hide without: they look ugly, horrible, like flayed men. It is the realization to me of dear old Brian O'Lynn—you remember:

"'Brian O'Lynn had no breeches to wear,
He got him a sheepskin and made him a pair;
The skinny side out—the woolly side in,
Pleasant and cool—said Brian O'Lynn.'

What terseness—what force—what a picture! We have lost in these degenerate days the power of writing like that. Healthy realism in every word. It would have ravished Goethe. . . .

"The [Crown] Princess has arrived. I was presented Sunday before last when she was at service at the Embassy. She has a pleasant, bright, intelligent face. . . . I never saw a face in which expression more replaced beauty. She conversed with me for a minute, 'How long had I been in Berlin—how I liked it—the effect of the cold on the poor.' I have met her once since at the baptism of Mrs Morier's girl, to whom she stood godmother. Jowett, who is Morier's oldest friend, baptized the child, and he preached for me the Sunday the Princess was in Church. . . . I saw a good deal of Jowett. I dined at

Morier's the day he arrived and met G. de Bunsen and others. I had a very pleasant evening and heard a multitude of stories—all of which I have abominably forgotten. Two days afterwards I breakfasted with Jowett and talked with him for two hours. It was chiefly a conversation on Robertson, and on certain letters of his, the expediency of the insertion of which I doubted. There is nothing of the suffering martyr about him either in appearance or in manner. He is a joyous person, and at first sight does not impress one with the idea that he could possess the great influence over young men which he does possess. Morier has an exalted opinion of him. He says that of the two intellects, Stanley's and Jowett's, Jowett's is the dominant one, and that Stanley's late move forward to the front is owing to J.'s influence; that J. is worshipped in Oxford, that he is the most unselfish man of men, that if there is a black sheep among the men of his College whom everybody avoids, who is a kind of publican and sinner, or who is remarkably dull in intellect, that is the man J. will single out as his special pupil, ask him to dinner, walk with him, personally instruct him, expend all his force upon him, till he has either redeemed him or drawn out whatever power may be hidden in him. That is very great—is it not? I am glad I have established a point of contact with Jowett.

"I have begun for the third time Mill's Political Economy. I have a German master and soon shall begin to read Ewald."

To William Brooke.
"Feb. 2, '64.

"There is a chance of my being compelled to leave this place. Some say that war is imminent in England, and others say not. I do not think it will come to that, but still our tenure here is so unsettled that I think it is better to wait before bringing out my furniture. I have taken a house for two years; it would be sad work if I had to pay the two years' rent and not be able to live in it. I do not know what I should do if war were to arise;

go on, I think, to Italy and see Venice, Florence, and Rome. . . . The Princess I have not as yet seen at the service in the Embassy. She has been ill, as you have probably seen in the papers. Her husband is off to the war. But my own opinion with regard to the war is this: that there is a private understanding between Austria, Prussia, and Denmark, and that after the first fighting matters will be arranged peaceably: and Prussia, laughing in its sleeve at the German Bund, will take possession of Schleswig as its own, leaving Holstein to Denmark, Austria having some sop or other on its own frontiers flung to it to fill its stomach. . . .

"The service goes on as usual. Some seem interested in the sermons, but it is still dead and dull work. Yet when I preach I always become full of my subject and forget that I am not at Kensington with a congregation of 900 people. Jowett's sermon was not much admired; it disappointed the generality, who expected great things. But it was wise and subtle in thought, and the text he chose a characteristic choice. 'Beloved, if our heart condemn us God is greater than our heart,' etc. . . . Both you and my Father seem to think that *I* would disapprove of Jowett's occupying my Pulpit: on the contrary, I was glad to see him there, and if I were occupying a church in London should have no hesitation in asking him again. I do not agree with many of his views—especially with those which he holds on the character of St Paul's writings; but with the main tendency of his views I do agree. I say this because I wish you clearly to recognize as I wish the world to recognize that, though retaining my individuality of opinion, I have deliberately thrown in my lot with that school which is called Broad Church, though I repudiate the name as given to us, not adopted by us. I belong I hope to the Catholic Church to which men of all opinions belong: my Father, myself, Stanley, Robertson, Maurice, Day, Gregg, Neligan, Archbishop Whateley, Canon Wordsworth, etc. I have chosen men of the most diverse opinions—in all worketh the one and the self-same spirit, dividing to every man severally as He will. Tell my

Father the name Broad Church was never 'self-assumed'—it was imposed upon us by Conybeare in his Essay in the *Edinburgh*; and most of the men I have spoken to abjure any party name."

"May 18, '64.

"I have resolved to return to England in two years, dating from 1st April last. Circumstances may possibly send me away sooner. The Prussians are furious with England; I can scarcely give you any idea how furious. . . . Prussians who have known Englishmen for ten years refuse almost to speak to them now. The King says he will give up the Duchies to the rightful heirs, but Bismarck wishes to incorporate them with Prussia, and that too is the wish of all the bourgeoisie here who are puffed up with more than Prussian vanity on account of the glory (!) they have won [in the Danish war]. . . . The Zundnagel rifle was fearfully destructive in the war. [A long description of the rifle follows.] The inventor keeps his secret [the preparation of the cartridge]. I pumped out this information thinking it might interest you."

"June 23, '64.

"We are now, of course, in the greatest excitement. War is 'imminent,' as the papers say. We shall know our fate on Tuesday. We shall then have 8 days to leave and to get everything ready. *Personally* I shall be glad—so glad. *Nationally* it would be a very sad thing that England and Prussia should be at war. It would be nothing but a war of aggravating reprisals. We could not meet the Prussians in battle on land. We have no army. At the most we could land 30,000 men in Jutland. That is a cypher—the Prussian army consists of 300,000 men. Grant that 1 Englishman = 3 Prussians: the Prussians could bring six to one. We must fight for the sea. You may see me in England in a month."

"Dec. 4, '64.

"I am going to send in my resignation by the next mail on Saturday. I wish to be free on Feb. 1, '65, in order that, if possible before returning to England, I may visit some of the German towns—Austrian-Tyrol. . . .

"Berkeley Chapel is again in prospect. . . . I like and at the same time shrink from accepting a post so full of difficulty and I think trial—but it seems thrust upon me, if I receive the offer; and though it has no parish attached, there are other things to do for the Church and for men; and God may be served even by preaching. This Berlin business has been such a total failure that I can scarcely expect to be so much in misfortune again—at least immediately after. . . .

"Lord Napier [the new Ambassador] has the character of harmonizing the Government of his own nation with that to which he is accredited. The Prussians are glad of this, for they do not in their hearts like to be in opposition to England. They think they will have a war with France through the Italian and Austrian difficulty, and they say: our interests are identical with England's, and England's and ours in opposition to those of France. There is no especial good feeling, however, lost at present between Austria and Prussia. There is a strong Liberal party at Vienna who are gall and wormwood to the Bismarck Schönhausen party here.

"I have read nothing of late but French and German; with one exception, Maine's Ancient Law—a most interesting book which you would vastly enjoy. Some pamphlets I have also read, lent me by the American Minister, as to what is doing for the freed slaves on the Mississippi. I will make notes of them for you. I have been delighted with Cairne's book; never read any *résumé* in my life better than the Career of the Slave Power—the V. chapter, I think. The prophecies for the future are not so interesting; however, Judd, the American Minister here, thinks they will militarily occupy the country till settlers from the North have largely filled it."

"Xmas Day, '64.

". . . Your account of the lecture was very interesting, and gave me great pleasure. Surely, however they may sin, God is on the side of the North. Broadly I may say so—not on the side of the excesses and murders which are committed here and there, but on the side of the Rights for which they are fighting.

"My whole being, down to its lowest depths, loathes slavery. I shrink from the touch of a slave-holder as I would from a rattlesnake. I could not shake hands with such a man, though at the same time I make allowances for their education and for the prestige under which the Institution has been fixed in their minds."

To his Mother.
"Feb. 5, '65.

"I write by this mail, though I have much to do, because I think you will like to know how matters went off at the Embassy last Sunday.

"First and foremost, very well. I was nervous because the last time the Princess was there I was deprived of breath owing to the heat of the room and could scarcely read. I feared, then, that this might occur again. But when the time came I was not in the least nervous. Just in front of me sat the Crown Princess, and beside her Prince Louis of Hesse—on her other side Princess Alice, and then the Crown Prince of Prussia. Behind them Ladies in Waiting—and ornamented Officers: then the rest of the congregation. I preached for fully half an hour, and as my congregation was larger than usual, with more spirit than usual. Indeed, I believe I was quite ardent. As you might like to see the sermon delivered to these very lofty people, I send it. I did not change it on their account. It was the same which a month ago I had arranged to preach on that day.

"When I had finished, and stood waiting for the exit of the big personages, the Crown Princess, who has a charming face, came up, grasped me by the hand and shook it cordially without saying a word. Emma and I went up to the drawing-room where we were introduced to the Princess Alice. She also shook my hand and said, 'Thank you very much for your beautiful sermon.' Then the Crown Princess came up, and said a number of compliments which I will spare you the narration of—they were out of bounds. 'She had never heard such splendid language,' etc., etc. She then requested to have a copy of the sermon which 'would I write out for her and her sister.' This laborious command I fulfilled some days afterwards. The Princess Alice has a nice, gentle, tender face and a cordial manner. The Prince of Prussia is, I think, charming —there is goodness and brightness in his countenance, but I like the Princess Royal. I like her for her very capriciousness, *i.e.* I suppose for her womanhood. I shall, I dare say, never see her again. There is to be a royal ball at the Embassy to-night—the King, the Queen, etc., etc., are all to be there. We were invited. I was going, but on hearing that I must be in official robes, I am not going; though Lady Napier says I ought, as the Queen has expressed a desire to be introduced to me. But first I have no notion of trailing about a clerical gown through the rooms and looking half a woman and half an ass, and secondly, I don't care for the Queen—so unless they send for me—I will not go. I am no longer a member of the Embassy, and it is not now, as it was, a duty to go once at least to these affairs."

To William Brooke.

"Feb. 27, '65.

"Perhaps you would like to hear an account of the last Sunday at the Embassy. I do not mind writing it to you, for you will not think me conceited. They were all there, the Crown Prince and his wife, Princess Alice and her husband, and ladies and gentlemen in waiting. The Princess Alice has a charming face. Nothing could equal the cordiality with which she shook my hand, refusing almost my low bow over it in order to kiss her hand, and said, 'Thank you very much for your beautiful sermon.' The Princess was just as cordial: regretted my leaving, at which I smiled, begged me to write out my sermon for her: 'such magnificent language.' 'I see two things,' said she, 'from your sermon, first, that you are a man of science, and secondly, that you are a Poet.' I disclaimed both. 'To tell you the truth I liked it better than many of Robertson's sermons, which I read continually.' 'Ah, Madame,' said I, 'if I am anything, I owe what I am to Robertson.' She then inquired when my book was to be finished, and asked me to send her a copy. She commenced then a conversation on the German poets—Goethe in particular, but she was called away by Lady Napier.

"The Crown Prince came forward and shook hands with me before the whole congregation, while I yet stood in my surplice after the whole service was ended. I preached, and had preached for some time, in a surplice.

"That is all I remember, and you must not speak of it, for all the Princess' praise is hyperbolical, and, though you will not, others would laugh if it were mentioned.

"There has been a great deal of fun at the fancy balls. At the Princess P.'s—the King, who changed his domino three times in order to be unknown, was accosted by some one, I forget whom, who poked him in the ribs and said, 'Ha! my friend, I recommend to you a course of Banting.' The King went into such a roar of laughter that he betrayed himself, and the unlucky joker fled in dismay.

"To-morrow I read service at the private Chapel of the Princess in the Palace. She thinks I am going at once, I suppose, and so pays me this compliment. . . .

"The book is finished, all except the Index, which is a few days' work. I have written a last chapter, a sort of Epilogue, endeavouring to condense into a brief space what is and should be the influence of Robertson's life upon England and the Church, and hitting, as far as I could, in brief sentences, several points, which ought to be well hit, in the conduct of all parties."

To William Brooke.
" March 10, '65.

"I have really some hope now of letting my house on the 1st of April. If so, I shall be, please God, in England in April. I shall look out for work at once, but I should like to have a geological expedition somewhere before settling down to a curacy. There is no chance of you or Arthur being in London in May. If not, I half think of running over to Ireland, if you or he can come with me to Galway or the North, or to the Shannon parts. I should like to see Dublin again and all my old friends. . . .

"Last Sunday I preached in the Princess' private Chapel at her request. It is a dark little place—fitted up in the Lutheran manner by the late King, and at 11 o'clock a.m. I preached by candlelight. The Queen [of Prussia] was there, and I was introduced afterwards. She talked for ten minutes incessantly. It was like a shower bath: and at the end seized my hand—'God bless you,' said Her Majesty, and ran away. I could scarcely help laughing, especially when she said—carried away about B.[1] in the middle of her speech—' God has many ways—and perhaps illness might remove Mr B.' She scarcely perceived what she had said, till the Princess came forward and said, with a naïve smile to me, ' Shall we poison him, Mamma ? ' I kept my countenance, thanks to my stolidity, but it was hard work. The Queen, however, is a clever woman, and spoke well of the relation of the English and German Churches. I had a conversation with the Princess afterwards, who was very kind. She told me she had sent my sermon to her Mother in England, and said—' Ah, Mr Brooke, if you were to stay here, I think you would do me good.' I am to see her again before I leave.

"What, in the name of the Antiquary, is this Westmeath canoe? You excite my curiosity to the last degree, and then break off suddenly. Where did you see it, who found it? What age is it of? Was there

---

[1] The minister of the English Church.

anything in it, implements or otherwise? What do you infer from it—how deep was it—was it in a bay, and how did it get there—or in the old bed of a river? What change of water and land did it testify? etc., etc. Send me your paper, for I am burning with curiosity."

CHAPTER X

ST JAMES' CHAPEL

1865-1866

"*Fight on, fight on, fortitude, the hoped victory, the certainty of it, the glory of the war—these I preach incessantly.*"—(Letter to the Rev. Arthur Brooke, July 30, 1888.)

BROOKE left Berlin in the first week of April, 1865, thus keeping the resolution he had formed twelve months earlier. His main object in returning to London was to find clerical work. In addition to this he wished to be on the spot when his Life of Robertson was passing through the press.

As a curate in Kensington he had drawn large congregations. He loved preaching, knew his power, and was determined to make it felt in the world. He had no false modesty, and in his search for opportunities, as in everything else, was perfectly frank and open. He held, all through life, that a good preacher should be well paid for his work, that he was entitled to a good congregation and should go where he could find one. The tendency to glorify failure, sometimes found among men of religion, offended his common sense, and he had no sympathy for incompetence parading as unrecognized merit. Nor was he fitted to play the part of a St Francis, and, knowing his unfitness for the part, he never attempted it. Unworldliness with him took a different form.

The way before him was not easy. He had been away from England for nearly two years; the appointments open to Broad Churchmen were not numerous, and he was by no means ready to accept the first offer that came his way. A proprietary Chapel in the West End had been virtually offered before he left Berlin, and the Bishop had signified his approval; but finding the place encumbered with debts and other drawbacks he promptly declined the offer. Country livings were out of the question, for he was resolved to live in London. He knew himself very thoroughly, knew among other things how dependent he was on external stimulus for the power to do his best work. He needed close contact with humanity to remind him of the battle and tragedy of life, craved for the presence of art, and for association with artists, to satisfy his love of beauty and to give direction to his passion for excellence. He dreaded finding himself in surroundings where he would be tempted to dream his life away—a temptation to which he was prone. He had not forgotten the hint his grandmother gave him as a boy, "You Brookes are too much given to soaring—I would clip your wings." In London, then, he was resolved to live.

He had some powerful friends, of whom the chief were Dean Stanley and Mr Henry S. King, the publisher. The latter especially never ceased to exert himself on his behalf, sometimes indeed with an eagerness which proved rather perplexing to Brooke. Mr King, who had been closely associated with him, had a very high opinion of his powers both as writer and preacher, and as early as 1865 was urging him to publish a volume of his sermons. Friends more powerful than these were in the background. While in Berlin he had won the esteem of the Crown Princess and the Princess Alice, and a MS of one of his sermons had been sent to Queen Victoria, whose disposition to the Broad Church party was by no means unfavourable.

Of formal testimonials he had very few, and those from clerical sources were not exuberant. Lord Napier, the Ambassador at Berlin, wrote of him that "the kindness of his manners and his ability as a preacher inspired all those with whom he was brought in contact with affection and respect." His first vicar had not helped him at all—far otherwise. His second vicar wrote of him in guarded terms. "He is of irreproachable moral character and of no ordinary abilities and attainments. He reads well, his sermons are eloquent, and he takes much interest in the well-being of the poor. In the present day there are great diversities of theological opinion, and he will at once explain exactly what views he holds;" from which the inference seems pretty safe that Brooke's promptitude in the explanation of his views had not always been acceptable to the writer of the testimonial. The Bishop's testimonial was less ambiguous. "He is a man of great ability, and during the whole time of his connexion with me, first as a curate in London, and afterwards as Chaplain in Berlin, has deserved my highest commendation." In which connexion I cannot refrain from repeating a story which I heard from Brooke himself. Complaint had been made to the Bishop about his heresies on the subject of Eternal Punishment, and an interview followed. After some beating about the bush, the Bishop, somewhat unwillingly, came to the point. "And now, Mr Brooke, what is it that you have been saying recently about Eternal Punishment?" Brooke, with his usual directness, at once stated his views, not mincing matters in the least. The Bishop listened with a grave but not unfriendly countenance, and Brooke, watching him closely and judging that his mind was embarrassed by cross currents, wound up his statement thus: "And now, my Lord, will you be so good as to tell me what *you* think of Eternal Punishment." "Perhaps we had better not discuss the subject," said the Bishop.

For nine months Brooke was without a settlement, biding his time. He was constantly preaching in London churches, and seems to have drawn large congregations. Five or six curacies were offered to him at various times, including one at St George's, Hanover Square, and another at St Martin's in the Fields. He declined them all, writing to his wife in reference to one of them, "I should not endure a curacy now without grave impatience." Various livings were being talked of, and both Stanley and King were interesting themselves in that direction. "The other day," writes Brooke (in a letter to William), "King goes to Stanley of his own accord and has a long talk about me, praising me to the skies, of course, and tells Stanley that he (King) 'has dissuaded me from taking a curacy.' 'Oh,' said Stanley, 'he won't do for a curate! He must not be a curate!' Stanley also told K., when the latter said an East End incumbency would not be a fair place for me, that he agreed. At last King said, 'May I ask plainly—have you thought of anything?' 'Yes,' said Stanley, 'I have—St Paul's, Covent Garden, and I will not let an hour pass without pressing the matter.' That Stanley should be ready to give me St Paul's fairly surprised me. It is one of the most important and difficult parishes in London. ... I should not like to have taken such a vast responsibility, and am glad such a big morsel is not for me"—an appointment, as it turned out, having been made already. In another letter to William he writes, "A. says that the Bishop will not give me anything: he thinks I have enough money to buy what I want and that I should do so. Jolly, ain't it?"

In the letter from which the last quotation is taken (June 19, '65), we have the first mention of St James' Chapel, York Street, destined to be the scene of Brooke's ministry for nine years.

"Lord Carnarvon has bought the East side of the road leading from St James' Church into St James' Square.... There is a small Chapel there holding, I conjecture, about 400 persons.... Lord C. does not want to be bothered about the Chapel, and has applied for leave to convert it into a warehouse.... W. B. proposes that I should take this chapel and offer Lord C. £100 a year rent for it. What do you think?"

Inquiries proceeded. It turned out that Lord Carnarvon was not prepared to accept these terms; there were many charges to be met and risks to be faced; an unsavoury past to be lived down, and there were difficulties with the neighbouring Church of St James', Piccadilly, only a few yards distant. The position was not tenable without the goodwill of the incumbent of that parish, and the practice seems to have established itself of "having fools in occupation of the Chapel. 'F. says of [one of them] that he was the greatest fool she ever met in her life.'" King was strongly opposed to Brooke having anything to do with the place, and the Bishop warned him that if he took it he would be a bankrupt in three years. Stanley was equally emphatic, and Maurice said the place was unsuitable for a man like Brooke. Plainly enough it was under a cloud—and a pretty dark one.

As events subsequently proved, Brooke was not the

man to be daunted by such difficulties, great as they undoubtedly were. But it so happened that soon afterwards he received the offer of another proprietary chapel, in Brighton, where his wife (Aug., '65), who had returned from Berlin in June, was then living. Brooke disliked Brighton, and, in spite of its association with Robertson, had no wish to live there. But he was moved by consideration for the health of his family, and King being very active and urgent, negotiations for the purchase of the Brighton lease were begun and all but completed by the end of '65. It was by the merest accident that Brooke's life was not thus diverted into a channel very different from that which it subsequently followed. At the very moment when he was on the point of closing the Brighton negotiations, he received a new and more favourable offer from Lord Carnarvon's agent. Brooke, who was then staying at his father's rectory of Wyton, wrote to his wife that he felt it useless to seek further advice in the matter. Moreover, he was "thoroughly disgusted with failure." So without consulting anybody he closed with Lord Carnarvon's offer, taking over the lease of St James' Chapel at a rent rising to £150 a year, for five years, with the option of renewal. King shook his head, and the Bishop repeated his vaticination. Even Mrs Brooke seems to have been alarmed at her husband's precipitancy, declining at first with characteristic reserve to express any opinion on what he had done. Unquestionably it was a bold move. But "he knew what he was doing"; and, anticipating somewhat the course of events, I may say at once that at the end of his first year's ministry, he had discharged the debt on the Chapel, cleaned and renewed it, paid his rent and all expenses, and had £12 in his pocket to the good. After that all was plain sailing.

Meanwhile an event had occurred which was destined to have influence on his future career. On November 23 he received a letter from the Dean of Windsor (Wellesley), informing him that "while he was in Berlin he was known and appreciated by the Crown Princess of Prussia, and she hoped he would come on Dec. 3 to preach at the Private Chapel at Windsor before her and the Queen." He accepted the invitation, and thus describes, to William, what happened—

"I wrote my sermon, which I send you, and went to Windsor on Saturday, to the Deanery. The Eburys were there, and I had a pleasant dinner. The Dean was kind; told me that the Princess had spoken frequently and cordially to the Queen about me, and in every possible way had proved herself my friend; that she was sorry to be compelled to leave Windsor before my arrival, and that she left to me the choice—if matters could be arranged, of a fit person to succeed me at Berlin. I had a charming room in the Deanery; the windows overlooking the slopes and terrace of the Castle, and the whole of that magnificent view of the sweeps of the river—the towers of Eton and the rich plantations of that lovely country. On Sunday morning at ten o'clock I went to the morning service in the Chapel, where the Dean read the service. At twelve we went again. The Litany was read. I read the Communion Service as usual, and then preached. I was not at all nervous when it came to the point, and preached without hesitation and with ease for half an hour. The Queen sent for the Dean to bring me to see her in the Corridor—a kind of crescent-shaped Picture Gallery—deliciously comfortable. Arrived there, we were told that the Queen would see us in the Prince's study—Prince Albert's favourite room. It is not large—looks out over the park: was richly but unostentatiously furnished and hung round with modern English pictures—Landseer's Sanctuary, etc., etc.

"The Queen came in, received me very cordially, and

talked for about twenty minutes to me about my sermon —Robertson's Life and Robertson's sermons—the Sabbatarian discussion in Scotland, and Prince Albert, asked me about my position in Berlin, and what I was doing, and various other things *quæ meminisse longum est.* She said that she was reading my book slowly in order to take it in well, and was very much pleased by it: that she found in Robertson's letters things so like 'her Prince's' thoughts that she almost imagined that she heard him speaking—that she had read one of Robertson's sermons that morning before church; and that she was able to read three of them consecutively in the train—not an easy thing to do—she said laughing—at all—especially if sermons were the reading. She thought the language of my sermon beautiful! and alluded to things I had said with pleasure. She looked cheerful and happy, her face has not lost its redness, she twisted a vinaigrette in her hand all the time she was speaking, and struck me as a shy woman. She seemed to appreciate her daughter's intellect, and rather amused me by saying that she thought the Crown Princess' head was getting clearer and keener every year. She then said she must have my sermon to read, and left us. She was exceedingly cordial and pleasant, and listened to me with interest. I hope that I did not—but rather fear that I erred against etiquette in talking too much. The Dean's bluffness entertained me. He is—they say on account of this uncourtlike manner—a great favourite with the Queen—whose private confessor and adviser he is—and who believes that she hears from him plainspoken truths which she cannot get from her Court. . . .

"I had a long talk with Lord Ebury on his hobby—the revision of the Liturgy. He is in earnest, in such earnest that he does not see the difficulties. . . . Did you hear that Stanley asked St Paul's, Covent Garden, for me? He has promised to exert his influence to get me a post in London, meantime I am trying for Dulwich Chaplaincy, £300 a year."

The year '65 closed with the death at a great age of Mrs Joseph Stopford, Brooke's grandmother, for whom he entertained a profound affection, and remembered none the less fondly for her attempts "to clip his wings." "So much of quaint kindness and old-world interest in things; she dwelt in many corners of my life."

On the whole, it had been a year of uncertainty, homelessness, constant wanderings to and fro, and of irksome separation from his wife and family. It had been marked, however, by one great event which formed a turning point in Brooke's career, the publication of the Life of Robertson. This, however, must be dealt with in a separate chapter.

The following extracts are, unless otherwise stated, from letters to his wife. She remained in Berlin until June.

"April 6, '65.
[Written in the train, Berlin—London.]

"It is unnatural to go anywhere without you, and that is the reason I feel these partings so keenly. It is erring against a natural law, and more against a spiritual one, so it is worse than violating gravitation."

"April 8, '65.
"Cornhill. [H. S. King's office.]

"I walked across the Park to Taylor's [The Rev. Isaac Taylor, afterwards Incumbent of St Matthew's, Bethnal Green]. The Park looked charming, the women prettier, the cabs decked out in the colours of Oxford and Cambridge. I saw more variety in the faces and attitudes in half an hour than I have seen during half a year in Berlin. Taylor was hurrying off to the Boat Race. I am much pleased with London, much pleased! It looked not only grand but very pretty. What horses! What houses! How I wish, and clasp my hands when I wish, that you were with me!"

He then goes down to Chigwell to stay with King, preaches at Chigwell Church "up a hill, the clergyman a dry bone," rushes off next day to his parents at Wyton, walks many miles, "plays cricket with violence all evening" and is knocked up. He has heard of a curacy in London "which would just suit you and me." Is going to stay at Wyton for a week to correct his proofs of Robertson.

"April 11, '65. Wyton.

"The primroses are out on the banks and round every tree root in the meadows violets, white and blue, are blowing thickly, making the air delicate with their scent. I shall gather you a bundle and wrap them up in this, and you must take their sweetness as a type of my constant love and thought of you. . . .

"My Father has just read my memoir [of Robertson]. I am glad to say he is delighted with it; and *that* even though he says he sat down prepared to feel strongly against it. He says there is nothing needlessly irritating. . . . This is valuable testimony as to what the better class of evangelicals will think. I do not want, as you know, by any useless broad-church partizanship to spoil the good which R.'s sermons have done to the evangelical body and to prevent evangelical curates from buying, as they do now, his books. . . . It bores me to death reading it again.

"A letter [from you] seems for a moment to supply the other half of my life, which is being lived in Berlin now. And you write so pleasantly—a charming *mélange* of pleasant gossip and quiet thought. . . . John Law [about whom you ask] was a great financier. He was the first to set on foot the great system of credit on which our modern commerce is based. . . . In the second volume of Mill's 'Political Economy' you will find an account of Law and his system.

"And my cigar case is gone! I cannot quite believe it. . . . All here send you their best love and I send you my whole heart!"

"April 12, '65. Wyton.

"All nature is rushing into life. I seem almost to hear and see the trees growing. I am well and fresh and am going to Ireland for a four days' spree. . . .

One of the chief things that carries me to the Green Isle is William's account of a quarry where a fossiliferous vein of the highest richness has been discovered. You will laugh at this, and say that I pay dear for my whistle, but who can resist, who has once loved them, the charms of a Cardiomorpha? . . .

"William gives me a bad account of the young English Liberals in the Church. Some of them seem to wish to get rid altogether of an Historical Christianity and go about saying that the great fault of the day is that there is too much reverence paid to the Bible. It appears to be, I think, the other way. I feel most deeply, and more deeply every day, the need of Veneration, and that it is the very ballast of the ship of Reason. All this pooh-poohing of the old beliefs simply because they are old, all this irreverent assaulting of what is held sacred by thousands is nothing more than a leaf out of the book of Mephistopheles, to whom nothing was venerable: who touched nothing which he did not scorn.

"We want men now in the English Church to bridle the young horses. . . . At the same time how useless would be wholesale condemnation. To guide this redundant energy, not to crush it, that is what we want. Oh, for a few more men like Stanley. Oh, for a man greater than Stanley who could grasp the time in his imagination and then mark out its needs and the limits of its thought, so as to make that thought not as it is now—a thought which must recede to find its true level, but a thought standing *at* its level."

"April 14, '65. Dublin.

"I went to hear Magee, Dean of Cork.[1] I sat with exemplary patience [through] a sermon intended to prove the Eternity of future punishment. It was very able indeed. He preached without notes, with a logical precision and force of thought that were astonishing. There were no repetitions, and no weak language. The illustrations were carried through without a flaw. The

[1] Afterwards Bishop of Peterborough and Archbishop of York.

only fault of the sermon was the subject. He enlarged —enlarged with what to me was a horrible gusto—upon the sorrows, sufferings, tortures and terrors of man, upon his iniquity and on the hell which his own nature was inevitably leading him into. If all he said were true there might be written, not only over the gates of Hell, but over the portals of the earth, 'Abandon hope, who enter here.'

"I met Tom Greene, my old College friend, after the sermon: 'Well, what did you think of that?' 'I think,' I said, 'that Eternal Death should be very much obliged to him.'"

"April 16, '65. Dublin.

"Old Dr T. preached the sermon—a mere repetition for the millionth time of the old arguments for the Resurrection being known to the Old Testament Jews, and for the fact of the Resurrection. The cool way in which he evaded every difficulty by saying that he would not enter into it, but that his view was right, and the audacity with which he ignored the fact that many of those who listened to him had read everything he said fifty times, and that there were a hundred new objections afloat which his argument did not touch—all this was the greatest impertinence I ever met in the pulpit.

"Is not this glorious news from America? Fancy Lincoln issuing proclamations from Jefferson Davis' house. I rejoice to think this great victory [capture of Richmond] will close the war."

"April 25, '65. 42, Upper Chapel Street [Lodgings],
"London.

"I preached last Sunday morning at Albert's Church [the Rev. Albert Sitwell]. I believe my sermon was liked. Then I met [John Richard] Green, a very gifted man, but in a state of theological 'yeast' which is curious and somewhat painful to see. We had some interesting conversation. . . .

"You see Lee has surrendered. One cannot help feeling sorrow at the fall of so chivalrous and determined a [soldier]. When I heard it Wordsworth's lines occurred to me—in his sonnet on the Extinction of the Venetian Republic :

> "'Yet shall some tribute of regret be paid
> When her long life has reached its final day.
> Men are we, and must grieve when even the shade
> Of that which once was great has passed away.'

"Half, and more than half, of our absence is over. It shall soon end. Till then we will pray God to keep us safe, and worthy of one another. Surely it is a high blessing that God has given us the power of loving one another so deeply, so sincerely."

"April 27, '65.
"London.

"This awful news [the assassination of President Lincoln] has convulsed London. It is too terrible to think about in a hurry, but I am seldom touched to the very depths, and I have been so, both yesterday and to-day. I could not help it, as I read for the fourth time to-day the account—the tears which would rush into my eyes. It is the foulest and darkest public murder ever done. I walk about like a man in a dream. It may be fancy, but it seems as if every man I met felt the same sick sensation of having received a blow upon some vital part. I look up in their faces to see if I can trace there the same shocked almost palsied feeling of pain which I know is upon my own face. It is most pitiable—most horrible. I send you the *Telegraph;* read the articles. The *Times* only feels its way in its article to public opinion. The *Telegraph*, though never a supporter of the North, has an opinion of its own and strives to lead, not follow, public opinion. Its articles to-day are good.

"I will write more fully to-night. I go this evening to the Curates' Clerical Club—a meeting held at Dean Stanley's. You shall have an account."

"April 29, '65. Wyton.

"Now to tell you some of my C. C. C. evening. The meeting was held at the Deanery. At the head of the stairs a tea-table was arranged at which stood Lady Augusta Stanley in morning dress, black with no ornament whatsoever. Stanley welcomed me back to England, and then introduced me to his wife. I talked to her for ten minutes. She is reserved and still, but courteous in manner; and has a certain stateliness which sits oddly on her aspect. We adjourned then, she going away into the large and pleasant drawing-rooms which overlook the Cloisters of the Abbey. A collect was read by Stanley, and then Fremantle, the Bishop's Chaplain, read his Essay on the Moral Basis of Christian Teaching. I fairly own that many things in it shocked me. Not only was it ultra-liberal, it might have been written by Strauss, only that it stated as matters of possible conjecture what Strauss lays down as proved. After the Essay each one was asked to speak. Some violent attacks were made upon it by the Orthodox party. Stanley strove to reconcile both opinions, vainly I thought. Some speeches were made by others which revolted me. I was asked to speak and attempted to say something, but many were, just as I was speaking, obliged to leave. I became confused and did not express what I wished to do. I have lost, if ever I had it, the power of speaking impromptu to an assembly. I must endeavour to gain it, and shall at once begin to try. Writing sermons always is all very well, but one loses rapidity of mind in seizing thought. I always did grasp things slowly—now I seem not to grasp them at all, except in the heat of conversation. After the discussion, which lasted till near twelve o'clock, we had supper—chickens, ham and wine, etc., very simple. Maurice was not there, but I met some old acquaintances. Llewellyn Davies among the rest."

To William Brooke.
"June 19, '65.
"8, Bolton Street, Piccadilly.

"I am sick of the delays from which my book has suffered. ... I am miserably disappointed at the letters I have received from Robertson's friends [to whom he had written for their memories and impressions of Robertson]. I have had to correct their English and to groan over their inability to give any picture of the man. The rarest thing in the world is a man with eyes in his head."

In September he went off on the geological expedition for which he had been craving all summer, first to Oxford, for the purpose of exploring Shotover Hill. He spent two days on the hill and in the adjoining quarries, coming back each time with a heavy bag on his shoulders laden with spoil—"I have found a glorious Plagiostoma (Linea) by the roadside—one blow of the hammer dislodged him." He spent much time in the Ashmolean Museum studying the Turners, especially "The Drowned Sailor," which he thus describes in a letter to his wife.

To his wife.
"Sept. 9, '65.
"15, Beaumont Street, Oxford.

"In the morning we went to the Picture Gallery, where I spent an hour and a half contemplating the Turners. I made the Curator get for me out of a box the 'Lost Sailor,' that wonderful etching, almost the most wonderful piece of pure imagination in any branch of Art. It ought to be known, but if it were would it be understood? It requires knowledge to comprehend it. Those who have only seen waves at Folkestone or Dover would pooh pooh it and pass on. A man must have seen and watched a real storm billow breaking on cliffs where the water even at low tide lies twenty fathoms deep to recognize the exquisite truth and courage of that drawing. It is unique even in Turner's outlining of the sea. Lashed to a barrel with outstretched arms and fingers still distended as they were in his last despairing effort to clench a rope, with his head fallen back in death, lies the sailor down in the trough between the fearful coast and the curling wave. Right over him in the distance—on the cliff—seen through a wild light of foam there stands the lighthouse—its saving gleam has shone in vain for the victim of the waters. It is the one touch of fine imagination which adds to the picture an infinity of human thoughts, pity, despair— all the past history of the ship which had struggled all the night against its destiny—the ship whose shattered mast is seen in the foreground driving on the rocks and on whose deck he had stood, and when he saw the light had pictured home and land and peace. And there he lies now—drowned in sight of shore. Everything else, in the room, of Turner's sinks into insignificance before this one print."

"Sept. 12 and 13, '65. Oxford.

"William has just gone to Wyton and I am here alone. I do not dislike it. I have plenty to do. I read Italian and German and write my essays; and worry my brain as little as possible about [St James'] Chapel.

"A most glorious sunset such as I have not seen for years accompanied my walk home from Shotover, and I pictured to myself as I walked how you would have enjoyed it with me. The only drawback was the immense weight of stones I carried. . . . On Sunday we took a charming walk to Iffley by the river. A yew of a thousand years stands in the Churchyard. The sexton, an old man, was filling in a new-made grave. About a dozen children were helping him, playing, laughing, shovelling in the earth over the dead who will smile no more. I lay on the grass thinking of all things which are done and suffered here."

"Sept. 15. London.

"Behold me once more in this irrepressible London. . . . I feel it as Home. It belongs to all my life with you and it has infinite associations. . . . I feel happier and more cheerful to-night, as if something were going to happen to-morrow to set right our long endurance of unsettledness. . . . I spent an hour and a half with the Turners this morning. Exquisite as a dream are some of the drawings on gray paper. The eye becomes wearied with gazing, though unsatisfied. Ah, when weariness cannot come through the body to the spirit! And yet I have no wish to leave this earth; I am too happy in my life with you; and when we do go it would be a happy thing to go together. . . . I am indignant about ——. She is very overbearing. Alack, alack, how I wish we could have XIII Corinthians interwoven with our very being. It is not difficult to me to be charitable . . . no more meritorious than keen sight in a falcon. My temptations lie in another direction. I wish I had some work to make the world real and not phantasmal to me."

"Oct. 18, '65.
"Wyton.

"The first copy [of Robertson's Life] arrived this morning [18] while I was in bed. It gave me a kind of jealous pain that I was not with you when it came. But, after all, the 28th, the day it appears publicly, I shall celebrate with you. I am neither rejoiced nor depressed by its being off my hands. I am so tired of it that I do not care about it."

"Oct. 23, '65. London.

"I am surprised by what you say of 'Maud.' I thought you knew it well. It seems to me that I *think* more of that Poem than almost any in the language. I do not need to read it, but it recurs continually and especially the 'timbre,' shall I call it, of its voice, to my mind. Do you know what I mean—it is not only the thought, the passion, the glance into the depths of the heart which chain me, it is also the ring of the language, the rataplan of the rhythm, the peculiar 'quality' of the arrangement of words. The non-appreciation of the Poem by the general public is a further proof that the public cannot take in any subtle Beauty. The creatures who cannot see Turner's infinitely subtle handling of colour, and call it unnatural, are the very people who cannot see what 'Maud' means. They cannot distinguish colouring which is insensibly gradated. They like a sketch like the Corsair. A huge blotch of black cloud —Conrad—with some gleams of tender summer lightning—but lightning still. . . .

"When my Father dashed down the *Times*, after a moment of bewildered silence and said, 'Lord Palmerston is gone,' I only said, 'Le roi est mort, vive le roi.' Still it is a great event, greater far in its consequences, I think, than men suspect. He was the last barrier against the next great stride of Democracy, and I believe he has been left so long that he might keep back the incoming of the next wave till the shore of England's national life was ready to receive it. The ministry with Lord Russell at its head will not long survive. Gladstone, leader of the House of Commons, will soon be Gladstone Premier : and though there may be a short Conservative Ministry before long, it will be succeeded by a Cabinet which will be forced to bring in measures likely to revolutionize England. I hope, I do hope, that sufficient caution will rule their counsels, and foresee a time when a wise reticence, a wise holding back will be very, very necessary; when liberals like myself will have *apparently* to adopt conservative views, will be, *i.e.*, obliged in the interests of true political freedom, to check as far as possible the eagerness of Reformers who will run in blind enthusiasm into the arms of Revolutionists."

"Oct. 24, '65. London.

"I shrink from the notion of the Chapel at Brighton, but I believe that God will order all things as He thinks best for me. If we are not to be in London for some time—well, we must bear it."

"Dec. 3 and 4, '65. The Deanery, Windsor.

"It is all over, and happily so. Curious—how one speaks of it as a kind of death. . . . I took courage and delivered my sermon with vivacity and force. . . . The Queen thanked me, asked for the sermon . . . and alluded to things in it. She looked shy. Spoke much of Robertson's Life, and asked me a good deal about him. . . .

"It seems the Princess spoke very much of me to the Queen, and 'is,' said the Dean, 'in *every* possible way your friend.'"

"Oct. 19, '65. Wyton.

"I will not enter on the occupation of the [Brighton] Chapel unless the Trustees know that my views are *not* moderate—know them at least for what they are, moderate *Broad Church* views. Else the usual fruits of suppression of the truth will follow. . . . I do not like these apparent subterfuges and *ruses de guerre*. . . . Why are all these chapels such dirty work? And yet I am more or less forced to try for them. . . . Dante has dreadfully flagged of late, and I suppose you are far ahead. I will not begin the *Purgatorio* without you.

"I am ashamed of my forgetfulness about the Prayer. I have written a memorandum of it in order to do it to-night. [This refers to Mrs Brooke's request that he would write prayers for his two little boys to repeat morning and night. I have found these prayers in a note-book of '65, and give them here :]—

"O God my Father in Heaven, I thank Thee for my pleasant sleep, and for giving me a new day. Do not leave me during this day, but be always with me, though I cannot see Thee. Help me to be good. Help me to be an obedient boy, and to be kind and gentle to my brother and sisters. Help me to be attentive to my lessons and to like to do what I am told. Teach me how to love Thee for all Thy goodness to me. Teach me how to thank Thee for the bright sun and the pleasant sea and the green land which Thou hast made to please me and everybody. O God, I like to think that Thou lovest me, a little boy, and hast saved me through Thy Son Jesus Christ. Amen."

"O God my dear Father in Heaven, I thank Thee for the pleasant day I have spent and for all the good things which Thou hast given me. Watch over my Papa, Mamma, and my little sisters and brother, and take care of them this night Watch over and take care of me also when I am asleep. Forgive me when I am not good and make me try to do better. Do not let me forget that Thou seest me always and wishest me to be a good boy. Help me always to think of others first and of myself last. Bless me, a little boy, for the sake of my Saviour Jesus Christ, who was once like me a little boy. Amen."

CHAPTER XI

THE LIFE OF F. W. ROBERTSON

1865

"There is now a sort of reaction to the 'sixties and 'seventies in the XX century brooding among men which, if it goes on, may make sermons of that time have some interest. As to Robertson's Life . . . it has an historical value in regard to that time. Its real value is in Robertson's Letters, not in my work. Its sale in 'Everyman's Library' would be problematical. It would depend on the interest above spoken of; and also on the deep attraction Robertson's personality and thought might have on the spirituality now awakening in the working men of England. . . ."—(Letter to Mr Ernest Rhys. November 16, 1915.)

"THE Life and Letters of the Rev. F. W. Robertson" was published at the end of October, 1865, six months before Brooke began his work at St James' Chapel. From the evidence before me, part of which has already been given, I conclude that he had been occupied in the preparation of this work, though with many intervals, for eight years. His diary records that he was asked to write the book in the summer of 1857, and in a letter of 1856 he says that he is reading Robertson's *manuscripts*, which suggests an even earlier date for the birth of the design.

There is no doubt that his equipment for the task was exceptionally thorough. His personal acquaintance with Robertson was indeed little more than a memory of his youth; but it was a memory which gave him a vision of essential characteristics. He had studied the letter of Robertson's teaching over and over again, and had revised his earliest impressions in the light of maturer thought; he had viewed the man from every possible angle of vision, and the fire of Robertson's apostolic spirit had mingled with his own. Moreover, access had been given him to a vast correspondence, and he had ample opportunities of consulting those who had been the friends of the great preacher. To all this he brought the artist's vision for essential truth, selecting from his material what was necessary to his purpose, and rejecting what was not.

In 1865 the Broad Church party were in the throes of the controversy raised by Essays and Reviews (1860), attacked on either flank by the Ritualists and the Evangelicals, and hotly engaged on their front with the growing forces of scientific materialism. It was a time of great religious excitement, not only among the clergy, but among the public at large, especially the middle classes. A rumour had gone abroad that certain learned men, with a Bishop among them, had proved that "the Bible was not true," and alarums and excursions were being sounded in the newspapers, and in the Churches and Chapels. Hyde Park, too, was exceptionally busy on Sunday afternoons. The public had not yet grown familiar with these controversies, nor tired of them, and a multitude of readers was waiting for any book which might affect the issues at stake. To the Broad Church party, therefore, the appearance of Robertson's Life was a momentous event. For there is nothing which helps a cause so effectually as the emergence or the re-emergence of a great personality at a critical moment of its fortunes. Would this be the effect? Would the book be a mere statement of Robertson's Broad Church opinions strung on a biographical thread, or would it present a great man, to embody the cause and give it life by his personal force? The first would be of little value, the second would be worth more than a thousand arguments. Such were the hopes and fears with which men like Stanley and Maurice looked forward to the coming Life.

When the book appeared it was recognized at once as a biography of exceptional power, and as a Broad Church document of great importance. With singular skill it combined the two aspects of the movement, the theological and the humanitarian, and the combination formed a picture which men of all parties were eager to study and, with few exceptions, ready to appreciate.

But the book showed further how Robertson's adoption of his views had its roots in the nature of the man. This was essentially a nature at odds with itself, in which religion had to sustain a severe conflict with a contrary principle. In fact, the very conflict which was then raging in the world of contemporary thought, between traditional Christianity on the one hand, and materialistic science on the other, was here exhibited as a human drama of which Robertson's mind was the seat. Robertson was the victor emerging from the contest, victorious, too, by virtue of the sword which he carried, that of a broad, humanistic interpretation of Christianity. To the theological interest there was added a dramatic and human interest, which gathered round the figure of a great spiritual warrior, a man beset by foes within and without, waging in his personal experience, and triumphantly, the warfare which it was the mission of the Broad Church to wage in the world at large. Thus the book had the character of a work of art, and of that difficult art which invests the career of a preacher and a theologian with dramatic interest. It was impossible for Brooke to write it otherwise.

That a portrait so painted would give an impression somewhat different from that which an untouched photograph of Robertson would have given was, of course, inevitable; but this is not to say that the photograph would have been the truer picture. Be that as it may, the immediate effect of the "Life" was that Robertson rose from the dead, and his name, his teaching, his personality became thenceforward a new power to the cause of which Jowett, Stanley, Kingsley, and Maurice were the protagonists. And this power was all the greater because Brooke had laid emphasis on that side of Robertson's work which made him "a friend of the people." Thus the book appealed to reformers as well as theologians. In twelve months four editions were sold out.

The Evangelical newspapers, especially the *Record*, were quick to perceive that a new and dangerous foe had appeared on the scene, not only in the book, but in the person of its author, and the vials of wrath and abuse were freely opened upon Robertson, upon his biography, and upon his biographer. As to Brooke himself, he certainly suffered nothing by these attacks, save for some outbursts of indignation which he was not always able to restrain himself from publicly expressing. It was a critical moment in his career, when he was about to make a new entry into the religious life of London, and whatever fame he may have won as the author of the Life was only spread further afield by the maledictions which were heaped upon his head. If new enemies were made on the one hand, the loyalty of old friends was deepened on the other. "The second edition of R.'s Life comes out to-day," he writes to William in February,

'66. . . . "Many people have spoken to me of its success; Stanley most kindly when I called upon him the other day. He said 'though I dislike applying for anything and to anybody, if you hear of an advantageous place falling vacant and wish to have it, write to me, and I will ask it for you.'"

Concerning the influence which Robertson had upon Brooke it is difficult to speak with precision. Brooke's own testimony on the question is contradictory. About 1900 he told me, as I have already reported, that he owed nothing to Robertson, and this is true in the sense that the main tendencies of his thought were rooted in his own nature. Had Robertson never lived Brooke would not have been essentially different from what he was. On the other hand, he said to the Crown Princess in '65, according to his own testimony in a letter quoted above, "If I am anything, I owe it to Robertson." If one considers the dates at which the two statements were made —widely separated—and the different circumstances, there is perhaps no real contradiction. Certain it is that Brooke always resented the imputation, when made by others, that Robertson was his model. Writing to his wife in '66, he says, " the only thing I do not like is what is implied in the last sentence [of a letter from a friend], *if* it is implied, that I am in a certain sense an imitator of Robertson. Its being so natural to say so makes it more distressing. For it is not true. I never heard R. preach. I used to be sorry for that. Now I am glad. I especially avoid following him, and I know that my mode of preaching and of seeing things is of myself alone. I speak my own nature into the things I say. It is a nature far inferior in many things to Robertson, but it is my own, and not modelled after another man's." This statement is also obviously true. It is not in the nature of a man like Brooke to adopt anybody as a model.

On the other hand, there is not a doubt that Robertson influenced him. He had travelled for eight or ten years in close company with the mind of this man, and influence there must have been. That the companion was to some extent an imaginary being would, in Brooke's case, only increase the influence, for it was precisely the beings of his imagination who possessed the greatest power over his actions and his thought. Unquestionably, too, there were resemblances between the two men —both were imaginative, eager, forceful, and daring.

But there were differences that went deeper. Whereas the two natures of Robertson were in conflict, Brooke could live in different worlds and constantly change from one to the other without the least consciousness of strife. There was "soul trouble" in Robertson from first to last and some of it was morbid. But no man ever lived who was less in trouble about his soul than Brooke. His attachment to the objective world was so strong and his interests in other people so various and eager, that a flower, a picture, a cloud, a breeze in the tree-tops, the entry of a human figure into the room would cause him to forget his own existence in an instant and to become wholly absorbed in the thing or the person before him. Like the rest of us he had his times of weariness and depression, but they never sprang from anxiety about his spiritual state, and whatever their cause might be he could usually throw them off by a week in Venice or among the mountains. Morbid he was not, not even under protracted illness. And though I have often seen him exhausted by work or by pain, I cannot remember him in the condition of a man who sinks under the burden of life. Between him and joy there was an irresistible affinity, and even in circumstances the most depressing he could find for himself a sunny nook and reflect the sunshine on those about him. In such a nature soul-troubles of the religious kind have no chance to develop, and they never did develop with him either in youth or in age. No form of teaching which required him to keep a finger on the pulse of his own soul could ever appeal to him, for the next thing that happened would sweep him out of himself. And so it came to pass that through all the theological storms and the inward conflicts thence resulting, which lay so heavily on many of his Mid-Victorian contemporaries, Brooke went on his way radiant and rejoicing, his soul unshaken by any doubts of its destiny, undarkened by any eclipse of faith. Of him it could not be said, as it could be of many of the others—

> "His brow deep scars of thunder had intrencht
> And on his faded cheek sat care."

Between such a nature and that of a man like Robertson there is a deep and impassable gulf. This is as much as to say that Brooke's originality was in no degree impaired by his studies of Robertson's mind and by his admiration for the man. That it was enforced, encouraged, and inspired is equally true.

Although it may be accepted that Brooke never took Robertson for his model, I think there are grounds for believing that the figure of Robertson, as portrayed in the biography, is, in *some* features, unconsciously modelled upon Brooke. Scattered throughout the Life are many passages, notably in the seventh chapter, which recall Brooke's most striking characteristics, and might be taken with very little alteration as descriptive of himself. It is of course conceivable that the resemblances between the two men were actually as deep as these passages suggest they were, but this is hardly borne out by an examination of the Robertson letters as cited in the biography, nor is there any collateral evidence to support it.

We here light on a feature which characterized the whole of Brooke's literary work, as well as his preaching, and may be judged a strength or weakness according to the point of view. Just because his personality was so forceful and vivid it impressed itself upon every object he studied or described. He illustrated the doctrine of *homo mensura* in a very peculiar way. With many men the doctrine results in a certain dragging down of the world to the human level; with him it took the form of lifting the world up, investing persons and things with his own vitality and irradiating them with the light of his own joy. "My joy shall be in you" expresses the principle which actuated his literary criticisms and his studies of men, books, pictures and natural objects. In literary and artistic criticism this tendency was a main source of his power. In reading joy and vitality into the artist's work he discovered the secret which makes that work what it is. But in his portrayal of Robertson I cannot refrain from thinking that it led him into the kind of exaggeration which the artist may freely indulge, but which the historian needs to hold under restraint. Up to a point there was, as I have said, resemblance between the natures of the two men, and there was enough of it to constitute a real danger to a man like Brooke who, just because he was so little introspective, was the more inclined to reflect himself unconsciously on the object before him and to dramatize his own inner life in the history of other men whose characters partially resembled his own. A careful reading of the letter of

Stanley quoted below may suggest that thoughts similar to these were moving in his mind. And a remark made by Brooke himself after visiting the tomb of Robertson in 1863 seems to bear out the same conclusion. "I found it," he writes, "and could not but think on all I might have been had he but lived. Yet perhaps he never would have influenced me so much had he not died."

That the book did not disappoint those who had most reason to wish it success we may gather from the two following letters from F. D. Maurice and Stanley to H. S. King. It will be observed that of the two letters Stanley's is the more guarded in its praise.

From F. D. Maurice to Mr H. S. King.

"My dear Mr King,—You will believe that it was from no want of gratitude that I have delayed to thank you for your invaluable present. I would not write till I had read nearly through the Life and Letters. I could have read them through more rapidly, but I have read them out aloud to my sick wife who has shared all my delight in them. I could envy Mr Brooke the honour of doing so great a work, and of doing it so entirely to the honour of his subject, with such noble carelessness about his own. I had trembled very much when I heard the book announced, and scarcely had courage to open it. But it is all that could be desired; no word in the letters too much; what has been suppressed I am sure ought to have been. And there is amply enough to discover the man in all his reality, and all his variety. The steps of the history succeed each other with such evident truth, and it is delightful to find Robertson often contradicting himself as every true man does, and his biographer resolved not to make him consistent with himself at the expense of his veracity, and to the destruction of the fullness and vivacity of his intellect and character.

There has been no book like it for a long time. You must look on it with profound interest and tenderness.

"There is no fear of its being sufficiently reviewed, and sufficiently praised. I am only afraid that some critic will get up such a phrase as 'morbid' and work it, and that the rest of the sheep, as they are wont to do, will leap after him.

"There should be some attempt to counteract that impression, while justice is done to it, by bringing out the continual struggle against morbidness which is manifest in every page of his life.—Believe me, etc,

"F. D. MAURICE."

From Dean Stanley to Mr H. S. King.

"MY DEAR SIR,—I have postponed thanks for your kind remembrance of me, in the Life and Letters of Robertson, till I had read enough to make my thanks worth having.

"I think, as I always thought, the narrative exceedingly well done; and whether it is that the letters in their completed form produce a different impression, or that they have been much curtailed, the objections which I made to the publication of many of them are very much reduced, if not altogether destroyed.

"I still think that the whole work is rather too long, and to me, deep as is the interest of reading it, the Sermons still seem the climax of the man.

"There are a few places where the biographer has, it appears to me, made too much of an effort to isolate the hero, and place him on a pinnacle, I do not say above, but apart from others, which to my mind, somewhat distorts the true historical position which he occupies in the nineteenth century. But as a general rule, I greatly admire the way in which he has met the temptations (*carpenti credc*) of the class (of biographers), and I cannot but hope that the book will do much good.

"Yours, etc.,
"A. P. STANLEY"

The following is a passage from a letter written by Brooke to his mother. It is an answer to his mother's criticism that the eulogy of Robertson was too extreme, a criticism akin to that contained in Stanley's remark that the book showed an effort to place its hero on a pinnacle.

To his Mother.

"Nov. 27, '65.

"Your letter about my book was very interesting to me from the extremely different point of view in which we look at the same subject. First you remark on the continuous strain of eulogy from beginning to end. I do not think this is quite true, though partially so. I have painted Robertson's weaknesses—morbidity, impassionateness—almost too strongly for many who do not wish, as they say, the effect of his sermons to be destroyed by the representation of an erring and ofttimes impatient heart and of a restless and speculative spirit. I have left in many letters which a biographer who wished to present a faultless character would have left out. Against the advice of many of my friends, against the advice of Stanley, I left these letters in and let these traits of character appear vividly. For if a man is to be represented as a living being he must not be seen as an Angel. No one thinking over what I have written—when he has finished—would say, here is a flawless saint, a perfect being. On the contrary, the reader must feel, here is a man of great trials and many failures, a man consumed by a morbid self-consciousness at times, a man of much weakness, of no religious calm, to the very end perplexed.

"But also a man who never ceased to fight manfully against himself, who never thought his doubts fine things, who recognized humbly his weaknesses, and whose greatest sadness was that he could not attain here that deep rest in God which to many a Christian like Robertson is not a present rest, but a rest that remaineth to be fulfilled. It is in this very noble battle against himself that Robertson's greatness consists, and in which is the teaching of his life.

"He is no St John, whose love never failed, whose character is always calm, who felt ever Christ in himself and himself in Christ. He is more what St Paul describes and what I have quoted of him—persecuted but not forsaken, perplexed but not in despair, cast down but not destroyed.

"It is this weakness and his victory, this inward martyr life, which I hope the world will see and draw strength and comfort from. It is the picture of a sensitive, passionate, often morbid and weak heart slowly winning strength and turning his agony into gain."

From this account of Brooke's relations to Robertson I pass to a brief indication of the form his message assumed during his first years as minister of a Proprietary Chapel, a position which gave him a certain measure of independence and freedom. From this the reader may further elaborate for himself the comparison with Robertson. I shall speak only of essential features.

The evidence we require for this estimate is contained in the volume of "Sermons" published in 1869, the first of a long series of such volumes which continued to appear at intervals till 1913, and by no means the least significant.

The core of the volume is contained in the four sermons on the Development of Christ, the mere title of which shows that Brooke had humanized his conception of Christ and departed from the Athanasian theory so far as to view the Second Person of the Trinity in the light of *growing* personality, and growing by the same stages and under the same influences as other men.

But neither this nor any other "view" of the Person of Christ gives us the outstanding feature of these four sermons nor of the volume as a whole. The outstanding feature is an intense human love for Christ as a personality—as a man. This personal love is a veritable passion, and has all the consequences as well as the characteristics of a passion, for it guides and dominates the form of thought under which Christian doctrine is here presented, and may be said without exaggeration to have begun already to play havoc on the field of orthodox dogma. Nothing is allowed for an instant to interfere with the free play of this overmastering love for the human Christ. Every form of thought which by exalting his divinity places a gulf between Christ and man is immediately swept away or dissolved into some other form in which the original features of the dogma are completely lost. To say that the *religious* adoration of Christ is absent would not be true. It is present but only in that form which can be expressed in terms of *human* imagery and *human* relationships. Mysticism is abundantly manifest, but its source seems to be rather in Nature than in Christ, who is represented as the glory of our common clay, but a glory which the common clay, of all things in heaven and earth, is the best fitted to receive and reflect. An effort, a sincere effort, to find ground of accommodation with orthodox theory is constantly apparent. Many passages are introduced with the phrase, "if it may be said with reverence": but what is said "with reverence" always leads up to some outburst of personal affection for the Man of Nazareth, and so returns to the point of its origin. This is the real *motif* of these sermons, perhaps unconsciously followed. It acts as a solvent of all theological forms, and the action goes on, with occasional hesitations, checks, and accommodations, but on the whole swiftly and steadily.

A THEOLOGICAL ARGUMENT

It is deeply interesting to watch Brooke at one of the points where a check occurs. For example, he has to reconcile the conception of Christ as a *growing* personality with the doctrine of the Perfect Man. How can we say of Christ that He was perfect, and yet that He grew? We can say it, Brooke argues, by drawing a distinction between two kinds of perfection: the first, which is Christ's, develops *from within*, and is perfect at every stage of its growth in respect of the stage then reached; the second, which is to be ours, develops by conflict with *outer* or alien principles—weakness, evil, sin. By applying the idea of growth to Christ in common with other men Brooke believed that he had bridged the gulf between the two and made a free passage for reciprocal love: he did not see that by making the growth of radically different kinds in the two cases he had restored the gulf in another form. But he saw it later—witness his sermons on the Temptation of Christ (in "The Early Life of Jesus," 1888), in which the struggle for perfection which Christ has to sustain is precisely that which faces us all

Of the four sermons, the one which throws most light on the mind of Brooke at this time is, I think, that on the "Development of Christ through the Influence of Nature"—a sermon otherwise remarkable for its mastery of prose as an instrument of religious expression. In this we see Brooke pursuing, with wonderful insight and immense ability of exposition, his central aim of effecting a synthesis between Nature and Spirit, art and religion. Nothing in his later writings is more finely said or clearly thought than the passages in which he shows how, in the absence of such a synthesis, we mentally drift either into scientific materialism or into the formless pantheism of Shelley.

I wish, so far as possible, to base what I have to say of Brooke on other evidence than that which is to be found in his published sermons, but there is one passage in this sermon at which we seize him in a moment of impassioned insight, and the essential mind of the man, as it then was,[1] stands suddenly revealed. This I shall quote.

"As we grow older, we unlearn the faith of childhood; and as science gives to us its teaching, we find that we can only explain phenomena on the supposition that nature is not living, but dead.

"But the fact is that our childhood is really right in principle, though wrong in its application of the principle. Nature is living, though not in the way we then imagine. We fancy that we are moving, the only living things, in a dead world; the fact is we are moving, the only dead things, in a living world. And there are moments, even now, 'when years have brought the inevitable yoke,' that we catch some glimpses of the truth; when we are freed from this incubus of a dead world, and realize the living world: when the old stars of our childhood reappear, and we learn a deeper lesson from them than childhood could receive; when the trees talk to one another in the wood, and we hear and understand their speech; when we listen to the voice of the great deep with the same awful joy as the child, but with a completer comprehension; when the mountains, watched by us at night, are not dead forms, but grey-haired sages, who sit in silence waiting for the dawn. These do not speak to us then of the old Greek humanities, but of *God*. We stand in His presence, and the trees and sea, the stars and mountains, whisper to us that it is not they which exist, but that invisible world of which they and their relations to each other are at once both form and symbol—the spiritual world of God's eternal love, enduring sacrifice, ever-moving progress, the calm of His order, the rest of His

---

[1] In 1867.

unopposed activity, 'His righteousness, like the great mountains, His judgments like the deep.'"

To this chapter the following letter from Ruskin may be appended, as suggesting another aspect of Brooke's development.

John Ruskin to Stopford Brooke.

"Denmark Hill.
"16 August, 1866.

"DEAR MR. BROOKE,—I have never received so much help from anything as from this letter of yours, and I need help just now; so you may guess if I am 'angry.' Indeed, judging of me as graciously as you do, I do not seriously think you could believe I should misunderstand your letter.

"It comes at a critical time, too, when I am wearily deliberating what is best to be done. You must come and talk with me :—I can't write at any length to-day, but I want to tell you more about the business than you can otherwise allow for. That sting of conscience in sitting in my comfortable room instead of going to cholera hospitals is indeed one of my hardest troubles; but only one of many, that you could conquer in me, and enable me to get peaceably to my own work. One may resolve to go on with one's work, whoever is fighting or falling in the street; but if a brickbat goes through your drawing! there is a necessary end—one gets up and says—I must stop this throwing of brickbats, at any rate—or get knocked on the head by one—as well as through one's drawing. And thus I have no joy in my work now. I meant to have written a careful book on the 13th century—two years after I had begun arranging it—Napoleon 'restored' every building I meant to examine, and there was an end to all my architectural work for ever. I hate the sight of a cathedral now, just as I do that of a dead body, however beautiful once. Well, also I meant to have etched a series of drawings of Swiss towns; I began, but again in the twinkling of an eye, they were all turned into railway stations. My very skies and waves are gone. There is not a river— hardly a stream—in Switzerland now left pure. This is *not* dyspepsia. I know clear water when I see it, dyspeptic or not. There is a clear spring at the head of the lake of Brientz, another in the valley of St Martens, I love them as much as ever. But the lakes are DESTROYED, and my *impression* is, that it is the perpetual working down of the liquid manure from the meadows in the new system of dung agriculture, together with the *steamers* and new quays and building mess.

"Well. Here I cannot see a pure sky once in two months. I want a *white* cloud just now for a sketch I'm doing of a friend's grave for her husband. I've waited a fortnight, and haven't seen one!

"I told you how my Turner work was destroyed, and what am I to do,—Crabs. Well, perhaps! if I had any corner of sound heart left for work—of the old sort of heart. But do you not see in the end of Modern Painters, that there can, at present, be no rest for me? Consider what it was to me, when the fact came full on my fairly examining thoughts, that the *only* work done of any good quality in my own business was by men apparently abandoned by God to their own ways; that on the whole religious people were powerless, that all painting and poetry, now, were done by men like Shelley, Byron, Keats, Turner and the like. And fancy all the troublous thoughts and hopelessness of darkness, following on that fact, reasoned out.

"Well, a man whose hobbies have all been taken away from him, and whose faith fails, may still get on somehow if he has any affections to help him, or anything like that other animal I showed you a sketch of besides the Crab. But from these, I through my whole life have nothing but restraint or pain, my parents never understanding me in the least, nor being able to guide me in the least, yet *loving* me so that I should have killed them if I had left them (else I should long ago have begun a series of studies from the Italian frescoes—

but then I must have nearly lived in Italy). And for other affections, they have been only distress to me—not slight, from my early youth till now. So you see how one is driven to fighting, as the only thing that one's hand finds to do, though the hand is weak and no wise meant for swordhilts, and it is no wonder you miss the old creature in what I write now, for the old creature is at least half of it dead, and half the rest changed. But it is still possible, perhaps, to do some remnant of the old thing once meant, and your letter helps me. I'll write again.

"Ever gratefully yours,
"J. Ruskin."

BOOK III

THE BROAD CHURCHMAN

CHAPTER XII

QUEEN'S CHAPLAIN. HOLIDAYS. A BEREAVEMENT

1866-1870

"Kings, emperors, sultans, princes have their wings clipped now—they are not much better than ostriches kept in captivity for the sake of their feathers. But even so, as they are continually trying to keep up the divine right abomination, with all the ills with which great wealth and personal influence afflict [the world] they are like ulcers in the body of mankind. I have no personal hatred of any of them; but my hatred of that which they represent—the despotic, the monarchical idea—deepens in steady wrath every day I live."—(*Diary*, November 19, 1894.)

"It is difficult as one grows older, to feel as much as one did, the importance to individuals of their individual trouble. So much experience has taught me to feel that sorrows and pain which once seemed overwhelming do not overwhelm and are turned by fortitude into powers of the soul. In us, or rather in us in God, resides that which if we are brave, if we keep love, conquers life. The soul is the master of all evil, outward and inward."—(*Diary*, January 7, 1898.)

HAVING closed with the offer of St James' Chapel in January, 1866, Brooke had still three months to wait before his work there could begin. In February, he succeeded in finding a house, No. 1, Manchester Square, which continued to be his London home for forty-eight years, until in 1914[1] he retired into the country at the age of 82. "What a joy it will be," he writes to his wife in January, '66, "to be settled again. Home! Blessed word!" Meanwhile he had no regular clerical work. Kingsley had asked him to act as *locum tenens* at Eversley for six weeks, but the prospect of Brooke's large family of children in the Rectory made an obstacle, and the matter was allowed to drop.

His friends continued to discourage him about St James' Chapel. When it was too late to retreat King wrote, "I earnestly hope you will not close yet with that miserable Chapel. . . . I beg of you remember your own previous opinion, confirmed as it was by Stanley's strong expression. There is no shame in your not having anything to do. The scandal of that belongs to the Bishop—let him bear it. As to that Cave of Adullam, for Heaven's sake let it go to the dogs rather than you touch it. . . . Just let patience have her perfect work. It will, it must, it is sure to come all right." In another letter King quoted Maurice as saying that the Chapel was "utterly unsuitable to him." On this Brooke writes to his wife, "entire idleness and living in lodgings is still *more* unsuitable to me. Our new life will require wary walking and more attention to business. The difficulties likely to meet me are calculated to teach me much and develop my character in a direction where I feel it needs development. . . . With you I fear not life." But Mrs Brooke was not immediately won over to an adventure so risky. "Your letter," he writes to her, "is so judicially calm that I cannot say whether you care or not." "I am sure it is better, bad as it is, than any curacy for me." "I dare say the worry of

---

[1] His retirement to country life began in 1911, but he did not give up his London house till 1914.

these Proprietary Chapels has been much overrated by people who make more of life's troubles than I do. Like the limpet I soon fix my sucker to the roughnesses of the rock and make them a tolerable dwelling place." To perplex him still more he had no sooner closed with the Chapel than he received the offer of a curacy at St George's, Hanover Square, which in spite of his objections to curacies in general was not without its attractions. He was worried also by the attacks upon him in the Low Church newspapers, and by a correspondence with King on the method of dealing with these attacks. However he was able to console himself. A day among the Turners at Cambridge, another day at Peterborough Cathedral, whose beauties he describes in a letter five times as long as any devoted to the Chapel worries, and he was himself again. "What joy," he writes after the visit to Peterborough, "what a sense of power, what a delight in the labours of his hands must have been this architect's. I fancied I could read the dancing exuberance of the designer's mind when his work was done. I came away thoroughly pleased and happy—so pleased that I forgot that I was chilled to the bone." After that he doesn't care a rap for the croakers : he will go on his own way—"and we shall see."

He preached his first sermon in St James' Chapel on the second Sunday of April, 1866. About 70 people were present in the morning and 12 in the afternoon. Two months later the morning congregation had increased to 200. In a year the place was full. In 1869 he writes of great difficulty in accommodating the mass of people seeking admittance.

Writing of the first Sunday he says, "I was slightly nervous but got over it. Curiosity must have brought half the people, and half of the other half will be frightened by the doctrine. I expect the 70 will drop to 20." In July " he has paid the quarter's expenses minus £3." "Men from the Clubs and the big West End houses are beginning to attend." On December 3, '66, he writes to his sister Honor, "The Chapel is slowly increasing in congregation. I have been preaching revolutionary sermons. 'Waving,' as Ardagh[1] says, 'the red flag of Revolution even from the pulpit.' Ardagh, as you know, is a virulent Tory. However, I am sure I am right in preaching against the widespread dishonesty of England. I do not mind Ardagh's denunciations." In February, '67, he is "preparing Lord Salisbury's daughter for confirmation." " These Tories haunt me. They take pews, they write me letters, they put their daughters under me, and all my radicalism goes down their thrapple without a wry face." In May, '68, after reporting a full Chapel, he says, " as a money business it does not pay. I get out of it about £50 a year surplus. . . . But I never expected it to pay well. Only, in spite of the pleasure of being able to speak one's mind, it sometimes touches me with a kind of dark anger that after 12 years in the Church I should be earning only £50 a year. . . . And I do not expect that I shall be promoted. They look on me as a dangerous person who speaks his mind, and to do that is the greatest crime of which a man can be guilty in this age. . . . Yet I cannot act otherwise. I should fall into self-contempt, and then it would be all over with me. I should never do anything in this world." In January, '69, the Bishop of Oxford (Wilberforce) asked him to take part in his Lenten Mission at Maidenhead. "I refused, feeling that I should be out of place there. I said I was afraid that if I went and expressed my

[1] The late General Sir John Ardagh.

opinions freely I should prove an element of disturbance, and if I suppressed my opinions I should myself gain no good but harm by attending."

Brooke was deliberately determined "to speak his mind." Being what he was, he was indeed incapable of doing otherwise—equally incapable whether his audience was a crowded congregation of West End fashionables, "swallowing his radicalism without a wry face," or a solitary woman with a love affair seeking his advice in the study of Manchester Square. His strength lay in his directness. And although his early sermons in St James' Chapel (of which the first volume was published in 1869) look moderate enough in the light of the much more "advanced" theology which the Church of England has since shown itself able to tolerate, we must not forget that in the sixties no clergyman could speak his mind as Brooke was doing without a courageous indifference to his chances of promotion.

However, St James' Chapel was not the only place where he could speak his mind. There was at least one other—the Chapel Royal at Windsor—a place where some men might find a difficulty in speaking their minds, but where Brooke, as it happened, felt himself singularly free. He was commanded to preach there on several occasions, and in January, '67, he was appointed Chaplain to Queen Victoria.

On March 11, '67, he writes to William, "The twelve o'clock service at Windsor is the Litany, the Communion Service to the Nicene Creed, and a sermon. This I preached. The Queen and [Royal Family] were right opposite me in an alcove pew. She looked much the same as ever. I did not see her afterwards. They were in a great fuss, and the Queen was in a greater fuss than anybody. . . . I suppose, however, that the

Queen liked the sermon, since she demanded it, though probably that is general. I do not think that the preachers are generally summoned into a private room to be buttered by H.M. . . . Stanley was in the Church [1] yesterday, and it is amusing that I mentioned him in the pulpit, and declared that his view of the [date] of the XXIII Psalm was in my opinion untenable."

On the next visit to Windsor he dined with Her Majesty. The event is recorded at length in the following letter.

To William Brooke.
"Nov. 24, '67.

"This is almost the first moment I have had since Sunday last to write to you. I have never been so busy in my life. . . . I have two lectures to prepare and deliver every week, and sermons. I have not even had time to write out my sermon for the Queen. I preached a quiet sermon—I think you have heard it, on the repentance of St Peter. The Chapel was unusually full; and the music as infamous as ever. I suppose H.M. intends it as a ceaseless dirge to the memory of the P. Consort. I had told the Dean that I must leave him at five o'clock for London, as I had to be in the City by 10 a.m., and I was packing up when he knocked at the door and said the Queen wished me to dine with her. I believe I said—'Must I go?' I know he said, 'You ought to go. I can get you off, if you wish —but you ought to go.' Of course I said I should go. Dinner at 8.45. I suppose the Queen thinks it right to be ultra-fashionable. We went into the long corridor filled with pictures and found Lord John Manners and his wife waiting. Soon 'a dignified menial' approached —'The Queen is coming.' We all drew up two deep in column and she came out bowing and smiling, and

[1] This refers to St James' Chapel. Stanley attended from time to time, and was frequently present during the afternoon lectures on "Theology in the English Poets."

looking as usual, a comfortable, good humoured, motherly little woman, followed by the Princess Louise and Prince Arthur, who is about 18, and who looked well with his black silk and garter and star and coat turned up with scarlet. He came forward and shook hands with everybody. The Queen led the way and we followed. A very handsome room with hideous pictures—historical—which I conjecture were by that prince of false sentiment, B. West—rich carpet with intricate royal device—cosy round table with gold chandelier—table-cloth with arms of England; the Irish Harp was just under my nose; *only silver* plate to dine upon; it should have been gold, I thought. We were a small party—Queen—then Princess Louise, Lord J. Manners, his wife, Dean Wellesley opposite Queen, myself, Mrs. Wellesley, Prince Arthur. Dinner very good and wine excellent. A gigantic butler, six feet three and slight, in full uniform—epaulettes, etc.—bore the bottles round like children in his arms. Another personage—short and stout, in full Highland uniform—hovered round as well as his age would let him—four or five other servants. The conversation was general and unrestrained, the Queen in an excellent humour laughing heartily and delighted with puzzling the Dean. She asked him with a laugh in her voice if 'the Infidel's banner was up yet.' He had no conception what she meant and obliged to answer—he answered something about Frogmore utterly apart. She was amused at his mistake and repeated her question. He answered something about some old houses in the Castle Yard. She went into a hearty ring of laughter and repeated her question, looking round the table to see if we were all enjoying the fun. He answered again all wrong, and she laughed more and more. At last I took pity on him and whispered to him 'the Sultan,' and he laughed and answered her. I was struck by her frank enjoyment. She seemed to take pleasure in putting everybody at their ease and did the Hostess capitally. Prince Arthur is very bright in look and manner, quite radiant, with his white teeth and fresh face. I did not see the Princess Louise well on account of the envious chandelier. A lovely Skye terrier, white and soft grey, amused himself by going round to everybody and looked a high bred voluptuous animal; every inch a gentleman! After dinner the Queen rose and went round to every one, talking to Mrs Wellesley and then to me and the Dean. She made me her compliments by saying to the Dean as if I were not present—how fine, etc., etc., the sermon was; I do not remember conversations, but she talked of Ritualism, and spoke *very strongly* against it, wishing as well as I remember that the Ritualists were out of the Church. That was the drift of it, at least. I said that I thought no greater blow could be given to the Church than the expulsion of these men; that the Church by its clergy ought to *represent* all phases of religious thought in England which did not absolutely deny its Charter, that these men did represent a widespread phase of thinking, and we ought if possible to retain them, that we should fix the evil into a sect if we expelled them, that in retaining them the good in the movement would be retained in the Church and the evil—through free discussion and through the slow influence of opposing ideas—be eliminated, and I recommended her—of course in a fitting manner—to read that essay in the 'Church and the World' which I recommended to you. There, I said, your Majesty will be enabled to see clearly into the inner force of the movement and how much more fullness it has than we imagine. I thought she took all this very coolly and I suppose it was rather audacious, but I could not hold my tongue because it was a Queen who spoke, when I should have said the same to another person. She brought me up against myself, and said it was a time to speak out and that we had heard, she said, this morning how we should be bolder than we were for Christ. I let her have the last word. I had said my say and she knows, I suppose, that I personally am as far apart from Ritualism in its ideas as a man can be. I told her that if we expelled the Ritualists we should probably on the same principle have to expel at some future time the Evangelists and the Broad Churchmen.

Our object should be to retain all whom we could loyally retain. The Church was not to be made into a small sect, but to be a true National Church representing the religious thought of the Nation within the widest limits possible.

"She said she was sorry the Princess Royal could not come over, and the Princess Royal would be sorry not to have heard me, and asked me to send her the sermon to send to Berlin. I forget the rest of the conversation, which was animated. In talking she has a habit of fixing her eyes upon you and they are very bright and clear. She then went on to speak to Lord John Manners and then left the room followed by the Prince and Princess. We filed out again and went to the Drawing Room where the Household were assembled. As the Queen had vanished etiquette did not oblige me to stay and I vanished, just catching the last train to London."

A year later he was again at Windsor, and on this occasion he had an interesting conversation with the Crown Princess of Prussia.

To William Brooke.

"Nov. 17, '68.

"I got on very well at Windsor. Every one seems to have liked my sermon. The old clerk who came to fetch me to see the Crown Princess said to me, and I was delighted with his praise—for it could not have been mere politeness or phrase—'That is the sort of doctrine we want, Sir, we do not get that often, it makes the 'eart vibrate.' I never met in my life so consistent a hater of H's when necessary and so consistent a lover of them when not necessary. It is so complete, so perfect a reversal of usage that one begins to think there must be something in it. I did not see the Queen, but I had half an hour's conversation with the Prince and Princess of Prussia. She looked as charming and pleasant as she could. The Crown Prince looked more worn and aged than he did three years ago, but was as fresh and frank as possible. I had interested them both by an allusion to the German bookseller who had done so much for Hamburg during its occupation by Davoust and afterwards, and I found them contending as to whom I meant. The Prince was right in thinking I alluded to Perthes. He said he was very glad to hear me again. As to the Princess she is always complimentary to a degree. She talked unmitigated liberalism; spoke of Mill's Inaugural Address at St Andrew's with enthusiasm—it is pleasant to see how her face and eyes kindle and flash and how in her excitement she rises from her chair, but it must make her a difficult person to live with, and I fancy her opinions are not well grounded, *i.e.* she holds them more by impulse than by principle. She spoke of Stanley's letter about Mill and how shortsighted it was to attack clergymen for showing interest in politics. Why should not they have rights as well as the rest? 'We intend to *claim* them,' said I. 'It will not be long before we sit in the House of Commons.'

"She wants an English tutor for her boys—to teach them, she said, 'liberal principles, the English Constitution and the growth of the nation into free government. Princes nowadays have no chance, Mr Brooke, unless they are liberal.' 'I should think not,' said the Crown Prince, but rather as if his wife had gone too far. She said she had heard of my success in London and congratulated me, and asked most kindly after the children and Emma, to whom she desired to be remembered. I ought to have put in a word for myself here, but I forgot all about it.

"I am afraid I speak too freely to these Royal people, but they always inspire me with a boldness and openness of speech which I have not in society and I say what comes into my head, breaking rules of etiquette which I only recollect afterwards. However, it cannot be helped. The Prince shook hands with me cordially when I went away and I kissed the little woman's hand. . . . I plumped this morning for the Radical candidate."

The following autograph letter from the Crown Princess contains an interesting reference, amid other matter, to the conversation reported above.

From the Crown Princess of Prussia.

"Isle of Norderney.
"July 26, 1869.

"The Crown Princess of Prussia thanks Mr Brooke for the volume of sermons she received two days ago, accompanied by his letter. The Book which she has been busily perusing she found very attractive, the Crown Princess admires both the matter and the language in which it is put, sincerely. The sermons on the "Baptism of Christ," the first one in the book, and the one on "Individuality" were those she thinks struck and pleased her most. The Princess takes a fervent interest in the course of *progress* and *enlightenment,* when this *sacred* cause is preached from the pulpit, words of glowing earnestness and of poetical beauty cannot fail to make a deep and lasting impression! And it is no doubt a pleasing task to illustrate the truths one has at heart, and is longing to impart to one's fellow creatures, from the words and acts of Him who is our Master, our teacher and our example!

"The Crown Princess ventures to call Mr Brooke's attention to two German books which must be very interesting to a divine, "Neutestamentliche Zeitgeschichte," von Hausrath, and "Die 5 Bücher Mosé," von G. Ebers, in case he has not yet read them.

"The Crown Princess is *very* sorry that no person has yet been found to fill the place the Princess spoke of at Windsor, but that the difficulties are very great she is aware of, still she does not quite despair of some one being found some day or other, perhaps in a year's time.

"An English Church is to be built at Berlin, and most likely a house for a clergyman will be attached to it. Money is now being collected for this purpose.

"The Crown Princess ends by renewing her thanks both for the letter and book, which she was very glad to receive."

Another landmark of this period is his first preaching in Westminster Abbey. The letter which gives the fullest account of this was written to his father. It contains references to some notable personalities.

To his Father.
" May 5, '67.

"You will perhaps like to hear something about to-night. It was really a grand sight, that vast nave crowded to the doors, and hundreds standing in the side aisles. Stanley said that there were somewhat more than 2500 persons there. I was greatly thrilled and excited—that strange electricity of a mass of men had its own way with me. The service is, as you know, held in the nave, while the choir is closed. The singers, Dean, Canons, etc., assembled in the choir, which was unlit. Over the screen, however, the lights in the nave threw a gleaming glow up on the glorious roof over our heads as we stood there in comparative darkness. I thought of all the thousand years in which God had been worshipped in that place, and a tremble of excitement made my blood dance. Then the organ rolled out its chords, the gate was thrown open, and we streamed in to our places. It was wonderful to see that mass of people stretching away into a mist of faces, and to know that you were going to speak to them. We sit in chairs in the nave at right angles with the people facing the north. The service is simple, though choral, the singers all volunteers, the Psalms are chanted to an easy chant, there is a short anthem, and every word of the prayers is heard. Stanley read the lessons well. It was astonishing how much voice his little frame was capable of. It is the perfection of a Church of England service. I looked round me as I sat down. There were a great number of clergymen whom I was glad to see—two bishops—one the Bishop of Chester, the other I did not know. I have always longed to preach to Bishops that I might let them know what the young Church is thinking about, and I felt a warrior spirit kindling in me when I saw their aprons. Behind me were a great number of various people, great and small, who had been admitted by tickets to reserved seats. Among them were Greg, brother of the editor of the Westminster, Gladstone's son and daughter, Hanna, the Scotch Kirk leader, who married Chalmers' daughter and wrote his life, and Coquerel, the French Protestant clergyman whom they call a heretic, and whom Guizot wishes to turn out of the Protestant Church of France. The hymn before the sermon was 'Rock of Ages.'

"When I got into the pulpit I felt, I must say, more than doubtful whether I should be heard by the vast mass of people down to the end of the nave, and a slight degree of nervousness came upon me, but it had all gone when I had finished the Collect, which I intoned. I think I must have been audible to the greater number, and my voice grew stronger and better the longer I preached. There was a good deal of coughing at first, but it passed away, and was succeeded by a deep silence which gave me confidence. They appeared to be thoroughly attentive, and I felt a mastery over them. I preached on 'the night is far spent, the day is at hand, let us therefore, etc., etc.,' applying it to the circumstances and religious condition of England, for forty minutes. I was much excited, but spoke, I think, with sufficient quietude. I am told it was a daring sermon, and I believe several clergymen were indignant. It was, of course, Broad Church, and you would not have liked it, except so far as you like, and have always taught, us to speak boldly what we think under all circumstances. Coquerel and Hanna expressed to me afterwards their pleasure quite enthusiastically. 'To think, I should live,' said Hanna, 'to hear such a sermon *in the Abbey!*' 'Twenty years ago,' said Coquerel, 'who would have believed that these arches would have heard anything like that! In France we accuse you English of preaching sermons so mild and sugary that they have no effect, but I change my opinion now. Nothing could be bolder than you were—and more pointed.' Lady Augusta said she was glad so many heard it, and Stanley thanked me. I had a conversation with the Bishop of Chester, who has a pleasant face and a pleasant manner. I was pleased to hear from Coquerel that he understood well, and did not lose a word, a testimony from a Frenchman who says he is often puzzled in listening to English, which was satisfactory to what he called the 'netteté' of my pronunciation.

"I tell *you* all these compliments, because you will like to hear them, and will not accuse me of self-conceit

"I was speaking to Stanley of his book on Canterbury, and he told a very characteristic story of himself. 'When I first got the appointment of Dean of Canterbury, I hesitated about taking it. It was leaving Oxford, and I scarcely liked adopting new duties. But when I said yes, my first thought was'—and here he rubbed his hands together with excitement as he spoke it, 'now I shall know all about the murder.'

"I was introduced to Miss Gladstone, who has bright eyes. . . . Greg, who is half a Unitarian, but with a tendency to us—said to me, 'I have never been so touched and moved in my life as by your sermons, and whenever I can I go to your Chapel.' It was he who urged Stanley to ask me to preach, as Stanley told me himself. If any of the Recordites were there I expect a row. . . .

"My rather grandiloquent writing in this letter is, I suppose, on reading it over—a reflection of the excitement I was in last night."

During the whole of this period he was working at a pressure which even his splendid physical constitution hardly sufficed to sustain. He had joined the promoters of *The People's Magazine*, and though he was not the nominal editor, it is evident from his letters that he was doing the bulk of the work, procuring and criticizing the articles of others, and writing articles of his own on a great variety of subjects: historical, literary, artistic, and scientific. He was also lecturing three times a week on English History and Literature at Queen's

College. He writes that he is "seldom in bed before three in the morning. Monday, Tuesday, and Wednesday are taken up with reading and preparation. Thursday, Friday, and Saturday given to sermons, of which I write two. . . . I get messages asking me to publish my sermons. It is possible I may do something of the kind, though my sermons are preaching, not reading sermons." He was also conducting an immense private correspondence, and "every other night we are dining out somewhere" to meet people, conversing with whom "puts a man on his mettle." About this time he was asked to take part with J. R. Green in producing a quarterly review of Liberal Theology. His letter to Green on this matter is worth study, as showing how little disposed he was to throw in his lot with the extreme section of religious Liberals.

To J. R. Green.

"I do not know of any one who would take shares without further information, without being sure of the Editor, and without the support of some well-known name to float the paper. When you mentioned my full sympathy with your proposition did you mention also that my sympathy went with the proposition as such, but that I did not guarantee my sympathy to the paper on its appearance. That would depend on the mode in which it is edited, and the spirit in which its contributors wrote. The very first principle of such a paper should be reverence for all that men truly hold sacred . . . a reverential mode of approaching all those opinions, beliefs and forms which are not pharisaically, but in truth of heart believed, and rested on. Let them be opposed if necessary, fairly, decidedly, but with the reverence due to things-held dear, and sacred by the heart. We have no right to hold up to contempt and ridicule opinions which are the religious life blood of thousands and it is pure folly into the bargain, and for one we gain by it we lose a hundred. Robertson, to speak of what I know, compared the evangelical theory of the atonement to the sacrifice to Juggernaut, and said its principles were derived from the heathen shambles. I think he was bitterly to blame in doing so, and that his language was as unfair as it was harmful to the cause of his argument. He forgot the pain, I may say the agony, which such comparisons would cause to men, who, whatever were their opinions, were as true followers of Christ in his life as he was himself. Granting that the comparisons were true he had no right to use them. Charity doth not behave itself unseemly, nor seek to win its cause by injuring the hearts of others. Now I do want to know if the spirit of the articles and letters is to be reverential. Let them be negative, and destructive if they will, though all negations and destructive efforts are pitiable things and no-things, and never did one hand's turn of real work in this world. But at least if they do try and knock down let them do it with some awe of what they are about, some veneration, not for the errors, but for those to whom they are truths, some tenderness and tolerance. I fairly own I am sometimes sick of the intolerant bigotry I hear talked by our liberals and of the growing cant of the Broad Church school. Again, if it is not errors but old-established beliefs which are approached menacingly in the paper, I do trust it will be done with reverence. Clergymen who have a smattering of Greg and Renan and Strauss approach, *e.g.* the subject of the Resurrection with the opinions of the three and of half a dozen others all mingled together in one lump, as if their points of view were not quite different, and ask questions, and propound theories which make me crisp all over; not at the discussion remember, but at the flippant way in which it is carried on. The hopes of nine-tenths of the religious world in immortal life rest upon the truth of the fact of the Resurrection, and yet doubt is thrown upon it, not with passionate sorrow for doing so, not with solemn awe, which remembers the faith of millions, not with that stern spirit of truth, which says to itself: if the Resurrection be not true I shall sorrow all my life, but still if it be not true—truth above all, but with a careless indifference to Truth itself and to the souls of all who believe in that historical fact, as the proof of the reality of the life of Christ and the witness of their own immortality. If that unreverential spirit is to prevail in the columns of the paper, if it is to be a field where every young enthusiast for new views is to shake out his red rag to excite his opponents, if it is to laugh to scorn old opinions because they are now proved to be untrue, forgetting that once they were true to men, if it is to encourage doubt and to suggest it, and not to teach that faith is the highest and doubt only worth a farthing when it is a necessary passage to faith, if it is to destroy like Colenso and not build up like Stanley faith in a divine revelation in the Bible, I could not sympathize with it. I dare say you are weary of my harping on reverence. But it seems to me the very thing we all want more than anything else in this world in our present contest, and I grieve to see so many in the liberal movement cutting the throat of all their efforts by the way in which they speak and write. The freest discussion on all points, as free and bold as you like, but how, the spirit in which it is to be done is the question."

With all his physical vigour and his marvellous resilience from fatigue it would have been impossible for Brooke to sustain these labours had he not been in the habit of taking long holidays in the country or abroad, which, being his own master, he was now free to do. A holiday with him was always a swift resurrection to another life. He was under no danger of carrying his working self into his leisure hours, or allowing the memory of daily preoccupations to interfere with his communion with Nature. He had only to cross the Channel with his face towards Switzerland or Venice—"Venice, the city of my soul"—and the whole of his

HIS POWERS OF OBSERVATION

London life would fall away from him like a dream. With "In Memoriam" in one pocket, the "Divine Comedy" in another, a sketch book in a third, a well-filled cigar case in a fourth, and the heart of a boy beating beneath it all he would leap into the train and before the sea was reached St James' Chapel, the College, the *People's Magazine*, the sermons, the lectures and all the rest became as if they were not. He flung it aside as easily as he flicked the ash from his cigar, and not a word of "shop" would pass his lips—if he could help it—till London saw him again full of health and joy and just as ready to put his hand to the plough as he had been ready three months before to leave it at the end of the furrow.

A separate biography might well be written of Brooke on his holidays. The mere enumeration of the places he visited would fill many pages, and if the descriptions and impressions which he recorded in his letters and diaries were to be printed, I believe they would exceed in volume all the rest of his published books.

To all the changes of the natural world he was extraordinarily sensitive and his powers of observation correspondingly alert. He had the Celtic passion for colour and always saw, or rather felt, the colour of his surroundings before noting their other qualities. His eye loved to dwell upon details and would pick them out in rapid succession at the very instant that his mind was forming general impressions of the object before him, and this no matter what the object might be—a landscape, a picture, the faces and attitudes of a group of people, the furniture in a room,[1] the appointments of a

[1] As an instance of his quickness in this kind of observation take the following description (written from memory after an interval of two days) of an uncomfortable room in which he was lodged at an

dining table, a woman's dress. A never ceasing inflow of impressions kept his imagination in "a white glow." Indoors and out of doors it was just the same. On entering a room he would see first, what so many people see last (or not at all), the pictures on the walls, and any small object of art the room might contain, a bit of carved ivory, a piece of lace, a bronze figure three inches high: the colour of the carpet, of the curtains, of the walls would be instantly noted. Or he would go into a dealer's shop, plant himself for a few minutes in the midst of the confusion, and before the dealer had time to offer his wares Brooke's eye would have ransacked the place of every treasure it contained. He was a great collector—especially during the sixties and seventies—and people used to say he had "the lucky touch"; but his success was really due to the complete self-detachment with which his powers of observation did their work. In the open air he was a living confutation of those psychologists who say that our senses *wait to receive* the impressions of the outside world. His senses *attacked* their surroundings on every side. They were in a state of boundless activity, searching out every secret thing.

Nor did he rest content with the immediate experience. It was his principle as well as his instinct

---

hotel when preaching in the North of England in 1898: "The room in which we sat had every kind of furniture in it; beds hidden against the wall, sewing machines, dreadful porcelain figures, appalling cushions, armchairs on which one slides as on a skating rink, lined with iced horse hair, and cupboards and shelves filled with every rubbish under the moon—dogs' muzzles, cord, samplers, coffee tins, photographs, flannel waistcoats, glass drops from Christmas trees, trousers, bodices, pamphlets, tracts, albums, a wig, a flute, songs, music hall scores, darned stockings, one toothbrush, four combs, small and large; a ball of worsted, four antimacassars, a plaster cast, a dog in floss silk, several greasy neckties, two paper collars, and I might go on for ever—but the page is at an end."

to cast his experience into form. Had he been a painter he would have transferred it all to canvas, as Turner did. As it was it found expression mainly in his letters, his diaries, and, of course, his sermons; and the form of it was always fresh. Throughout the many hundreds of pages in the diaries that record his communion with nature he hardly ever repeats himself. The same objects, or the same class of objects are indeed described over and over again—the racing clouds, the sound of wind, the curve of swirling waters, the movement of birds, the appearance of the heavens at night, the rising and setting of his favourite stars, the roses in his garden, the doings of his dog, but it is a different story every time, differently told and differently interpreted. "I know you do not care for descriptions of scenery," he wrote to his wife, "but I simply cannot help myself." The power to describe nature, or rather to interpret her, was inborn: signs may be found even in his schoolboy letters. It was of course considerably developed at the time of which I am now writing, but did not reach the fullness of its development till a much later period, when new influences, not yet mentioned, had come into operation. It was only when he had withdrawn to some extent from the theological atmosphere of his early and middle life that his natural religion and his power to interpret natural objects in spiritual terms gained a perfect freedom of expression. Vivid and copious as are the descriptions of nature in his middle period we find in his later language an ease and a penetrating force not present in the earlier letters. For the evidence of this the reader must be content to wait until we come to the diaries of Brooke's old age. By that time the proportion between "work" and "holidays" which prevailed in the sixties had become reversed.

The following letter records his first impressions of Venice, and will serve to illustrate what I have said.

To William Brooke.

"Venice, Sep. 23, '67.

"I know that you will like a line from me from this city, so I write, though I have but little time, being out of doors from 9 A.M. to 10 P.M. except at dinner.

"First, I am not disappointed, it is even more interesting and varied than I imagined. The extreme novelty, the irresemblance to other cities is a constant, unconscious surprise. The noiselessness, the absence of carriages and of horses, the strangeness of always living in a boat, come with 'a gentle shock of mild surprise' upon the mind continually. One seems out of the world, in another planet, where life is led under different conditions.

"Again—there is the extreme variety. Two artists entirely new to me to study, and both magnificent—Tintoret and Giov. Bellini; the architecture of 800 years in perhaps the finest examples; an ever-changing sky and moods of weather; new views of an unique type of scenery at every five minutes of your gondola's progress; and the nightly excitement of killing and erecting defences against the mosquitoes.

"The prevailing feeling is that of sadness touched into greater tenderness by romance. Everything is going to ruin; again and again I think of Ezekiel's chapters on Tyrus; his human sorrow and pity for the fall of the Queen of the Seas, and yet his stern declaration of the indignation of God against her. Tintoret's pictures are rotting on the walls of the Schuola di San Rocco; St Mark's is crumbling away in portions. They are restoring both, and the ruins worked by restoration are greater and more pitiable than those which are worked by time. They have put skies into half of Veronese's pictures, because his were not blue enough. They are taking down the precious old Byzantine mosaics in the roofs of St Mark and restoring them, Heaven preserve us, right and left, with frantic and

FIRST VISIT TO VENICE

villainous energy. Titian's celebrated picture of the Doge Grimani presented to the Virgin, I could not see, it was rolled up and being, I suppose, repainted. What surprises *me* in all this, is the profundity of impudence which it reveals as possible in the human subject. Here are creatures, who cannot paint even a finger correctly, whose notions of colour are those of a sign painter, whose landscapes are inconceivably insolent to Nature—and these men, who, I am told, think themselves the best painters in the world, these men lay their coarse academical paws upon Tintoret, G. Bellini, and Titian, and amuse themselves with the destruction of the finest pictures. I should like, for every picture they have ruined, to drag them at the stern of the gondola in the water, all the way up and down the Grand Canal, towing them as Duncan Knock Dunder threatened to do to the 'sincere professor'—who should for conscience sake oppose even for a moment the will of the Argyle in the election of Reuben Butler.[1]

"Ruskin seems to me in certain instances to have exaggerated the merits of Tintoret; but I do not think he has in the slightest exaggerated his merits—or rather his genius—as far as imagination is concerned. In *that*— the highest thing a man can possess—there is no painter whose works I am acquainted with, who approaches him, except Turner. Turner stands above him, I think, in the quality of his work, and in mastery of his subject, landscape painting—but Tintoret and he stand side by side in the white glow of their imaginative power. Everything these two touch with all their power is made a new thing upon earth. I say, with all their power, for both now and then do weary and conventional work, Turner however less than Tintoret. I feel before him, at times, that feeling of inconceivableness which is stirred by Shakespeare and Turner. 'How could human powers be so great, so all embracing—I cannot conceive it—it is unapproachable.' Tintoret's 'Paradise,' *e.g.*, covers a whole wall, and has in its glowing profundity about 900 figures. I did not see a

[1] In "The Heart of Midlothian."

weak one in the whole, and some of the figures were inexpressibly grand, magnificent in dignity, force, and solemnity. The composition of this enormous picture was as simple as its parts were suggestive, and its idea profoundly religious. Without any desire to exaggerate, I should pronounce it the greatest conception ever born in any man in any branch of art.

"Nothing can be more charming than to wander through the rooms of the Ducal Palace; walls, ceiling, gorgeous with colour, and alive with the noble thought of men; a thousand associations crowding round you, not as phantoms, but as dignified scenes and forms of beauty and greatness, the sunlight pouring in from a heaven of cloudless blue, perfect quiet, the exercise of thought to find the ideas of the pictures, the pleasure of discovering them, the analogy of all the pictures with the character of the city itself; and when one is a little exhausted by gazing, to take refuge on a balcony and look out upon the Piazza of St Mark where the Campanile cleaves the blue sky like a mighty arrow of flame, and the Lion of St Mark looks from his column of Egyptian marble out upon the dancing waters of the lagoon, and the faint lapping of the water, where the gondolas rock in the ripple, comes up to the ear as it leaps up and down upon the marble steps, and the deep orange sails with black patches go by like tropic birds of giant form upon the sea; and to people the quays and the Piazza, not with the vulgar Venetian of the present day, nor with the hideous iron rams which lie now beside the Riva dei Schiavoni, but with argosies from Tripoli and the Levant, and with sailors from every clime, and with the forms of the grave Senators, and the graceful and dignified women, dignified with the sacredness of great beauty and moral power, which burn in colour and move with nobility, and look the Masters and Ladies of the Ocean Queen upon the canvas of Tintoret and Veronese.

"Hours go by like days and days like hours, and the charm does not decay nor the passion of living grow weary. It is not mere sight seeing, it is the entrance of new thoughts, the refreshing and recasting of old conceptions, the kindling of imagination, the constant and easy exercise of mind and feeling together, and the pleasurable delight of being brought into contact continually with men infinitely above oneself, and receiving from them seeds which you feel must germinate into something in yourself afterwards because they are living seeds—which redeems all this from mere sight seeing. Moreover, at any moment when the works of man fail to interest, you can turn aside and read a new leaf in God's book of Nature. In a moment you are on the sea and beneath the sky, and both are decked continually with His Beauty and His Variety in Infinity. It is not so in any other city. The roll of a single cab over the stones is destructive to the religion of Nature.—Ever, dear boy, Your very loving Brother,

"S."

Between 1865 and 1870 he was twice in Switzerland (once with J. R. Green), and twice in Venice, first in '67, and afterwards in '69. He was several times in Ireland, making a long tour of Donegal and Sligo in '68 with his brother Edward, subsequently staying with Lady Castletown in Co. Meath. On this occasion he spent much time at Kells studying Irish antiquities. He made several geological tours with his brothers William and Arthur, one in the Yorkshire dales, another in Derbyshire, another in the district round Whitby, another from Milford Haven. I find him also at various country houses in Yorkshire and Northumberland. In '66 he was at Allenheads, the seat of his brother-in-law, and explored the lead mines in the neighbourhood, of which he wrote a long description. In '69 he took two holidays, one in the spring at Llanberis ("a place I dearly love") and the other in Switzerland.

That year—'69—was marked by one of the deepest

sorrows of his life; it was in fact a year of many troubles. One after another his children, of whom he had now six, were attacked by dangerous epidemics, and his wife's health was causing him anxiety. In April his second son, Graham, a bright and beautiful boy, of whom his parents had many hopes, fell a victim to typhoid fever. It was a bitter loss, his first experience of the intensity of grief; and the memory of it, and of the victory he achieved over his pain, opened a fresh fountain of tenderness in his nature, and enabled him in the coming years to stretch out a helping hand to many a stricken soul. And yet the pang was too sharp to be easily translated into the terms of his own moral benefit. To a friend who offered him the cheap comfort, "that his loss was intended to educate him," he replied, with well-merited asperity, "Your theory about my education may be true; I suppose it is true; but I do not like it. It has further extensions which are too terrible to think of. After all, why should I be of more importance than Graham, and his education not be of more importance to the world than mine? I see the answers to these things, but only intellectually. Still I am content to be puzzled. Few things produce more intellectual scorn in me than the impatience of the human race under enigmas. For my part, if life had no puzzle it would have no pleasure. It is true *this* pleasure is always drifting or darting into pain. But he who has not in some sense recognized the inner coincidence of pleasure with pain has learnt but little of the secrets of the soul."

Mrs Brooke never recovered from the blow; the spirit was brave, but the flesh had less resistance. "She kept these things in her heart," and sorrow preyed upon her vitality. On May 19 he wrote to her from his father's rectory, where he was often in those sad days, "I look forward with a shrinking of heart to seeing that chair empty and to have S. coming into my room and no companion with him. As long as [the children] are all away I half feel that he is not dead but with them, and find myself expecting him back and thinking of what he will say to my room. For you it is far worse. You have no regular work which you must do and you have let your health sink to that point at which grief is apt to accumulate itself and its pain. Moreover, it is your nature, like Mary's, to keep all these things and to ponder them in your heart. If you were more expansive by nature you would get better sooner, but that is not belonging to you, and for you to attempt it, even if you could do so, would be wrong because unnatural."

To William he wrote, "Emma cannot get over this loss, and it has become worse to *me*, since all the children came back, than before. It has left a dreadful uncertainty over all life, and I am in continual fear of something else. It has made me feel several years older. . . . I look behind and see a gulf impassable and profound between now and the past." And in another letter written from Llanberis: "This sunshine and tenderness of nature suppress the pain of the thought of that quiet grave at Kensal Green and that empty bed at home, but at night it comes back to me and I live over and over again those last 24 hours till they enter into my dreams. His birthday was the 23rd of this month and all through his illness he was looking forward to it. . . . It is pitiable to think that he spends his birthday in his grave, pitiable to us however much we believe, and I *do* believe it, that he is at home in the fullness of joy. . . . You must come and visit his grave with me when you are in London." And again to his wife, "I thought of you on the shore ... and then I thought of Venice and its peace, and then of Graham and the gulf which his loss has opened between this year and that year of happy wandering. What *is* that line which I used continually to say to myself for a week after he went away, 'You cannot tell how ill's all here about my heart—but no matter'?[1] I wish I could find it."

We return to the brighter side. In the summer of 1866 he was geologizing on the north-east coast of Yorkshire and writes thus to his wife from Runswick on September 15:—

"I like the Yorkshire people here. They are a manly conversational race. Yesterday we met an old sea captain on the road who told us all his life. We were arguing to-day about the mode of using the herring net. We stopped a pretty girl and begged her to explain it. She was astonished at first when I said we could not agree about the nets and wanted to know from her, but she was very communicative and clear. An old man employed in the alum works for 47 years—'poor old Jem' he called himself—asked me for some tobacco. I gave it to him and sixpence, for which he all but embraced me. He could scarcely get up the bank. Arthur gave him his arm to help him up. He said, 'Oh, Jem, you were a mon once, now it's ower.' He too entered into the history of his life. He was quite contented, had always had good health till the last year, hoped the Lord wouldn't forget him, nor the help he had given to others when he was young. He was receiving 2/6 from the parish. I do think that these large landowners and manufacturers should give a pension to a man after 30 years of labour and good conduct. They send an old

---

[1] "But thou wouldst not think how ill all's here about my heart. But it is no matter."—*Hamlet*, Act v. scene 2.

horse into a fat paddock. They send an old man to the workhouse."

The following records a conversation with Woolner, the sculptor, in the study at Manchester Square. It is highly characteristic of Brooke's manner when opposed in argument.

To his wife.

"April 17, '68.

"Etheridge dined here last night and Woolner came in for an hour. We had a geological and medical and artistic conversation. I sold my Spicifer Princeps, that large fossil shell on my chimney-piece, to the Government for a pound, with which pound I bought a picture! That was a nice exchange, for the picture is a good one.

"Woolner depreciated the drawing of the sea in my big Turner and compared it to the sea in the shipwreck in the National Gallery to the disadvantage of the former. I said it was at least as truly drawn and that it was a magnificent rendering of the sea near a rocky coast.

"W. 'It is good, but' (very obstinately) 'it is not done, the thing is not given.'

"S. (Brooke). 'It is the very thing that *is* done, it cannot be truer.'

"W. 'Perhaps you have not seen and studied the sea, as I have, if you had you would not maintain that. I have been six months at sea.'

"S. 'And I have lived twenty years by the seaside close to a rocky coast, and have seen ten times every winter the sea breaking upon a cliff-bound coast and on long reaches of sand, and the sea of the shipwreck is true to the forms of waves breaking on sandbanks out at sea, but it is not true to forms of waves such as break on rocky precipices, and this sea is [true to that]. As to your six months at sea that does not supply you with a particle of experience as to the way in which waves behave under the conditions represented in my picture. On this point I have a hundred times your experience.'

"We had a sharp passage of arms, but Etheridge

chimed in with me, having himself lived for months on Lundy, and seen also the sea breaking on Land's End. And indeed I know I am right and Woolner wrong.

"Hunt's picture is magnificent. The conception is as great as the execution and the drawing of the figure is finer than anything he has done. As to the colour, it is subtle beyond conception. But he never will have Millais' touch, that touch which only a few men in the world have ever had, it is the only thing in which Millais excels him. In sheer force of intellect, in feeling, Hunt is infinitely superior, but Hunt wants that spiritual fire of feeling which, in a picture, raises it to the first rank. He has feeling, but it is elaborated, not flashed out like the burning glow of noon."

A letter to his wife from Wyton shows him in one of the characteristic moods I have mentioned above.

To his wife.

"May 5, '68. Wyton.

"As usual, I write to you on the grass of the pleasure ground taking all the advantage I can of the blowing wind and happy sunshine. There is a sea-like freshness about this place which always pleases me, the wind comes over so wide and so flat a country that it is especially free in its movement. It is exquisitely sweet at present, for it brings with it a subtle scent, not of any one flower, but of the whole essence of thousands of faintly scented things. Spring has come dancing down here as young and as lovely as she was four thousand years ago.

"'Lord, how all creatures laughed when her they spide.'

"Everything gives one to-day the choicest pleasure, the shape and glimmer of the sward grass, the glance in the water of the glorious golden green, tender as the last hues of sunset, of the limes, the mystery and joy and ravishment of all things in the embrace of May.

"To exist alone is enough and I sit beneath the trees, listening to the larks and the breeze in the chestnut-nave, and quaffing the soft wind and seeing colour come and go, like blushes on a girl's cheek, over the face of meadows and wood, sit doing nothing, thinking of nothing, and almost caring for nothing."

I regret that space forbids me to print with adequate fullness the long series of letters written by Brooke to his wife during his Irish tour with his brother Major Edward Brooke in August and September, 1868. Together these letters would fill a fair-sized volume, and would form a delightful guide-book to any person intent on following his steps through the wilds of Donegal and Sligo, or investigating the antiquities of Co. Meath. They vary through every conceivable mood from deep depression when he is wandering in dark and rainy weather among treeless hills and bogs to wild and elemental joy when the waves of the Atlantic are breaking beneath him on the sunlit cliffs. There are many amusing pictures of Irish life by the wayside, in the markets of the small towns, and of the Irish hotels of the period. There is a lively report of a conversation with a chambermaid at Bundoran which turned on the problem of how two stalwart gentlemen were to take their baths in a pint of water and dry themselves with a towel the size of a lady's pocket-handkerchief. There is an account of his visit to Leix Castle, the seat of his ancestor Hector Graham, "the wickedest and the most daring of men. It is beautifully situated in a bend of the river Barrow, rising above it on a great limestone mound, now covered by masses of broken masonry, large and grass-grown like scattered boulders in an Italian glen. This ruin is the work of Cromwell, who blew up the castle, once one of the noblest piles in Ireland." Then for several days he is a guest in a Bishop's palace, "a good pious man, with a look of St Patrick; but his two daughters are a brace of hippopotami." Then for a week to a country house where he is "bored to extinction." Finally, he arrives in Dublin and there makes a "strong speech to the Church Congress" defending the Liberal party from the charge of infidelity, which "must have made me a few enemies, though not personal ones of course." "To-morrow evening to my regret I am to preach at Bray. I am sure to let something heterodox slip out, and it is a pity to destroy the beautiful impression of orthodoxy I have made."

One letter to his wife which reveals him in a part which he could play to perfection when he was minded must not be omitted.

To his wife.

"The Impayrial Hotel, Enniskillen.
" Aug. 10, '68.

"Me darlint, here we are, in the Impayrial Hotel with the bright wathers of the river Erne straming smooth and tindher in the distance; a beautiful chain of mountains curves from west to south just foreninst us, and behind rises shublime and extramely noble, on the top of a hill covered with threes, the pillar erected to the hairo of the place—Colonel Cole—who commanded the Enniskillens in the Peninsular War. He wears along with his hair a lightning rod on the top of his head, and looks mighty proudly out from the imminence across the country. And, by the powers, it's a fine view entirely which the ould man sees with his sthroug eyes, at laste, it was so, this evenin' when me and the Meejor was there. The southern sky was black with clouds and rain and the big hills were barred with white mist, which came slowly creepin' on over the dark brown bog-land; jist at our fate lay the town, arching up and over and down the hill, and in the middle the Church with its tall spire and a clump of dark yew trees looking over the low wall—then to the west, the sun setting over a purple sweep of hills in golden bars of clouds, fringed with angry scarlet. Below the river winding among islands, glassy calm, a boat rowing upwards made a long ripple, but beyond a pleasure yacht with its sails spread, lay like a sea bird on the smooth water and set its image there. The clouds gathered thicker and thicker; rain began to fall and we came back to beefsteaks and to tea."

I append two letters relating to public matters, the Irish Church question, and the action which Prussia was then taking on the Continent.

"Aug. 28, '66.

"We had a very interesting discussion on the Irish Church Question at the C. C. C.[1] Maurice introduced the subject and said that the Irish Church was not a national Church, *i.e.* did not grow out of the national life of Ireland, and that having failed in its *raison d'être* —which was to make Ireland Protestant—it was doomed to fall, God would not suffer it to live. He especially referred to the Placards offering money to any R. C. to find proof for certain doctrines as disgraceful, and to the violent ferocious controversy of the proselytising societies as destructive of religion. I replied that had the English Government acted with wisdom in the time of Elizabeth the whole of Ireland would have probably been Protestant, but that the blind ignorance which forced the English language on an Irish speaking people drove the people back to Popery: that the Church had never had a fair chance, for it was always looked upon as a portion of a State which enacted the most tyrannical penal laws against the R. C. religion. . . .

"There was a very interesting discussion. To my surprise the feeling was very general that the Irish Church should *not* rashly be abolished, that it needed reform not dissolution, that it would be a perilous measure to the English Church, Wales being instanced and Scotland, that the question of what was to be done with the Endowments was all but insoluble, that English feeling would never permit the handing over of these endowments to the R. Cs., that the English people in general, no matter what Parliament might wish to do,

[1] The Curates Clerical Club.

would not suffer the Irish Church to be dismissed, that its abolition would tend to make the attitude between Protestant and Roman Catholic in Ireland still more violent, that the Church was a protection against, and not an incitement to intolerance, etc., etc.

"These points were maintained by men like Green, Llewellyn Davies, Wace and others. Maclagan made an admirable speech in favour of the Church, and made a great impression."

"July 16, '66.

"[The newspapers] are now (about America, about the Reform Bill, about the war) all grovelling in the mire, and eating dirt together. There cannot be a strong German Confederation; . . . they, the little Kings and Dukes, are such poor creatures, fifty years behind their time, thinking the chatter of their little state is the great movement of the world. Why, Morier told me it was impossible to get into even Prince Alfred's head any large political idea: if there cannot be this confederation, which more than anything else I should wish, if it were not a vain hope, what is there left but Prussian Hegemony? I believe at present it will be far the best for Germany. The finance system of Prussian Government is the most economical in Europe. They are without exception the most energetic, vital people in Europe. They are steady, brave, prudent, and full of ideas. They are eagerly interested in commerce: they will soon be free traders. They are determined to push their manufactures. They talk little, they do much. Their army is the best managed in Europe, better I believe than the French. The whole people have the same dogged perseverance in work as the soldiers have in battle. At present I see nothing better for these weak little Kingdoms and Principalities than being absorbed into Prussia and gaining strength by union with that which is strong.

"It is true the Government of Prussia is illiberal, etc., etc. But that will change as time goes on. I believe in my intellect that when a nation can bear a liberal government it will get it by the onward motion of things themselves. The Crown Prince will be more liberal than his father, but not so much so as people expect. Perhaps towards the close of his reign, if the Prussians care for it, he will be as liberal as need requires.

"With all this I do not like the Bismarckian *régime*, have no sympathy with it; but I believe his policy is best for Prussia, and I believe nothing will be better for the Peace of Europe and the well being of Northern Germany than that all these little states should be united together under a strong head, whose sympathies in some years will be with free thought, free trade, and free government"

CHAPTER XIII

EVENTS AND OPINIONS. LETTERS TO HIS WIFE

1870–1875

"I have heard many political prophecies [in my time]. None have ever come true."—(*Diary*, January 21, 1916.)

WHEN the Franco-Prussian war [1] broke out in the summer of 1870, Brooke strongly espoused the cause of Prussia. His admiration for Prussia at that time was by no means unqualified; he had seen the growth of a dangerous spirit during his stay in Berlin; he had an intense dislike for the autocratic system, and no high opinion of the reigning monarch. But he regarded all this as temporary, and believed that the German spirit would ultimately declare for peace, liberty, and popular government. Moreover, he had seen something of the Crown Prince and Princess, admired their characters, and hoped that under the coming rule of Frederick Germany would step into line with democratic tendencies. France, on the other hand, appeared to him to have entered upon a stage of decadence. Under Louis Napoleon, whom he despised, she was setting a bad example to Europe. As between France and Prussia he had no questionings as to the side to which his sympathies were due. He agreed with Carlyle. Mrs Brooke held a contrary view, and some interesting

[1] See note at the end of the chapter.

letters are extant in which he argued the matter with her, for it was one on which he felt strongly. But she, too, had lived in Berlin, and she held to her own opinion with a prescience, based on her impressions of the Prussian character, which in this instance was sounder than his. She knew the faults of France, but believed that a yet more virulent poison was at work in Germany.

Soon after the war broke out Brooke preached a sermon in defence of the Prussian cause which for the time became the talk of London. It was read with approval in high places, and reproduced in the German newspapers. It brought many letters from that country, including some from royal personages at the Court of Berlin in which he was thanked for what he had said.

Of the many prominent Mid-Victorians who advocated the cause of Prussia, he was one of the few who lived to see the dire events of 1914. He did not repent of what he said in 1870. Judged by the evidence then forthcoming he believed that he had been justified in expecting that the influence of Prussia would be beneficent. But he recognized that the evil tendencies, which he knew to be in existence in '70, had suppressed the good ones on which he had based his hopes, and he looked upon the action of Germany in 1914 as the most signal instance of wickedness in high places the world has ever seen, an illustration of the pride and covetousness which of all qualities he held to be most detestable, whether in nations or individual men. All the more because he had seen the immense possibilities of good of which Germany was master in her earlier growth did he deplore the moral fall of her maturity. "It was a tragedy too bitter for speech."

In this connexion we may recall his conversation at Windsor in 1866 with the Crown Prince and Princess, already reported, in which a hint was given him that he might, if he would, become the tutor of their children, and explain to them what liberty meant. If he had taken the hint——? It was, perhaps, a fateful moment in the history of modern Europe when Brooke, addressed by the Crown Princess, adroitly turned the conversation.

On receiving a copy of his sermon the Crown Princess again wrote to him, in terms which will be read with interest and sorrow at the present time.

From the Crown Princess of Prussia.

"Neues Palais, Potsdam. Aug. 23, 1870.

"The Crown Princess of Prussia thanks Mr Brooke very much indeed for his kind letter and for his fine sermon, which she has forwarded to the Crown Prince to the seat of war, as she is sure it will give him pleasure. The sermon has created a great and pleasurable sensation here, and has been mentioned in strains of unqualified praise in the Prussian Press, at a time when the tone of the same Press towards England was one very painful to a true English heart to read. The sermon has *really* done good, and has been of use.

"In such awful times as these, when the whole nation feels itself injured, and excitement and just indignation prevail, it is not to be wondered, that when a feeling of annoyance once arises it should spread so quickly and become so intense that it almost becomes a little unjust; this was the case. I trust this will wear off, and that the two Protestant countries will be firmly united, and maintain the peace of Europe, working *together* in the cause of progress, enlightenment and civilization. A merciful Providence will surely bring this about; the truth must always be victorious in the end, and the good triumph over the bad. Germany and England are so necessary to one another, one can only feel *how* much this is the case, when one is equally devoted to both, and loves the one and the other, understanding their common greatness and characteristic differences.

"THEOLOGY IN THE ENGLISH POETS"

"Every individual is at this time passing through a fiery ordeal in Germany, the anxiety is not to be described, may God in His mercy bring this war to a termination which may be good and useful to the world!"

In 1872 Brooke began, in St James' Chapel, the Lectures on Theology in the English Poets which, published two years later, gave him a position, unique at the time, as a reconciler of things secular and sacred. At the present day, when this type of address has become not uncommon in the pulpit, and when the line between "sacred" and "profane" literature is less sharply drawn, it is not easy to realize the courage that was needed, forty-five years ago, to launch out in this direction. By making English Poetry into the text of his discourses it was evident that Brooke was adopting a heresy, regarding the nature of Revelation, then regarded as highly dangerous. He was severely criticized, and indeed threatened. In a cutting from *The Inverness Courier* of March 13, 1873, I find the following statement made on the authority of its London correspondent:—

"The leaders of the Church of England are considering whether they should or should not take steps to bring up the Revd Stopford Brooke on a charge of rationalistic preaching. The rev. gentleman is delivering a course of Sunday lectures on the Theology of the English poets. The heterodox preachers are, it seems, making enormous strides in the metropolis. The majority of the orthodox preachers address small congregations and empty pews, but their heterodox brethren —the rationalists as they are called—lecture every Sunday to crowds."

The Bishop might prohibit Colenso from preaching in Brooke's pulpit, but he had no power to interfere with the lectures, or, if he had, it was not exercised: and the threats came to nothing. The lectures disclose nothing new in the mind of Brooke with regard to the nature of Revelation, in which he had long included extra-biblical elements, but they mark a distinct turning point in the history of English preaching, and may be justly described as the work of a daring pioneer. "I wished," he says in the preface to the published lectures, "to claim, as belonging to the Christian ministry, political, historical, scientific, and artistic work, in their connexion with Theology; and to a greater extent than I had hoped for, the effort, so far as I have carried it, has succeeded." This shows that the lectures were a step to the fulfilment of the resolution he had recorded in his diary for 1860, the words of which may be here recalled:[1] "I wish I could make this an object of my life—to preach the reasonableness of Christianity as shown in the identity of its principles with the principles of human life and human knowledge."

The first volume of his sermons had turned out a success, and the Chapel was well filled by the end of 1870. Expenses, however, consumed the receipts, and left only a negligible surplus. "I have no news," he writes in January, "about my Chapel. Motley has taken a seat. The cash is as low as ever. The sermons still sell, and have gone to a third edition." The sermons had dwelt largely on the Humanity of Christ as essential to a right conception of His Divinity. To his brother William, who had had a theological training, this seemed a dangerous tendency: he rightly perceived that the balance could not be held in the manner indicated in the volume, and that the Divinity was in danger. In answer Brooke writes as follows:—

[1] See p. 120.

To William Brooke.

"I am always on the point of writing to you in answer to your letter about my sermons, but I still should prefer to *talk* over the whole question with you. I keep your letter carefully and have read it more than three times. I do not think I ever saw the other side of the question put more forcibly or better. But the difficulty of answering it is that we have no common term. You say that my opinion with regard to Christ's nature takes away from you your God. Exactly the opposite; I could also say, your view takes God away from me. Well, when this is the case how are we to answer one another without misunderstanding? But your criticisms were most valuable to me, and I will keep them in my mind in order to give me balance."

The close of 1868 had been marked by the beginning of a friendship with the Hon. George and Mrs Howard, afterwards Earl and Countess of Carlisle. It was a friendship destined to exercise a vital influence on Brooke and on the character of his work. Mr Howard was a man of many parts, a highly gifted painter, a free spirit, and, as Brooke was wont to say, "a universal person." With him Brooke had much in common, and the friendship between the two men remained of the closest until the Earl of Carlisle's death in 1911. In the summer of 1870 he was the guest of the Howards at their Cumberland seat, Naworth Castle, and from that time onwards we find him, for many years, spending a part of his holiday at Naworth. Some of his most charming letters to his wife are dated from that place; extracts from them will appear in due course.

The following extract from his "Studies in Poetry" refers to an incident which occurred, I believe, on the occasion of his first visit to Naworth in 1870. The Castle and the surrounding country always reminded him of Sir Walter Scott, to whose writings he was passionately devoted.

"I went north and found myself in the early morning looking from a height over a castle famed in Border minstrelsy, and beyond it lay the Solway and its hills, Lanercost, Askerten, Bewcastle, Liddesdale, Teviot and Eskdale, and on the right the ridges of the Roman Wall, the valleys, the rolling rig and flow of the Border mosses and the Border hills. There was scarcely a single name of river, mountain or sea-estuary, castle or farmhouse, which was not known to me from the poetry of Scott. I leaned over the gate and looked long upon the poetic land, and it seemed as if all the dew of youth fell upon me again, as if I were again in the ancient world of adventure, romance, love and war, which we have replaced by science and philosophy, trade and misery, luxury and poverty. But it was to Scott I owed the pre-eminent pleasure of that hour, an hour the impression of which I kept like a precious jewel, and which I have never lost."[1]

On February 27 he again dines with the Queen.

To William Brooke.
"Feb. 28, '70.

"I dined with the Queen yesterday and had a very pleasant evening. You will see the company in the Papers. She was very kind, said she had read my sermons with much pleasure—I wondered if it was true —spoke of my Chapel, and asked if it was not in York Place and very crowded and large. I said it was crowded, but so small that it was easily crowded. The Dean proposed that Rev. —— should be asked to preach at Windsor. But I settled that question by telling the Queen he belonged to the Ten Days' Mission against the Devil. 'Oh that dreadful Mission!' says her Majesty.

[1] "Studies in Poetry," p. 58.

I described his favourite attitude, sinking in the pulpit till nothing but two wavering hands and his head are seen over the parapet. 'That would scarcely do for the Royal Chapel, Madam.' 'Oh no!' But I told her that Mr Gladstone was a great admirer of ——. Capital dinner, servants in all sorts of clothes, scarlet, tartan plaids and kilts, etc., etc.

"Princess Louise asked to be introduced to me. . . . A tall stately girl, with a pleasant spring-tide face, bright teeth, blue eyes and chestnut hair. . . . She said she wished much to know me, her sister had spoken so much about me. I had a most pleasant talk with her for a quarter of an hour.

"When Princesses are pretty girls and are very civil to one, it tickles one's Radicalism, and some effort is needed to get out of the carnal state of royal worship and to feel the truth again of the flesh and blood theory. I don't quite wonder at Kingsley falling a victim to it. But there are two guardians which protect one against falling away. First, Christianity—secondly, resolution not to talk about one's royal experiences at all, to any one. . . .

"I say to you, but do not talk of it, that scarcely a day passes that I do not hear of the influence that small Chapel is having upon men and women in London society. It is very nice, but I keep myself in readiness for a crash. I suppose I shall by and by share the fate of Polycrates."

In May he again preaches in Westminster Abbey.

To William Brooke.
"May 23, '70.

"Enormous congregation in the Abbey. Aisles and nave all full, a sea of heads. Sermon not liked by Dean and others. I am always breaking my head against the leader of my own party. I am one who pleases a few, not many, which proves plainly I have only a talent, not a genius for preaching, but I have learnt to be content with mediocrity, and only try not to fall below *my* mediocrity.

> "What's the use of sighing
> When time is on the wing?"

"Emma and the baby blooming. Oh! why was it a girl?"

In the spring of 1871 he reports a change in the financial affairs of the Chapel. After five years' hard work he is now anticipating a surplus of £600 a year. In May he published his "Freedom in the Church of England."

To William Brooke.

"18 May, '71.

"The book is out to-day.... I fear you will not like it at all. But read it from my point of view and feel the protest I was obliged to make, as guardedly as I could, against portions of that judgment which seemed to traverse and almost destroy everything I had been doing and saying for the last four years.

"I could not agree with the general silence of the Liberal party, with Stanley's and Davies' cry of 'Do not move the waters.' When the waters are moved what is the use of saying they are still? If I succeed in stating my views and yet retaining my position in the Church, I shall have saved many a liberal clergyman from feeling himself a lie.

"One of the things sorest for me, indeed the only thing, for I do not care a straw for the general opinion of the orthodox party, is the thought that you and others dear to me may be vext or troubled by the book. But there are times when one must act independently of Father, Mother and Brother."

From the following extracts, which require no further introduction, an idea may be formed of his opinions and movements between 1870 and 1875.

To William Brooke.
"May 30, '71.

"That Napoleonic conception of the place of France has never left her. Whether under the First Empire or under Kings or under Republics, it has always been the same. Under the present Republic it is rampant. Gambetta is the very embodiment of it in a vulgar form.

"Therefore I deny that the honoured name of a Republic is to be given to France at any time through this contest. She has been consistently Napoleonic in ideas.

"As such, and till she gets rid of this view, which makes her separate from Mankind, liberty cannot safely be entrusted to her. She will do as she did before, place the head of freedom on a body of Slavery and call it a Republic.

"Germany is twice as free. Her institutions are absolutist, etc., etc., but she has within them the idea of the Revolution, in the sphere of the intellect. An intellectual Republic existing within a political absolutism, would be my definition of Prussia, but the idea will be too strong for the institutions and will finally overthrow them.

"I place the cause of liberty in the hands of Germany.

"1. A federal union of States cannot long exist side by side with imperialist institutions—one must destroy the other.

"2. The *People* have felt their *unity* and their *force* in this war, for it is not only the standing army but the Landwehr who have done the work. Having won the unity of Germany, they will next take up the idea which has been long the cherished thought of Germany, of constitutional liberty, and the people will be too strong for the King and Junker Partei. It will be Mrs Partington and the Atlantic dream.

"But not while this old Gentleman lives. The Germans will make no disturbance while the old King exists. They are a patient people and will say, Liberty will be none the worse for waiting. They are a kind people and will say, the old King has done his work well, we won't disturb him.

"3. The Crown Prince is a Liberal, and so is his wife, and he will slowly diminish the militarism and the exclusiveness of the aristocratic party, and probably with the assistance of Bismarck, whom now he hates, for I think B. is a radical at heart."

To his wife.

"June 19, '71.

"It is too bad that Jowett will not preach on some interesting or useful topic. Fancy instructing that congregation in good manners. It is the only part of Christianity which the fine world possesses as a tradition, and the worst of the sinners are the most courteous and kind. They want to be told that good manners are not everything and that to be a Christian in life means something more. It makes me impatient when Jowett has, I suppose, so much to say that he does not say it. At least he believes in Immortality. It is largely doubted and decried. Why does he not give us his reasons for accepting it? But no! he prefers the domestic-cat religion and he purrs away over the fireside and the social board, till I am disgusted."

To William Brooke.

"July 24, '71.

"I saw the Princess Royal at Stanley's; she asked him to invite me to meet her. She was very nice, and looks quite unchanged. . . . I had five minutes' chat with her, and then made way for a tribe of celebrities asked to meet her. Stanley's home is thus not only a bridge between Dissent and Church, but also between Royalty and Literature. An immense congregation at the Abbey. I preached a simple sermon enough, and was heard as well as can be expected when there was not even standing room in any part of the place. The Dean thanked me very cordially and was pleased."

To his wife.

"Aug. 1, '71.

"The Louvre as far as the Hôtel du Louvre was gutted and the stone above the windows blackened by the rush upwards and outwards of the fire. Opposite St Germain l'Auxerrois another fire had taken place in the Palace; but the most desolate thing was the Hôtel de Ville. The street which runs past it, the rue de Rivoli, was even yet impassable: one had to go round. The whole courtyard was filled with shattered stones and masses of bent and twisted iron, and of staircase and rooms, pillars and roof, not a vestige was left. It rose, an eyeless ruin, without a shred of the beauty of ruin. Everywhere on its walls were marks of shell and shot and bullets. These marks increased as we drove down into the rue St Antoine which continues the line of the rue de Rivoli into the Place de la Bastille. Barricade after barricade had filled this street, and the walls of the houses on both sides had been literally sown with bullets. I counted 30 marks of shot between two windows alone. When one got into the Place de la Bastille, it was worse. You remember that a number of streets enter this Place as a centre. The houses at the end of nearly all these streets were almost levelled with the ground. The very bronze of the pillar in the midst was pierced with holes. Turning aside down the Seine, we passed the Grenier d'Abondance, the great storehouses for the goods which come up the canals and the Seine. It was an absolute and frightful ruin. Some of the interior pillars which still stood were calcined to the depth of an inch, and a mass of hideous rubbish filled the interior. It burnt, my cocher told me, for a month. We went into Notre Dame, but could not get into the Sainte Chapelle. The former had suffered a little in its outer sculpture, the latter was untouched. From the Palais de Justice we went through the rue de Lille, which leads down to the Chambers past the Cour des Comptes and the Légion d'Honneur. In this street the most furious fighting must have taken place. On both sides not a house was left entire. The barricades were up to the first floor, and as they were carried the houses were set on fire. The Cour des Comptes and the Légion d'Honneur were mere shells. It was horrible in the bright sunshine, and the advertisements stuck up on boards of So and So removed to —— etc., jewellers, drapers, porcelain sellers, clothiers, etc. etc., which one sees all over Paris, gave one a sense of the enormous loss of property. Passing the Exhibition Palace in the Champs Elysées, the whole of the glass roof looked as if a tornado of hail and wind had visited it. All over the front deep holes showed where cannon balls and shells had gone through the stone as if it had been paper. Passing under the Arc de Triomphe the stone was all starred with marks of balls from Mont Valérien which rose grimly in the distance, white against the blue sky. All down the rue St Honoré the houses were stained with the white patches which marked where the bullet-holes had been repaired: the mullions of the windows snapped off: the plate glass of the shops patched in the oddest manner with lines of paper crossing and recrossing like a web where the bullets had gone through. A mass of houses near the Madeleine had tumbled in ruins. High up on the wall of one of these, on the fifth story, there hung upon a peg, fluttering in the wind like a flag, a woman's shawl. She had left it there, when she fled, and the whole house tumbling in ruins had saved it from the fire. But it was the most suggestive thing I saw in Paris. It had been there for more than six weeks, and I wondered if its owner had been there to look at it. I never saw Paris so empty. Nearly half the people were in black. The streets, once so brilliant at night, were badly lighted and few people were about. It seemed as if the city had received a shock which it would take years to repair, and that it was also half depopulated. But no one seemed particularly to care."

To his wife.

"Zermatt.
"Aug. 20, '71.

"An immense number of dull English are here, so dull that one asks what possible reason brought them to this place. They are varied by Alpine bores, the most fearful portions of the human race. Some are slow and solemn bores, others are jerky and good humoured, but all are loud and roar like bulls of Bashan. They defile the woods and degrade the mountains. I met a man called ——, an old member of the Alpine Club, at the Riffel Hotel. You should have heard this self-constituted lion bellowing in the passages, growling in the bureau, and gnawing his bones with roars of vacant laughter at the Table d'Hôte. They assumed, that is, he and two others, the whole space of the doorway, had their coffee in everybody's way, smoked their pipes in everybody's face, and spoke of their comrades in the high Alps as if they were the only real existences in the world. Their talk was like their literature, if one may give that honoured name to the hotch potch of bad jokes and maimed descriptions, and overstated dangers and villainous English which fills the pages of Peaks, Passes, and Glaciers."

To his wife.

"Aug. 26, '71.

"We parted from the ——'s. He brought his brother to join us and his brother-in-law. His brother is Chaplain of a lunatic asylum where 5000 lunatics are under his care—a delightful parish! He is a molly-coddle of a man, always wailing about something, always frying with some anxiety, trembling if he walks on a road without a railing, terrified at the absence of any of the party for ten minutes, utterly unable to make up his mind, whirling from one opinion about his journey to another, till his mind puts me in mind of a teetotum in full spin. —— at last resolved not to leave him, but to go homewards with him. What they had read of the Monte Moro put him into a state of abject terror, and, indeed, I think he would have fainted had he crossed it. The only way to have got him over would have been to place him in a state of coma and carry him across."

To his wife.
"Aug. 30, '71.

"The Lago d'Orta is everything and has everything a man needs for his best enjoyment. As I walked down yesterday I thought I should have cried, so beautiful was the colour on its surface, not brilliant, for the day was dull, but it was glassy calm, and there was not a tint, not the most fleeting, of the hills and banks which was neglected in its mirror. A ceaseless change played upon it, and the infinite degrees of blue from deep violet to turquoise, and all mellowed into an inexplicable tenderness, would have made Dante's heart leap as he wrote the Paradiso."

To his wife.
"Venice.
"Sept. 5, '71.

"It is as bright, as lovely, as attractive, as sunny, and as unspeakable as ever, and I have wished for you a hundred times since I have been here, where you are connected with every campo, with every island, with every wave, with every table at Florian's. . . . Green is quite right about 'Chaucer's Landscape'[1] being 'thin,' but what else could it be? I never intended it for more than a pretty article on a pretty little subject, and its only object is to make people look a little into that part of Chaucer's poetry which introduces landscape. So far as that goes it is exhaustive enough, and touches all its characteristics. And it will attain that object, and to load it with the elaborate knowledge which I dare say a Chaucerian student would have put in about Feasts of Roses and symbolic significations of daisies, and the growth of such poems as the Romaunt of the Rose would have been tiresome if I could have done it. The great mistake of such writers as Freeman, Green, etc., etc., *when they write in magazines,* is that their articles are not *thin.* They are loaded with the fat of knowledge, and no one except the initiated knows anything about what they write, nor carries anything away from it."

[1] An article written by Brooke.

To his wife.
"Dec. 4, '71.

"What do you think of 'Middlemarch'? It seems to me inferior to any other of George Eliot's works. I have always said that her efforts at Poetry, in a sphere where she is wholly out of place, and *forced* to search painfully for expression, would spoil her English style, and so they have. It has lost all its charm, except here and there in the conversations; it is now laborious, creaking like an overloaded waggon, and there are here and there detestable expressions, such as produce a sensation of nausea, like a 'glutinously indefinite mind enclosing some hard grains of habit.' How odious is this 'glutinously indefinite'! and the whole metaphor, so far away and so difficult, is only one of a number in the book. They all come of the effort to concentrate, which blank verse demands of persons who can't write it, and of the effort to find poetical phrases where there are none to be found in the mind itself. Nothing is then produced but expressions which smell of labour like a workman's coat and which create a thoroughly bad English style, devoid of all simplicity when the would-be poet takes again to prose."

To William Brooke.
"Dec. 11, '71.

"I cannot say how much I feel this mortal illness of the Prince. It mixes itself up with my memories of Graham so forcibly that I seem to be going through the whole thing again, and I could not do my work on Saturday. When he was taken ill, he gave himself up and said, 'I shall die the same day my father did,' the 14th of this month. And nothing can be more probable.

"I met Dilke at dinner the other day. A mild-looking person, not dull, and somewhat heavy about the forehead. It was an unlucky moment for him to begin this republican starring round the country. Indeed I am not a Dilkian. He spoke like a discontented greengrocer and in the spirit of one. I thought it odiously put. If we can't be gentlemen as well as republicans, I think the price too high to pay for a republic."

To William Brooke.
"July 4, '72.

"I ask myself again and again, Is the position tenable? Can we long go on, as a community, asserting that we subscribe to Articles and Formularies, or rather to the general body of doctrine contained in them, when it is plain, that the Evangelical subscribes in one sense, the Ritualist in one totally different, and the Broad Churchman in another as different from both as they from one another? Do you know, it looks to me as if a few sharp letters in the *Times* from a hard-hitting man would knock the whole thing on the head.

"It has now reached a climax, it seems, of untenableness, and if it can stand it will be very curious.

"But this is plain, that never before in history did there exist a religious community, purporting to be at one, which had practically no dogmatic basis at all. For that is what it comes to. We agree to act and live together, each of us holding contradictory schemes of doctrine, on a basis of mutual tolerance, and owning union in one thing alone, obedience to the spirit of Christ.

"Nothing has ever been like it before, and I am mortally curious to see if it can continue. I believe it will have to go on in comprehension and to include the Unitarian, and when it goes on to that, it will smash."

To his wife.
"Naworth.
"July 8, 9, '72.

"It was pleasant to walk in the woods again and to feel the wild grass under one's feet. The foxglove grows here in broad spaces and looks like patches of azure sky, even in this gloom, let fall upon the earth; and the woodbine climbs to the very summit of the holly trees, and hangs down in breaking spray of flowers, and the meadow-sweet and the elder tree are in the richest flower, only that through want of sun they have no scent. It is the silence which is so delightful after London, and already the whole of the preaching business is far away from my mind. . . .

"The whole livelong day out on the moors. It was quite a perfect day. A moorland wind was blowing, and the clouds of yesterday, not yet totally dispersed, were blown before this wind over a blue sky, and light and shadow interchanged themselves without end upon the hills. We drove through broken roads up hill and down dale; rude stony paths at times, just wide enough for the carriage, and bordered by grassy slopes or brown moors. Of course I walked most of the way. Nothing could be more Wordsworthian in its way than one little scene when, looking from a one-arched bridge which spanned a tawny little torrent, one saw a space of meadow of about two acres, lying flat among the hill sides, and one white cottage standing on it, quite alone in the world. A decrepit hayrick, the scanty produce of the meadow, stood in a small farm enclosure; one heard the routing of cattle in the byre, and that was all. Not a single human being appeared, and yet the whole solitary place took a delightful human-heartedness to itself from the associations which the cottage created.

"'Roof, windows, floor,
The very flowers are sacred to the poor,'

and as one looked up out of the hollow to the heaven above, of which, so deep was the nook, only a small space was visible, one knew what Wordsworth meant when he said of such another little treasure cottage among the hills, that it had 'almost its own sky.'"

To his wife.

"Naworth,
"July 15, '72.

"In the afternoon we drove to Scaleby Castle, of which I know nothing. . . . We had a series of adventures driving there. The pony was not much accustomed to harness, very difficult to turn, and no power of persuasion would induce it to back. I was driving Mrs Howard in a small gig, with this tempestuous animal, and the first thing it did was to shy at a great branch torn by the wind of Friday from a tree, which lay across the road; but when Mrs H *would* go down riding lanes with this creature, we found our difficulties multiplied. First, the wheel got against a gate in a field, and it took five minutes to make the pony retreat enough to get it loose, then we knocked down a donkey in a narrow lane: Mrs Howard's merciful disposition to beasts wishing to investigate its hurts. As for me, the donkey was such a donkey not to get out of the way that I drove on without pity. . . .

"I am anxious to hear how the Chapel got on, on Sunday, how Stanley preached, and Loftie read, and whether the collection was a good one. I went to Church here at Lanercost and really enjoyed the service, which I have not heard, as an attendant, for more than nine months. It is seldom I get a taste of any religious emotion, but the hymn was beautiful, and I felt it very much, and wondered to myself if my whole work would not be better, if I could give a little more piety to it and feel spiritual emotion a little more. My sermons for the last year, now I look back on them, have been, for the most part, only analytic, and more and more removed from the religious sphere, properly speaking. Don't you think, if I could do it truly, that it would be better to change, to take a text, rather than a subject; and to work at it and its meaning, spiritually, rather than intellectually? It strikes me, almost painfully, that my sermons have been far more Theistic than Christian, and that Christ has nearly altogether disappeared from them. If there is any real reason for this, it is better to look it in the face. I do believe that Green, if he were to preach now, would be far more emotional than I have been of late. I thought much of all this yesterday. I wish you would think over it also, and talk of it, when I get back, to me. It is not without its use, sometimes, that one throws off the parson, and looks at one's parsonhood, as I have done here at Lanercost yesterday, from the layman's point of view."

To his wife.

"Naworth,
"July 19, '72.

"I write this in the garden, looking down the grassy walk to the yew trees in the centre and the dial, and seeing over the tops of the fruit trees the red tower of the Castle rising into the blue sky. It is not strange, and yet it is, how entirely this place is apart from modern life, and its associations, when one is outside the house, and even inside. G. H. is so unlike a mere modern gentleman, and so much one of that artist band who belong to all time, in manner and in thought, that the illusion is still supported. I suppose it is on account of this, that this place rests me more than any I know except Venice."

To his Mother.

"Oct. 16, '72.

". . . You will never go back, thank goodness.[1] Once out of that marshy monotony of misery, you will never go sopping down into it again. It rejoices my heart to think of my father with his friends about him and plenty of people to talk to, instead of sitting like an owl in that gloomy study, and with the sea to look at from the open window, and a bath-chair, if necessary, ready to go to the end of the pier with; and I think of you going as of old into Kingstown to market, and in the evening walking on the pier and remembering old days, and seeing the sunset light over Howth reflected from the west, so young, like God, when we have all grown old, except our hearts, and I picture the girls laughing, talking, in tearing spirits among the grey granite rocks and revisiting the old places, Killiney Hill and Dalkey Island and the homes where we flirted, and knowing in their hearts that they have not come

[1] His father was leaving Wyton, in the Fens.

for a visit, but are at home at last, after a drear parenthesis to which they must look back with a shudder. Never let a false feeling of tenderness creep into your hearts towards Wyton. It was a hateful burial, and it was only exceedingly healthy hearts which could have borne it without turning sour or wicked. . . .

"The Queen has made me Chaplain in Ordinary. I had a civil letter from the Empress thanking me for my sermons. I am going to deliver the Inaugural Lecture at the Philosophical Society in Edinburgh on the first, a great compliment, I believe. I rather fear the experiment. Emma comes with me, and we stay at Dean Ramsay's."

To J. R. Green.

"Oct. 24, '72.

"My lecture for Edinburgh is all but done, and when it is published you shall have a copy to knit your brows over and to spit your gall upon. I have sent in my resignation to Queen's College, and as soon as ever my work there is done, and before, when I return from Edinburgh I shall begin my book. Eight o'clock every morning, Sir, since my return, sees me among my infants at the breakfast table and the *Daily News* in front of me. Nine o'clock sees me in my room, and two o'clock or three has the happiness of beholding me in clerical costume issuing like Apollo from my door for my afternoon walk. From five to seven I amuse myself with lighter books, and the rest is as usual, only I go to bed earlier. Is not this virtuous? I dared not tell you till now, for I feared it was but a flash in the pan, but the moral conduct has now lasted so long that I begin to hope it is becoming a habit, and what is more, Emma has some glimmerings of faith in it now. You, the child of a sceptical time, will distrust me, but evidence shall be furnished.

"You have heard, I suppose, that we came home by Lyons. It is a dirty city, foul is the right word, but if only we had had a little sun, and not a filthy sky and filthy rain, it would have been a glorious sight from the heights, with those two great rivers rushing through it, and the steep cliffs behind under which the old town with its spires clusters. . . .

"I send you a Poem I wrote on the children at Lucca lying on the grass, which Miss C. tells me was received with great laughter and delight by the children at Bognor.[1] Isn't it lively? Oh, how in this 'tenfold concentrated gloom' in London, where I have been driven to buy an umbrella, I do regret the sun of Italy!

"'Misery, oh misery,
The world is all too wide for thee!'

"Good-bye, dear boy."

To William Brooke.
"Edinburgh.
"Nov. 5, '72.

"I walked up and down the terrace and through the woods by the side of the Tweed and peopled the place as well as I could with the figures of those who came to visit Sir Walter. I sat down again and again where I thought he must often have sat and talked, and thought how he should untwist the fates of those whom he created. I came back by the meadow and looked up to the house standing under the ridge of wood and I fancied I could just see his tall figure standing at the library window and then passing down the staircase to the lawn of the terrace. It was all as sad as it could be, to the imagination. I cursed the stupidity of the Constables, and as I counted tower after tower and thought they were paid for by work which made all his later years a dreadful mechanism of literature, the words which came unconsciously to my lips and which I spoke aloud, were 'paralysis and death, paralysis and death.' When I came back to the terrace, four hideous tourists were peering and grubbing about and trying to look in to the lower windows, and their coarseness drove me away. It

---

[1] The poem mentioned in this letter was found among J. R. Green's MSS and published as his composition. The mistake caused Brooke much amusement. See "The Letters of J. R. Green," edited by Leslie Stephen, p. 207.

added to the sadness of the whole scene that I knew that Hope Scott [1] was dying in London, and that, as a keeper told me with a break in his voice, 'he will never see Abbotsford again.' Then I walked across the back of the place to the Ferry, intending to get to Galashiels by the road in time to catch the train for Dryburgh. It was a pretty bit of water and wood at the ferry. The river, brimming over with the rains, rushed like an arrow, and the bright sunlight made it blue, as I stood and shouted for the ferryman. Poor old man, he could get across only with difficulty, so swift was the current, and when I asked him how much I was to pay as I stepped out at the little cove, he answered, 'Wall, I do chairge a penny, but when the stream is full, a stranger sometimes gives me a wheen mair.' So I gave the poor old body fourpence, and his surprise was touching. If he had known I was a clergyman he might have called me what the old attendant at St John's called the Dean when he gave him half a crown—'Oh, your Royal Reverence.'"

To William Brooke.

"Edinburgh,
"Nov. 7, '72.

"They listened, about 900 of them, with great attention considering the demand on their patience and that it was past ten before I had done.[2] I stopped all applause, for I knew I had no time for it, and whenever they began, unless I was out of breath, I talked through the clapping, and this was successful on the whole. Lots of the small literary world of Edinburgh were on the platform and in the room, and I was heartily congratulated by men like 'Rab and his friends,' and the rest. I wish they had left the MS. in my hands. I could have got ten pounds more for it from the Magazines. But this, alas! is mussenary.

"I had a delightful day on Saturday, took Emma all through the old town, under the Castle into the Grassmarket, up and into the Castle, down the Canongate and

---

[1] He married Lockhart's daughter, Sir Walter's grandchild.
[2] The subject was "The Philosophical Aspects of Poetry."

into half a dozen of its slums—by-the-by they are pulling down the old tall houses—then into Holyrood, through rooms where Chastelard still rustles after Mary when night falls, then over the Chapel, and then hey, for Arthur's Seat. I left Emma and went quickly to the top, and spent four hours roaming about, saw a most wondrous sunset from Salisbury Crags over the uncultured breast of Blackford and the Pentlands and home to dinner, at which I met a number of nice people.

"I preached at St John's on Sunday, and it was to you I owed what the Dean called the 'unmixed satisfaction' which my sermon gave. Do you remember a sermon I preached on the Action of God in Temptation, 'There hath no temptation taken you,' etc., etc. You said you liked it. Now, said I, what William liked will probably just suit the cultivated orthodoxy of Edinburgh, and it did."

To William Brooke.

"London,
"May 5, '73.

"My afternoon congregations are now very large, and the lectures are becoming a success. I see others are following my lead, and in St James', Piccadilly, on Sunday afternoons lectures on such subjects as the Drama are being delivered by men like Lightfoot. I do believe I have given a new idea to the Church of England. I shall have it written on my tomb. I hear that my Father, to whom my dearest love is to be given, is well and that his sermons are one of the sensations of Dublin."

To William Brooke.

"May 12, '73.

"I am going to publish my Oxford sermon, not a very worldly-wise thing, but that wisdom is of the devil, or at least I think so. But I heard that all sorts of things were said about it by the Professors, etc., Liddon, Mozley, etc., and they may as well have the original to spit their rheum upon. It will do them good to get rid of it."

To his wife.

"Naworth,
"Aug. 3, '73.

".Lady A. I thought charming. She was very nice to me, and she had lost that insouciance and preoccupied air which she has had in London when I have met her before. She talked now with a natural *naïveté* which I was delighted with, though now and then there were sentences which one felt were said in order to find out something about the person she was speaking to. But these are traps which are easily avoided. But after a time she let herself go, and I recognized soon in her that which has always proved to me the charm of all these Stanleys, and which one sees traces of in their mother, a natural impulsiveness, a desire to commit themselves to the wave of the moment, a kind of surprised delight when they find themselves rising with the wave and then, a throwing of their whole self into the impulse for the sake of the pleasure it gives, so that they double the rapidity of the ascending wave, and then as their pleasure grows double the swiftness of the ascent again, and so on till the crest is gained."

To his wife.

"Naworth.
"Aug. 10, '73.

"So Ayrton is out! Hurrah! But there is no use strengthening the Government. It is doomed sooner or later. There is no use turning Ayrton out now and transferring Lowe; it should have been done before. I believe in my heart that it is its short-sighted economy and its dirty savings that have killed the Government, and I thank Heaven for it. When men like Lowe or Ayrton are the mouthpieces of English feeling, may I be sitting in my grave. Let us have real large economy, by reducing a multitude of useless officers, by paying smaller salaries to the asses we keep, by organizing public offices on scale more like the Prussian, and with a real eye to everything that is done, being worth the doing, but not by taking off our workmen at the docks, or reducing the grant for science, etc., etc., or digging up the flowers in the park—the cursed fools! Excuse this language but I *do* hate and abhor a man like Ayrton with every drop of blood in my body."

To his wife.
"Naworth.
"Aug. 11, '73.

"I sat up till near 3 finishing 'Old Kensington' and going off into trains of thought on that I read, and when I went to bed of course I could not sleep, and I lay in a quiet restlessness till past 4, till the dawn came and the birds awoke, and the sound of the beck in the glen grew less loud in the air. It was bright moonlight as I walked to bed through the long hall, and the moon was high and shone through the upper windows on the armour and tapestry, and lay in bars on the stone floor, and it looked more like the old times than I had ever seen it, for the armour did not look as if hung for show, and the banners did look as if they had just been tossed aside after a fight, and the little modern appliances took an antique air in the antique-making light of the moon, that hides so much to the sense and reveals so much to the imagination. Though I sometimes think, all the same, that it is not the moonlight which makes things look antique, but that there is a dim half-unconscious association of scenes in the theatre that it awakes which, by recalling castles, halls, ruins, banners, and glints on armour, and all the properties of your mediæval scene, really does the work of bringing the thoughts back to antiquity.

"However, all this high-falutin romance has left me dead tired this morning, and only caring for solitude and to be let alone. I should like to go away and walk about the whole day till 7 o'clock by myself, for this is one of those days when the desire to be quiet, and to have nothing to say or do with anybody in the world is quite overpowering."

To his wife.

"Naworth.
"Aug. 18, '73.

"I am sorry about Miss R. I told you I knew the type. And I should not be one bit surprised if when she got well enough, she went away with the first person who showed to her a little passion. Do find Manon Lescaut in my bookcase, a small blue book, top shelf, I think, on the right of the fireplace. It is a matchless study of that class of girl, and a classic bit of work. I don't believe she—Miss R.—would have ever left her life if she had not been driven for a time into the Hospital. You are right in saying it is in the blood, only it is not in this case sensual passion that is in the blood so much as the habitual pleasure of giving way from want of any will to the excitement of the moment, which may happen to be religious or sensual. If I chose, in ten minutes, I could induce that girl to be my mistress, or I might lead her to weeping confession of her sins, and adoration of the love of Christ for her. But the latter, so induced, would seem to me as bad as the former. I hate religion induced by playing on weakness of temperament. And though I can't help emotionalizing people when I preach I think there is nothing I so resolutely set myself against doing, and a good deal of the disappearance of 'pious' talk out of my sermons is due to the knowledge I have of how much I can stir people, if I choose, to tears or excitement, and I have a contempt for that sort of thing. . . . You say that you wonder, being great friends with the Howards, I do not wish to be as much with them as possible, and that you would be otherwise. Well, I do not know whether you would understand, but when I am too long with any one except those to whom I am tied by a vast number of interlinked associations, there is always with me the danger of change or weariness, and I hate this element in me, which even now that I am past youth is nearly as strong as it used to be. I am now far more constant than I was, far more affectionate hearted all round: there is far less chance of my altering to anybody, but there is always that suppressed dread in me of finding no more interest, no more to look into and search for. And I do not like to risk that . . . by staying too long. . . . There is a nice little bit of private feeling, which I dare say you knew was in me."

To his wife.
"Bolton Abbey.
"Aug. 6, '73.

"There is no rest to be got out of English air and English scenes. It is not enough of change to do one good, that is, when one has got a higher idea of what holiday life should be. It is the worst of being on the Continent, that one is ever after dissatisfied with the life and air and skies of one's own country, in vacation time. I had rather have a week of Switzerland at any time than six weeks of England. I want *excitement* of scenery. It is all very well to try and get it up at Naworth, in Wales—though Wales *is* better—in Yorkshire, but it is getting it up. It does not come naturally, and the labour of trying to wake a wild sensation of beauty and so make the heart leap, spoils the sensation itself, and tires, so that when one gets low in spirits one hates the past beauty, which has given one so much trouble. There is never enough of it. In Switzerland and Italy there is always more than one can grasp. I can always take what I like, excite myself to the very edge of the precipice of satiety, then stop, and yet there is more to feel and see, if I should get the power of grasping more, and the next day, it is not the same sort of thing, but something quite different, and there is ceaseless change. And one may find all this at a place like Zermatt and within the range of five miles round, during the space of ten days, not a shred of weariness, not a suspicion of being bored, not a single effort needed to work up excitement. That is what I like, I never get it in England. And that is what really rests my brain. By and by, when I am old and need repose for rest, and not excitement as I do now, I may enjoy England and its scenery, but these placid hills and streams and the unstimulating air and the life which calls for no strong exertion, and the apathetic way in which the mountains develop their curves, do not rest, but worry me. I get angry with them, as I am now."

To William Brooke.

"Feb. 23. '74,

" Here is a parody I made the other night.

"' Bob Lowe was too much with us, late and soon
Getting a surplus we laid waste our powers,
Few seats we see in England that are ours;
We have given the income tax, a sordid boon!
Young Radicals like dogs that bay the moon
Non-Cons—that will be howling at all hours—
For this, for everything I am out of tune,
They move me not. Great Heaven, I'd rather be
A Tory suckled in a creed outworn,
So might I standing in St Stephen's, see
Some chances that might make me less forlorn,
Have sight of office coming fast to me,
Or welcome Sinecure with plenteous horn.'"

To William Brooke.

"London.
"March 4, '75.

" I find to my great surprise that the Lease does not run out till Michaelmas, so I shall have all the end of the season, nearly four months, to make efforts for a new place of worship. . . .

" You heard, of course, that the Queen insisted on my having the Canonry,[1] and that Dizzy said he *could not* appoint a man of my principles. So one really is a bit of a martyr. Hurrah!"

NOTE ON GERMANY

Since these pages were in print, I have discovered the MS notes of a lecture given by Brooke, soon after the surrender of Sedan, which contain a remarkable prophecy. The following are a few extracts. Whether they confirm or refute his own remark about political prophecies printed at the head of this chapter I must leave events to determine.

[1] Of Westminster.

A PROPHECY

"Prussia [stands for] absolute monarchy, Divine Right of Kings, vast standing armies, government which crushes people. But the people are not crushed at all. It is absolute monarchy indeed—army ruled by men who despise people, a nation of two classes—army and civilians. . . . All these are hateful things. But [I have] hope—a kind of certainty that Prussia's success will not establish absolutism; that . . . her restrictions on liberty will end in a freedom as great as our own, that events will be too strong for absolute monarchy. . . . (1) This war is being waged against Napoleonic ideas. . . . The [German] people will say 'What! are we to be oppressed by the very ideas we have overthrown for Europe at the cost of so much blood?' (2) This has been a people's war: that is the name it has in Germany. . . . The [German people] have grown so great they can't grow little again. . . . The next idea after the unity of Germany will be constitutional liberty. . . . Before the steady impulse of a determined people like the Germans, the party of personal government must go to the wall. . . . (3) The influence of the States in unity with Prussia as head . . . Prussia will have to give them free constitutional laws—and then can she refuse them to her own subjects? Here the logic of events will be too strong. And Bismarck is too clever not to bow to that. (4) The Crown Prince [Frederick] is a very different man from his father, and he has a very different wife. He loves liberty . . . is in opposition to Bismarck, to his father's policy and [trusts?] the people.

"Some of you will live to see my prophecy fulfilled. A monarchy in Prussia as constitutional as our own. More power in hand of king and upper classes but a power self-limited . . . towards the establishment of perfect political liberty . . . I see in the midst of Europe a great Federal Republic of Germany from which Liberty will radiate led by prudence, by strength of reason, by a hatred of violent and hurried change, over the whole of Europe. *We* may not see that—but it will come."

CHAPTER XIV

THE DEATH OF MRS STOPFORD BROOKE

1874

"I drove with E. to Hampstead, and saw the grave [of my wife] and made arrangements for the summer flowers. It is a quiet old-world spot, waving trees and rustling leaves and grassy mounds, where her body lies, oh, so fast asleep. Had she lived she would now have been 77 years old, and I often wonder how she would have looked, how spoken, how thought and felt, and how she would have enjoyed her children. But to wonder is not to know."—(*Diary*, June 21, 1907.)

THE shock of Graham's death in '69 undermined the naturally sound constitution of Mrs Brooke. From that time onwards there were recurrent periods of failing health, and on each occasion her power of recovery seemed to diminish. Strong and resolute in will she made light of her weakness or concealed it, anxious most of all that no shadow should fall on her husband's life. It was not till the end of '73 that Brooke perceived that a dark cloud was gathering on the horizon. In the spring of '74 his wife was unable to leave her room. Surgeons were called in, and though the result removed the gravest apprehensions and gave a glimmer of hope, it was soon evident that life was ebbing away.

Needless to say, these were days of agony to Brooke. He wrote to William that every form of work was hateful to him, and yet it was only by furious and incessant work that he could retain possession of himself.

Early in June, '74, hope was abandoned, and on the 19th of that month Mrs Brooke was rapidly sinking. She was still conscious and able to recognize those about her. Towards midnight physicians and nurses were dismissed and Brooke remained alone with his wife. When the sun rose next morning the dark waters of death lay between them.

She was buried in the cemetery attached to the old parish church of Hampstead. On the morning of the funeral Brooke, accompanied by William and Arthur, went up early to Hampstead Heath. It was a glorious June day, and for a long time the three brothers walked hither and thither in silence, Brooke with a spray of heliotrope in his hand. At the graveside a great thunderstorm came on, in which he seemed to rejoice, standing bareheaded in the torrent of rain. When the coffin was lowered he cast his flower into the grave and swiftly departed. He did not return immediately to his home, but went back to the Heath with one of the brothers, spending some hours there, silent as before.

Thus ended the years of his married life, sixteen in all. Chronologically his wife's death divides his life almost exactly at its middle point; he was in his forty-second year when she died, and he lived to his eighty-fourth. He was left with a family of seven children, one son and six daughters, of whom the eldest, his son, was fifteen years old and the youngest two. As was natural in the multitude of his preoccupations, their upbringing hitherto had mainly fallen on the shoulders of Mrs Brooke.

Soon after his bereavement his sister, Miss Cecilia Brooke, came to live with him, and remained in charge of his home for many years, earning, by her gracious character and self-forgetful devotion, an undying gratitude from his children. It was a beautiful home, adorned with rare furniture, pictures and tapestry, which he and his wife had collected together. But the central presence was gone.

In an earlier chapter I have described the marriage of Stopford Brooke and Emma Beaumont as a union of opposites. It was so at the beginning and it remained so to the end. His was the Celtic temperament strongly marked; hers the English equally distinct; the one expansive, fluent, dynamic; the other reserved and still; each with its own charm, but differing in strength and beauty as the flowing river differs from the placid lake.

It is not in a nature like that of Mrs Brooke to make many friends; but those she made were close and devoted; some are still living to bear witness. She had strength for her own part in life, and she could give strength to others. Her influence upon Brooke, acting through deep mutual devotion, was of the most salutary. She steadied and restrained him; when his imagination was most restless her judgment was calm; she was not only sagacious but practical in her sagacity, and that with a will of her own, which, though gentle, was firm in its pressure. She encouraged his friendships with men of the world, which he would otherwise have taken no pains to cultivate, much as he needed that kind of contact. Among all his admirers Brooke had none more fervent than his wife; she understood his gifts, beyond all others she was proud of his genius; but she saw the limitations as well and knew that natures such as his suffer harm when the devotion of those who love them is blind. Of all this Brooke himself was fully aware, and hardly ever wrote a letter to his wife without thanking

God that she had been given to him. "With you," he had written at one of the critical moments of his career, "I fear not life." And there is not a doubt that though she was taken from him when his own course was only half fulfilled, her influence remained at work to the end. To many Brooke appeared as a man on whom the past had little hold. His rush into the future was so rapid that the past seemed, at times, to slip away from him as he advanced. But this was an illusion; for though in the long years that followed he would often say that his past had become a dream, it must not be forgotten that he was one of those men for whom the dream is a guiding light. At the time of his wife's death he was still a young man attacking life; endless possibilities remained to be fulfilled and influences of many kinds were yet to urge him in this direction and in that. But however powerfully these may have operated, their effect was far other than it would have been had he suffered the waters of Lethe to pass over the memory of his wife. He never forgot.

What Brooke owed to his wife he never chose to tell. It may be gathered, in some measure, from the character of his work and of his message, in which there was ever a great tenderness. His silence on the subject is also eloquent. Only now and then is it broken, by some ejaculation in a letter, by some phrase in a diary which fall upon the ear like rare sounds heard in the night and remind us that even in the darkness nature is awake.

In the correspondence of the period I can find only one direct reference to his grief. It occurs in a letter to the Rev. Arthur Brooke, who had been with him during the last days of his wife's illness.

To the Rev. Arthur Brooke.

"Clovelly. July (?) '74.

"I am thinking of not going abroad this year. I am tormented as I travel. I cannot get rid of one desire, one expectation. I look round in the train, in the carriage, and there is no one there, and all that I have known in travel, when we have been more together than at home, comes by like Tragedy. I shall stay at home, I think, and perhaps go and see my old parents in Ireland."

And again he writes to William Brooke on April 13, '75, "I am not very well and I cannot feel as time goes on the bitterness of my loss one atom less."

In August, 1876, he is in Switzerland and makes this entry in his diary: "Near the little Chapel (at Ouchy) where in '71 I wrote my letters. Much has passed since then, so much that the previous years to that date have become one of my quiet dreams. And now I have for ever closed another book and put it on the shelf. It too will pass into the dream world by-and-by. What books shall I open now? Where is the new volume? I ask to-day with a bitter but excited curiosity. I shall be sure to find one. I am of those who find."

In a Swiss diary of a yet later period (1886) the same mood and the same thought recur, only now the expression is somewhat more direct.

"We walked beside the green flashing of the Reuss—saw the stars abide in it where the rush was smooth from very speed. The river keeps its life the same though its waters change. . . . This year my anchor is up and I am sailing free, whither I know not: it may be to behold the Happy Isles and see the face of Goodness, whom I knew."

The close of Brooke's married life seems the fitting moment to mention his profound insight into the mind of woman and his reverence for her character. There was something in his own nature which gave him a clue to that intricate psychology which few men are able to follow, and this gift it was which made it easier for him to cultivate the friendship of women than of men, and rendered him also more dependent on their sympathy. His intuitions on that side were indeed exceptionally acute, and in nothing more so than in the admission, many times repeated, of a secret in a woman's soul, akin to that of Nature, which neither he nor any man could penetrate. There used to hang outside his study a copy of Leonardo's Monna Lisa, before which he would often pause and say, "that face reminds me how little I know about a woman's soul." Perhaps it was true that he knew "little"; but it was far more than most men know. Yet even within its own province his knowledge was not without its limitations. Mary's part he understood so thoroughly, and thought so incomparably the better, that the necessity of Martha's would escape him now and then. He was apt to treat the charm of life as though produced by the touch of a magic wand, as indeed it sometimes is; nor did he always perceive, what is surely a fact, that in the actual world Mary is often another name for Martha off duty.

More than any other of the works of God women appealed to his imagination, to his artist soul. They were living poems of the Creator, to be read as such, to be loved as such. To him, as to Dante, woman represented Nature at the climax of creative power. No surroundings could be too pure and joyous, no setting too fair for a being so wonderful. He loved to see women exquisitely dressed, radiant and adorned with jewels;[1]

[1] Precious stones, of which he was an excellent judge, had a great attraction for him. In his diary for 1894 he writes: "The attraction

VOL. I.

and for the same reason nothing afflicted him more bitterly than the thought of the multitude of wives and mothers who, under present social conditions, are condemned to joyless, loveless, sordid lives—exhausted by toil, ill-treated by brutal husbands, wearing out their wretched days in dark homes and filthy slums. The miserable lot of these women lay constantly on his heart; and any incident of woman's wrongs, learnt from conversation or the newspaper would burn itself into his memory. I have seen him roused to a fury of indignation by the story of a poor governess flung aside like a worn-out shoe by some heartless employer when she was too old to work. As for the outcasts, his pity for them knew no bounds.[1] These things represented to his mind the supreme outrage which man commits against the loveliness of the universe, and to mitigate its evil he was at all times willing to exert himself to the uttermost. There is not a doubt that among the many causes which made him a rebel against the existing economic system, this, the present lot of women, was the chief. When he spoke of the poor—and he hardly ever preached a sermon without speaking of them—it was poor *women* who had the chief place in his thoughts, as the context of the passage will generally show.

"Woman," says the diary of 1898, "was made directly out of Nature and has her change and charm . . . but man was made out of what is not nature, with one or

of gems is curious. There is more in it than their money value or their rarity. They have a magic of their own, a mystic character of light and colour which is wholly independent of commercial value. I subscribe to their wizardry. But I don't care for those that have no colour like the diamond. In the colour lies most of their imaginative worth, and in the changing of light in the colour. It is as though spirits dwelt in the stone."

[1] See "Justice" in his volume of Poems, 1888.

two faint touches of woman in him—and the rest? Let woman try to say. She never can—never can understand a man. And, of course, a man cannot understand a woman. Curious that things should be so arranged. It seems unwise, but then it keeps both continually searching, continually pursuing; and that keeps each of them alive, eager, passionate—and so the work of the world is done" (September 21).

In all this there is an element of mysticism. He was in the presence of a secret which stimulated his spiritual curiosity; the more so because he discerned a connexion between this secret and his central doctrine of Love as the master-principle of life. In nothing was this mystical element more apparent than in his relations with his daughters, who became his constant companions after the death of his wife. It was a relationship in which natural affection and romantic idealism were deeply, and strangely, mingled.

On the last day of 1901 he wrote in his diary—

"I read, to close the year, the XXVI and XXVII cantos of the Paradiso—beautiful things. What an exultation, what a spiritual intensity of rapturous love (so high that it can scarce be borne) thrills through all these closing cantos of the Paradiso! There is nothing that even resembles it in literature. Beatrice, of course, in this book of the Comedy is heavenly Love—the ardour of God—but all through the phrases that describe her his ancient love for the woman raised to the highest spiritual point also flames and glows. What a phrase is this—

"'Ma ella, che vedeva il mio disire,
Incominciò, ridendo tanta lieta,
Che Dio parea nel suo volto gioire.'"[1]

When Brooke left the Church of England, six years after the death of his wife, he placed on record his belief

---

[1] But she, who saw my desire, began, smiling so glad that God seemed to rejoice in her countenance.

that she would have approved of what he had done. And yet there are grounds for thinking that the bereavement of 1874 and the secession of 1880 are not wholly unconnected facts. The immediate effect of his loss was to create in him the sense of a profound breach with his past; not in any theological sense but in a much more intimate and personal form. The fragmentary diaries of the period between the two events show very clearly that during these years a new future was dawning: and that, when he looked back upon the past in memory, it seemed to be the life of another man. The chapter was closed and he was waiting for a new impulse and ready for a new departure. The following passage from a diary indicates his state of mind.

"*Jan.* 7, '76. We left Dublin early and got to Killiney in an hour. As we left the train the whole sweep of the bay burst upon us. There were the old well-known mountains, dark blue under a canopy of livid clouds. But through the rifts of the cloud the sun rays broke and beneath their impulse the green sea seemed to boil like molten silver. We walked along the strand where the sea raced in loud waves under the pressure of a wild north-easter. It was cold, but fresher than anything I have tasted for a long time, and I ran along the sand like a boy till my blood began to grow warm. Then we climbed the hill through the furze and larches and over the granite rocks and grass, and rested by the low wall I remember so well where the broad road of grass rises from the gate. The whole plain below, and the strand cut by the silver line of the stream, and the dark mountains were traversed in different places by the ladders of the rays of the hidden sun, and when we came to the obelisk and I sat down in one of the old seats and heard the wind lashing round the stones and over the grass of the hill I felt like a boy again. And then as I thought of all the twenty years that had gone by since I was last there, and of the gulf which, within me in character and without

THE GRAVE OF THE PAST

me in life, divided me from that half-forgotten past, I seemed to look on the life of a youth that was dead. I stood like Wordsworth, ' Mute—looking on the grave in which he lies '—only the dead on which I looked was myself. We walked home by Glengary Hill and the Shady Avenue, and went over the whole of Ivy House. Dead, dead Youth! Whither is it fled, the glory and the gleam? I am weary of the present, and I do not see the future."

CHAPTER XV

BEDFORD CHAPEL

1875-1880

"Over the site of Bedford Chapel a huge scaffolding rose with a lofty crane upon its summit. . . . That time has dropt into the past eternity. London has had thirty years of me. . . . Let them now put into practice what has been truly worth the saying."—(*Diary*, November 29, 1898.)

WHEN Mrs Brooke died in '74 the work at St James' Chapel was drawing to a close. The lease would expire the following year, after which the Chapel was no longer to be used as a place of worship. His future as a preacher was therefore again uncertain. About that Brooke did not trouble himself; indeed, in the desolation of the months which followed, he found preaching difficult, and would have been glad of a respite from the incessant demands it made on a heart sad and weary as his was at the time. But work he must have, and he found it in literature.

John Richard Green was at this time editing the well-known series of Primers published by Messrs Macmillan. More than one person had attempted to write a Primer of English Literature, and found it impossible to accomplish the task within the limits allowed. Green thereupon turned to Brooke, who at once closed with the offer. Within the compass of 160 small pages he was to write a complete guide to English Literature from its earliest beginnings to the Victorian Age.

Into this task, as difficult perhaps as any which a man of letters could undertake, Brooke plunged with the full force of his intellect and will. A vast amount of information had to be given, and accurately given, within a narrow space. This by itself was a task which any diligent hack-writer, with dates and facts at his elbow, might have accomplished. But Brooke was resolved that the Primer should be, what Matthew Arnold afterwards declared it was, a real guide to English Literature, which should inform the reader of the paths to be trodden, and at the same time kindle his desire to follow them. Not merely to give a catalogue of facts, but to set the facts in such a light as to arouse a love of English Literature and an eagerness to read its originals—this was the object which Brooke never lost sight of. It involved innumerable problems of compression, selection, and proportion, which had to be solved without damage to the essential character of the book as a living whole. The knowledge of the scholar, the skill of the artist, the insight of the poet were all required; and to these there must needs be added, since Brooke was to do the work, a touch of prophetic fire. The risks of failure were enormous.

But because of the difficulty, because of the risk, it was the very work to meet the moral conditions in which Brooke found himself at the moment, and perceiving this he grappled with it eagerly. In the long retrospect of his life which he was able to take in later years there was nothing which gave him greater pleasure to remember. He has often spoken to me of his Primer as the "hardest thing he ever did." Undertaken at a critical turning-point of his life, and amid the shadows of a great bereavement, it gave him when he needed it most a new sense of power won by a difficult exercise of the will. Hundreds of thousands of copies of this little book have been circulated through the schools and colleges of the Empire, it has been translated into many languages, and its readers may possibly be counted by millions. It were well that its readers should know the circumstances in which it was written. It represents a great effort of self-mastery.

The first draft of the Primer was finished by the end of July, '75. In ten months 25,000 copies had been sold. The total number printed in England up to the summer of 1916 is 444,500.[1] Matthew Arnold wrote to him, "You have made a delightful book, and one which may have a wide action—the thing which one ought to desire for a good product almost as much as its production." In Arnold's volume of "Mixed Essays," one of which is devoted to the Primer, there occurs the following passage:—

"A GUIDE TO ENGLISH LITERATURE.

"Mr Stopford Brooke has published a little book entitled a 'Primer of English Literature.' I have read it with the most lively interest and pleasure. I have just been saying how very desirable is a good guide to English literature, and what are a good guide's qualifications. Mr Stopford Brooke seems to me to possess them all. True, he has some of them in a higher degree than others. He is never dry, never violent, but occasionally he might be, I think, clearer, shorter, in more perfect proportion, more thoroughly true of judgment. To say this is merely to say that in a most difficult task, that of producing a book to serve as a guide to English literature, a man does not reach perfection all at once. The great thing was to produce a primer so good as Mr Stopford Brooke's. It is easy to criticize it when it has

[1] I am indebted for the figures of this total to the kindness of Messrs Macmillan, the publishers of the Primer.

BROOKE IN 1876.
From a photograph by Elliott & Fry.

[*To face page* 286.

once been produced, easy to see how in some points it might have been made better. To produce it at all, so good as it is, was not easy. On the whole, and compared with other workmen in the same field, Mr Stopford Brooke has been clear, short, interesting, observant of proportion, free from exaggeration, and free from arbitrariness."

In the letter which announces the completion of the Primer he tells William that St James' Chapel is to be closed in August, and that he is going to Rome for the winter. A number of his admirers and friends had resolved that he should not be without a pulpit in London, and negotiations were already afoot for purchasing and presenting to him the lease of Bedford Chapel, Bloomsbury. There is evidence that the first move in the matter was made by William Brooke, who was afraid that his brother might follow the example of J. R. Green in abandoning clerical work, and was determined that this should not come to pass. Brooke himself was not greatly interested in the design, and seems rather to have submitted to the wishes of his friends than to have encouraged them. In a letter of July 27, '75, he says, " I have fixed not to take Bedford Chapel at present. I may be *driven* to it in March, but not before." On August 18 he writes to Miss Howard,[1] " To tell you the truth, I am not sorry to have a time of silence. . . . For I feel as if I were drained dry. Nevertheless, a letter like yours gives me hope that I have done some good somewhere." And in the spring of the following year he writes to Green from Rome, " I feel as if all the trouble of thought and the pain of life were over for a time. . . . Things do not look to me happier in the future for my

[1] This lady subsequently edited the collection of extracts from his sermons called "Sunshine and Shadow." She had no family connexion with the Howards mentioned above.

profession." And there are other references in the letters of these months, which all tell the same tale—that he was *tired* on that side of his nature, and that he was shrinking from again having to face the weekly crisis—for such he always felt it—of unburdening his soul to a crowd of his fellow-men.

St James' Chapel was finally closed in August, '75. The following account of the congregation there and of the preacher is taken from the charming volume of "Memories" by Sir Frederick Wedmore, one of Brooke's friends in after years.

"Stopford Brooke was more ornate than the preachers I have already discussed. His temperament—his Irish temperament—caused his work to be bedecked with flowers of fancy. To say that he was more emotional than the [Bishop of Ripon] is not to say at all that he was not intellectual. To say that would be ridiculous. Thought and meditation, and meditation in high mental latitudes, in regions peopled by the great constructive poets—Wordsworth and Coleridge perhaps the chief of them—were the very basis of the fabric he raised. He had the courage to face modern problems, and he could preach a sermon that was a criticism excellent and final of the 'Melancholia' of Dürer. This variety, this range of mood and mental action, accounted for the range and variety of the audiences that crowded the little chapel in York Street. Opposite me in the gallery, I used to see Mr Justice Mellish—one of the subtlest lawyers of his time—Mr Justice Mellish sitting with open mind, and a countenance trained to express nothing.[1] After the sermon I have seen Matthew Arnold walking thoughtfully down the staircase, detached and analytical. Neurotic women of fashion and great place have I beheld, enraptured and enthusiastic, in the front seats. The young man about town was present occasionally, and you would hear him, after the *sortie*—as he stood

[1] Samuel Smiles, the author of "Self-Help," was also a frequent hearer of Brooke at St James' Chapel.

on the street pavement waiting for the Fair—wondering whether Stopford Brooke was a 'humbug,' and deciding that he was not But so much emotion seemed unnatural to the young man—his own heart scarcely aroused—and he remembered besides, that, like Charles Honeyman's, this was a proprietary chapel, and that, as at Charles Honeyman's, there were wine vaults underneath it. Still, the verdict was favourable. Then there were active members of Parliament, busy professional men, and quiet men of Letters, pretty ladies, and here and there the anxious young man, still troubled, because of his youth, to solve, or not to solve, the riddle of the world. Moreau's 'Sortie de l'Opéra' might have found its counterpart, or its pendant, had some observer of Life —a Frith with great power to 'spot' the characteristics of the refined world—or a Jean Béraud who could grasp the English type—recorded the *exeunt* from York Street Chapel in the 'Seventies.' On the pavement, there was the clash of secular tongues: but in the pulpit all had been earnestness, reflectiveness, eloquence, reverence.

"What a contrast it was—how different everything except the congregation—when one Sunday morning, unexpectedly, instead of Stopford Brooke with his atmosphere of poetry and feeling, we had as sole ministrant, an elderly, bald-headed little gentleman, dapper and prim, who read to us a sermon of the very neatest, a benevolent essay of the most precise, which nevertheless here and there wandered for a moment into regions of wellbred satire, so that we were able to recognize, not the face only and the piping treble voice, but the hand also, the individual mind, of the Master of Balliol—Jowett."

In the above extract Sir Frederick Wedmore speaks of the impression made by Brooke on the young man about town. I have been fortunate enough to recover three contemporary letters from a young man who was about town at this time, not as a pleasure-hunter, but in the sense that he was earning his living in a public office and seeking such food for his soul as the London

Churches of that day could provide. The letters were addressed to another young man in a similar position to that of the writer. They help us to understand the hold which Brooke had upon hearers of this character. I give a few extracts.

"Dec. 7, '74.

"Dear Charlie,—Where wert thou yesterday? I was all alone. . . . Brooke continued a sermon which he preached some years ago. His discourse yesterday, as he himself called it, was the Faithfulness of God. [Here follows a full analysis of the sermon.]

"We long for faithfulness without alloy, for a more perfect, indeed for an entirely perfect, manifestation of fidelity, and till we look to Jesus, we look in vain. Christ's faithfulness he divided thus :—1. Faithfulness to duty and 2. Faithfulness to truth. The one the outcome of the other, the hidden source whence all His actions sprang. The main truths to which Christ was faithful were: The Universal Fatherhood of God, the Brotherhood of man and the possible unity in spirit of the two —man and God.

"On each of the sub-divisions he enlarged eloquently. I am sorry that I can give you no more of it. The fact is, I took some notes in my little Prayer-book and then, like an ass, actually went and lost the book."

"Jan. 6, '75.

"Brooke's sermon on Sunday was a review of the past and a prospect of the coming year. He spoke of the frightening sermons usually preached about this time, and said that such sermons, if effectual at all, resulted only in evil. The year that has gone, he said, was comparatively uneventful—the only two notable events—at least the only two of which he took any notice—being the increase of brutal crime and of preventible losses of life. On each of these he enlarged saying—as regards the first, that men have senses which will have satisfaction of one sort or another—purifying or depraving. The spread of education is the only remedy for it. This education must not be by a very long way only scientific or technical—we must not always ask, as now we too frequently do, will such and such a thing be useful to the learners in their work? The masterpieces of literature can alone ennoble a man's life—communion through their works with the great men of the past. . . .

"After this came a forcible denunciation of mammon-worship which must have hit his hearers pretty hard. He used two illustrations to show what he meant by the temper of worldliness. The one of a young man going to a friend for advice. He had been offered a situation, but it was impossible for him to accept it unless he hid his opinions from his employers. He wanted to know what he should do—which way went your counsel? . . .

"Of course, Brooke said a great deal more than I have written both in the way of additional thought and of enlargement of what I have already given. He wound up by placing before his hearers two pictures—the one of a man whose whole life was a frantic pursuit of gain—the other of a man who, purified and ennobled by the Spirit of God, had lived always for others and had found his only joy in the advancement of his fellows.

"How goes it with you? Shall you be at Stopford's on Sunday?"

"June 4, '77.

"How do you feel without Brooke? I feel 'mortial' empty. Indeed, I have had serious thoughts of perambulating the leading thoroughfares on the 'Sabbath,' with a placard on my breast, 'bearing the strange device': 'I am starving.' But, seriously, it is a great pity that such an accident[1] should have happened to him. . . . Yesterday evening, in my hunger, I went to St Margaret's, Westminster, to hear Farrar: and was exceedingly sorry, after the service, that I had done so. He took as his text Solomon's words, 'Righteousness exalteth a nation, but sin is a reproach of any people'; and from them delivered an historico-moral discourse—so different from what Brooke would have made of it. Farrar has one of the cast-iron voices: strong and clear

[1] A sudden illness.

but *seemingly* heartless. He seems to me to say (at least this is, in substance, all he said last night), 'Do right'! and there he leaves you. He does not, as dear old Brooke always does, fill you with the thought of the beauty of holiness, or with the idea that he (the preacher) is full of sympathy with the worst of his hearers. Farrar preaches petrified (and, I fancy, petrifying) righteousness: Brooke preaches—well, let some more presumptuous youth than I say what! at least in a word or two."

Soon after the closing of the Chapel he went to stay with the Howards at Naworth. He was much depressed. "The house is full," he writes, " of Cavendishes, Stanleys, Abercrombies, Howards—and creatures who have to do with elections. There will be a hundred at dinner to-day in the big hall, and I suppose dancing till twelve. So we are gay enough. It is all remote from me, and I live not in it nor for it. I write steadily some hours a day in old Lord William's Library overlooking the Glen. It is handed over to me. I have just finished off Wordsworth and the end is at hand of my book. [This refers to a revision of the Primer.] I sometimes wish the end of all was at hand. I have but little left to live for; though I hope I shall not get into sulks with life. That is what I have been of late afraid of, and there is nothing of which I have a greater horror. Death would be better. What a pleasant time we had [with the family at Wyton]! How sunny and fair it all was, and how harmoniously we lived together! It will always be one of my delightful recollections, and I felt when I left you as if I were leaving a happy dream that had been put into the midst of a difficult life, for the sake of comfort."

He did not go to Rome for the winter, but spent the months in London. A letter to William on Dec. 27 shows with what feelings he looked forward to the new work at Bedford Chapel. "The negotiations with regard to B. C. have been at last closed, and they have bought the Chapel for me and given it to me. I don't like it, no, not one bit, but I suppose I must accept and work it. It looks to me—as I look into the future—dull beyond expression. I have not much spring now: not what I had when I began the other, and I do not see where or how I am to get spring. Autumn is coming, perhaps the set gray life and apathetic soul. I hope not, but I suppose it must be borne if it comes. I would rather die than decay. . . . Dear boy, I wish you every blessing." And again in the same month, "I am miserably depressed, and for vague reasons. Why I should feel homelessness so severely now I cannot tell, but I do. Well, it will pass away, and I dare say to-morrow I shall be better. I look forward now with no interest or pleasure to going to Italy and would rather be at home. I hope this will not last."

In the spring of '76 he was able to take his long-anticipated holiday in Rome, in company with Mr and Mrs George Howard. He appears to have enjoyed himself thoroughly, and though he was still apathetic about his new chapel, it is evident that the deep depression which marked the end of '75 has passed away. The following are extracts from three letters written from Rome to J. R. Green:—

To J. R. Green.
"March 8, '76. Hotel Costanzi. Rome.

"I wish I could write to you about Rome as I should wish, but what can one say? When you were here you did not write, as far as I remember. What is the use of saying a little, when that little cannot be a sample of what one would like to say? It would only be a sample of one kind of grain, and when one has been a month in

Rome, half a dozen sacks are filled with different kinds of grain. It is easy to say something about Florence or Venice or Siena, for on the whole the impression made is one. But here the modern town is nothing, and there are three or four other towns that one has to look for underneath the modern one, and each of them makes a separate impression, so that I, who do not know enough of history to keep them at first distinct, became utterly confused. Then I turned to Archæology and Ruins, and I soon found that everybody contradicted everybody and that only a few outlines were at last left clear. Only in order to get the outlines one had to go through the previous labour and dismiss the antiquarians. I know enough now of the Palatine and the Forum and the other Forums to reconstruct certain aspects of Rome at different times, and I can now fairly give myself over to associations and not bother myself as to whether the Comitium were here or there. Enough for me now to feel that what was done and said in the Forum made half the European world. Still, I never liked the Romans—in fact, their type of character is one that I naturally hate. And I cannot feel the tithe of the interest here I should feel at Athens, because there is no affection mingled with my interest. I confess, however, that I did feel a thrill of excitement when I stood on the site of the early arx or temple that was probably built by the first settlers on the Palatine, and still more when I saw the substructures of the temple that they say Fabius dedicated when Rome had made herself chief in Italy. As to the mighty ruins of imperial Rome on the Palatine and in the town, the Baths of Diocletian, Caracalla, and the rest, I hated their hugeness, and I hated the minds that conceived them. The ruins of the Flavian Palace did interest me, and especially the Basilica, where I saw what had excited you so much; but I was far more interested in the beauty of the view, and my eye rested with a pleasure, which was greater than that given me by anything on the Palatine, on the Romanesque apse and tower of S. Giovanni e Paulo, which I saw opposite me on the slope of the Cœlian. And then I longed for a stroll through Siena or Perugia. No amount of historical association overcomes in my mind the depressing influence of ugliness in these big buildings, and it is worse when I see behind them ugly characters. And that the ugliness is on so enormous a scale as to give an impression of vastness does not improve it. I have never liked giants because they were giants; on the contrary, their hugeness makes one hate them the more. And they are all stripped of the weeds and wallflowers and lovely things with which Nature tried to make them pretty, and I regret their clothing; foolishly, you will say. Well, I can't help my folly. I have enjoyed, and completely, the Campagna and felt its special charm. And the Villas have delighted me, and the landscape, and the historic towns and hills around, the archæology of which has not worried me. I see them through a mist of association and no more, and the mist itself is in harmony with the vaporous blue air that floats above them. As to the Art of Rome, one day in Venice or Florence is worth it all, with the exception of the Sistine Chapel. That is like the discovery of a new world. The Stanze have not made me change my opinion of Raffaelle. He is still the master of the divinest expression, but his pictures themselves have no unity or idea such as intensely felt would make them into a whole. They are more truly ostentatious, though pretending not to be so, than any other pictures in the world, and the Kingdom of Art, like the Kingdom of God, cometh not with outward show. . . .

"I wish you had been here. It would have given greater zest to everything, though I have not wanted for zest—no, not a bit. Your book has just come. Many thanks for it. I think it looks charming, and I shall soon read it through, and tell you how I like it as a whole. Write to me soon.

"Ever yours affectionately, S. A. Brooke."

"March 13, '76.
"Hotel Costanzi.

"I am very much pleased with Furnivall's approval of my book [the Primer], very much. I think I shall write to him. He is great fun about 'the Flower and the Leaf.' You know it was only after long resistance I gave in to the opinion that Chaucer did not write it. I have often said to you, 'If Chaucer did not write it, who was the great Unknown who did?' And I put Lydgate's authorship of it hypothetically. For I did not know whom else to give it to, and then Gray had praised Lydgate highly. And, here and there, there are such pretty things in what I had read of him that I thought he might have blossomed *once* in his life. Some men have.

"Some few serious errors that he mentions must be corrected. I wish I had sent him the sheets, but shyness has stood in my way all my life. In many ways I have never been a man, but remained a boy. It is an *accursed* error, as I have found not seldom in life.

". . . The Campagna is becoming most lovely. The willows are becoming green by the side of every stream, and the grass will soon be quick with flowers. I have never seen such sheets of daisies. They are like snow on the hill-sides. And when I get alone into a valley with a flock of sheep wandering by me, and a tomb looking down upon me, and the asphodel tossing in the wind, and a swift stream rushing by and reflecting the blue sky, I feel as if all the trouble of thought and the pain of life were over for a time. It does not last long, but while it lasts, it is great happiness. Things do not look to me happier in the future for my profession. It may be better when I get to work, but at present—no. I heard a friar preach the other day to a large congregation. I stood against a pillar and heard all the old things. They fell on my ear like drops on a stone. I asked myself what these thoughts were, these images of thoughts, what meant to me what he was saying, and I could not feel as if I were one of the crowd who listened to St Paul on Mars' Hill. It is a sad thing to have a hard heart.

"This Rome is a wonderful place, but it is not a good place for a man who is ill at ease within. It chimes in with shadows, and I am, like her of Shalott, half sick of shadows. With that enigmatical sentence I bid you good-bye."

"March 20, '76.
"101, Hotel Costanzi, Rome.

"I send you back your proof.[1] It has given me great pleasure, and nothing can be more vivid than the picture you have painted of our ancestors. Here and there I have found fault, as you will see, but the only large fault I find is with the introduction, the two paragraphs before you come to the account of the Aryans. They are the porch to the Temple of the whole book, and they are too short, too abruptly written, wanting in dignity. It is like entering a great Palace by a back door. They must be made more important and have a more stately style, and be impressed with the sense of the great history which is coming. The germ of what you might say in them is in your paragraphs, but only the germ. It will have to be wrought out in at least two pages more.

"Why, when speaking of England's work, [do you] not hint at her literature, since literature is to be taken up in the book, why not at the growth of her liberty in the burghs, why not at all the main points on which you will enlarge? Why, instead of relegating it to a preface, not make this portion of your book contain your statement of what you intend to do and of the ideas which will rule your book and of the lines on which you will lay down English History?

"That would not only prepare people for what is coming, but would also boldly assert your own position in its differences from that of other historians, and though it might alienate some would draw others to your standard. There is never anything lost by hanging out our colours and letting them blow in the wind.

"And then you must make the beginning more dignified and full than this. It is like the introduction to a primer! not to a history of five volumes."

Like many another man who has a long career as a preacher, Brooke was subject to recurrent moods of depression and apathy about his calling. Sometimes he

[1] The first volume of "The History of the English People," 1877.

felt that "he was drained dry"; sometimes he would wonder if his message was bearing fruit, and again he would take a detached view of the preacher's office and ask himself whether he could not serve his generation in some more effective way. These moods might be associated with ill health or domestic anxiety, or they might be caused by some strong personal influence which appealed to the imaginative and romantic side of his nature.

When actually engaged in preaching no man enjoyed it more than he, whether in composition or in delivery. Nevertheless he would often shrink from it as a thing in prospect, and feel, as he would say, "unutterably bored" on looking forward to a whole winter of preaching in London. His rich nature was deeply susceptible to the attractions of other interests, and there were times when it needed a stern effort of will to turn aside and set himself going on the lines of his prophetic calling. Yet when once the effort was made—and he had schooled himself to make it—and when he had felt the response of those who waited for his message, he would plunge again in the preacher's work with immense ardour and joy. This is what happened when in May of '76, after so much reluctance and misgiving, he opened Bedford Chapel and found it crowded to the doors. Little by little the mood in which he had written to his brother that he did not like the prospect, "no, not one bit," passed away, his lost "spring" gradually came back to him, and came back with a vigour which was to carry him through another twenty years of almost continuous preaching activity. To say that through the years that followed his mood of reluctance never recurred would not be true. It recurred with greater violence and had a longer duration in the early eighties, as we shall see.

The history of the years that followed till 1880 will be carried on, as before, by a series of extracts from letters and other documents written in successive years.

To his sister Honor.
"London,
"May 25, '76.

"My Chapel gets on well so far. The offertories for three Sundays have been nearly 60 pounds; that is the ordinary offertories—and the evening congregation keeps up to about 5 or 600, which is double that I expected. The morning is full. But I do not expect these will keep up. I have but little hope left for anything, and I don't care much about it.

"As to Pre-Raphaelitism, I don't think it a subject worth going into. The thing has been proved and found wanting. It is a dead theory. Why handle the dead? You will find heaps about it in 'Modern Painters.' But, as I said, why touch a corpse? . . .

"I wish I were in Ireland for a time. I should like to recover some of the old days when I was a boy. But that is no use. I can write no more. I am out of the humour for writing, and I am in an hour of depression in which everything seems so ghastly that I know not where to turn."

To Edward Brooke in Algoa Bay.
"June 5, '76.

"When I came back I found my Chapel all in scaffolding. I got into it while the paint was still smelling, and the first Sunday it was full to the doors. Since then I may fairly call it a success, but not a startling one."

To William Brooke.
"July 21, '76.

"Read the 'New Republic' in *Belgravia*. It is an amusing, but over-clever satire. Still amusing it is. Second part not nearly so good as the first. . . .

"Oh, I have been so lazy for the last ten days, so lazy —and with so much to do, it is criminal. But neuralgia and fate, that convenient scapegoat, have been against me. And the wandering madness is on me too."

To William Brooke.
"Aug. 1, '76.

"The Bishop will license me on sending in the proper papers. It is all right. The scaffolding still deforms the Chapel, and I cannot say how it will look on Sunday. I have but little heart for it, but heart may come like appetite *en mangeant*. If I feel that it is succeeding, that the horses go under my guidance at a good gallop, the movement itself will invigorate me and give me more interest than I have. But I am somewhat troubled with life, and I do dread terribly being bored. That may seem to you fantastic, but it is a real terror. I do not care for things, for anything, as I used. I will go and look at the chest of drawers at Pratt's."

To Miss Howard.
"Aug. 8, '76.

"You ask a question which it does not seem to me difficult to answer. It is difficult to answer when one believes, as the Evangelical theory of the Atonement teaches, that God needs to be reconciled to us. But that is not the truth. He is always loving, always fatherly to His children. But His children needed to be reconciled to Him. They saw Him as angry, as jealous, as unloving, as fanciful, as arbitrary, as passionate. They strove to propitiate Him to give up His anger, and to let them off their punishment. Then He sent His Son to tell them what He really was; a Father, just, good and loving. I cannot let you off your punishment, He said, for sin must reap its fruits, but when you know that My punishment is given in love and not in anger, given to educate and not to confound, given that you may use it as means to be like Me and not to sink you into a hell apart from Me, surely you will not hate Me because of My punishment, but draw near to

Me through it, seeing Me smile upon you and knowing that I love you so infinitely that I cannot but be just to you, nay, hope that you will say to Me, 'My Father, I could not love you so well, did I not know you were just.'

"See what My character is, He says, in My Son's life. It is goodness, purity, righteousness, self-sacrifice. It is infinite love that dies for the sake of Man. Know Me better now than you have done. Be atoned to Me, reconciled to Me. Surely when you know Me as Love and Righteousness, as Christ, you cannot fight against Me any longer. He is the way to Me. You know Me through Him. No man can come to Me except through seeing Me as Christ has shown Me. What other way can there be to Me except by believing that I am that which He has shown Me to be?

"And so it is. God was in Christ reconciling the world to Himself. That was the objective side of the Atonement. The subjective side is—that having conceived this idea of God through Christ, and loving God in Christ—we cannot help striving to be like that which we love, by passionate feeling to draw near to God, to do all things for Him, to die rather than offend His Character, to adore Him as the one Being with whom we wish to be united body, soul, and spirit. That is sanctification, a slow thing, but to be won at last. Then will our At-one-ment with God be perfect.

"And it will be done through Christ: through belief that He truly is that which He said He was, the very image of the Character of God. So it was not to appease God that Christ lived and died, but to make known God to us, not to reconcile God to us, but to reconcile us to God."

From a diary written in Switzerland.

"Aug. 27, '76.

"St Maurice with Arthur, on the wall, past the Bridge. The grey Château and its towers stand beside the Bridge under whose lofty and bold leaping arch the stately Rhone flows by. The grey walls of the Castle are hung with ivy, green trees enclose it from behind, meadows spread behind it down towards us by the side of the road, and in them grow richly walnut and poplar and sweet chestnut and acacia; on the other side of the river the high rock is edged with trees, and above rises out of vast slopes of limestone the snowy ridges of the Dent du Morcles. The sun broke out and lit the head of the cone-shaped mountain that beyond the town fills up the end of the valley. We went into the old Abbey and heard the organ play the end of the service. Returning and going in the train one wild dream after another, one picture out of fancied life after another beset me and made my blood rush fast and warm. But as the rain fell on us it seemed to wipe them all out with a sponge. 'Dreamer,' it said to me, 'why not try the possible, not the impossible?' And I answered, 'I have always hated the possible all my life; I will hate it to the end.'"

To William Brooke.

"London,
"Dec. 11, '76.

"I have sold 25,000 of my Primer in about ten months. Good! isn't it? I am going to do a Primer of the Bible, as a Primer of *Literature*. I wonder shall I do it well. Anyway one can try."

To William Brooke.

"Dec. 18, '76.

"Yesterday I had a quarterly collection and got nearly £80 towards the debt. I hope to pay off every penny by May next, but I do not think I shall have got anything out of it for this year. But I see my way to making a £1000 a year; or at least £800. That will be nice. I can buy prints without a pang of conscience then."

To William Brooke.

"Dec. 26, '76.

"Were I at the head of the Government I would send the Fleet to Constantinople and tell the Turks they would have to reckon with me as well as Russia. It would be the best policy for the interests of mankind, and it would be the best policy for the interests of England and it would satisfy Liberals and Conservatives alike. Otherwise we throw the Christian provinces into the hands of Russia. But Turkey would have to give way then and to give up these provinces, and we should have the credit as well as Russia, and there would be no war."

To his sister Honor, with the Howards, in Rome.

"Jan. 15, '77.

"It is wonderful how much breaking up a long stay with other people and a crowd of new interests work in one, although I do not think one understands how much of this has been done till one gets back to the old life. As for me I should like to be broken up every year. I hate being kept close to any surroundings. I love change with all my soul. The only thing one likes to keep unchanged are affections, but even there I like to have plenty of surface changes. You wish me happiness and content, and I wish you happy this year, but not quite content, for, with quite sweet content, I do not think there can be happiness. The manna kept till the morning grew corrupt; and the aspirations in poetry and pictures which keep us from the contentment of the cottager, are the first element in happiness, for they make us work. . . .

"Being over here in Ireland I feel how hard it is for any one to do any work, such as literary work. There is an atmosphere of laziness which seems to infect every one except professional men, and on them it works so far as to take ambition out of them. The whole world here is an hour late in everything. Perhaps I know this all the more because it is my own tendency, because I am so eminently Irish in this. Had I not lived in England, I should never have done anything except as a dilettante does it. . . .

"Those children [1] are interesting, and there is a vivid

[1] The children of Mr and Mrs George Howard.

individuality about them all. I am very fond of them. Some only amuse me, but others I am exceedingly fond of. I like their natures and I am pleased all over to be with them alone and to have them about me. I like their talk and I like talking with them, and I am not very shy with some of them as I am nearly always with most children."

To Mr Gurney.
"March 26, '77.

"You are quite mistaken if you think I do not appreciate Southey. I had in the original draft on my Primer characterized three of his poems with some fulness, Thalaba, Kehama, and Roderick. But I was obliged to cut down, and as Southey in my mind was a less figure than Byron or Wordsworth, or any of the rest, I cut him down. I wish now I had said something about these poems, for my silence does not mean contempt, and it is somewhat false for it does not represent my view, nor suggest to any one all the pleasure I have had with Southey. Roderick was my favourite reading when a boy. It is still a favourite book with me, and I go with nearly all you say on the subject. As to Kehama and Thalaba, I was never tired reading them and they have supplied me again and again with illustrations for my sermons. I not only admired them. I loved them.

"But for all that I cannot rank him as highly as you do. He had not wings. And to put him alongside of Wordsworth seems to my feeling for Wordsworth something like literary blasphemy. I allow his moral splendour, but it is too cold. I allow his pictorial power, but it is too antiquarian. Roderick is the only poem in which he rises into passionate intensity of any kind whatever, and even there he is over historical, or quasi-historical.

"All the same I confess my sin. I was not true to my own admiration in my silence, and if I can I shall repair it in some future edition. Had I had room I should have given half a page to Southey, but you have no idea how I was obliged to condense. The length of the remarks on Shelley and Wordsworth were caused by the fact that they were not only poets, but men who created a school, who embodied a time, and who revolutionized poetry."

To Miss Howard.
"Dec. 28, '77.

"Do not trouble yourself about the doctrine of the Atonement. What is it to your heart, you who believe that God loves you through Christ, in what way the theologians quarrel over it? You have got the reality. Let the shadows of it which the intellect casts, fly away. Look at the sun and it will warm you through and through.

"God wished to see human nature perfect, and the conqueror of sin. He saw that in Christ, and He sees now the whole race, as it will be, in Christ. That makes Him at one with man.

"What more can the intellect want to give to the spirit?"

To William Brooke.
"July 23, '78.

"I have been close at work on Milton and done two-thirds of it in a few weeks. I shall finish that Primer in two months, and I have liked working of late, and it is the first time for more than a year. It is really delightful to me to get back interest in things, and in life again. I feel like a dead man come to life. I only hope it will continue. I preached in the Abbey last Sunday evening to an immense congregation, and I said :

"'There has been much discussion of late as to whether Eternal Punishment be true or not. It ought not now to be a matter of discussion at all. That intolerable doctrine ought to be clean swept out of the English Church. Not only would religion be the better for its destruction, but society, and government, and literature and art.'"

To William Brooke.
"Oct. 20, '78.

"I am well and have been working since I came home. I have promised to examine for the Civil Service Commission in English Literature. I suppose I shall get a good cheque for this. I am getting on with my Milton. It will be finished by the close of the year; and I have undertaken to write one of J. Morley's series of Men of Letters. I think they will give me Keats, and I shall like to do him. So I have work cut out for the first months of next year.

"I had a very pleasant time at Naworth, and met Lady Rachel Howard, who was Lord Cawdor's daughter. She used to live at Stackpoole, and I had a long talk over the place with her, Don't you remember visiting the Stack Rock with Edward and all the fun we had wandering over that lovely place?"

To William Brooke.
"Nov. 22, '78.

"I have been working very hard, astonishingly hard for me. Eight hours or so a day; getting my Milton Primer finished. And I am going to edit a selection of Shelley's Poems and to write a preface, and I am thinking of editing on a plan of my own some of the old Plays, leaving out all that is not good poetry or is coarse, and putting in the good bits, and filling up the story with prose, and writing an Introduction about the Author—getting three plays or so into an octavo volume of small size, a good plan? What do you think?

"And I want to do Shakespeare's Plays on a new basis. In fact, I have work cut out for two years: and I feel as if I could do it."

Extract from an Address to a meeting of working-men, '78.

"I have been forced to win all that I believe at the point of the sword, and I shall speak to-night of what faith in God is, of its foundation and growth, and what, when it is won, are its results.

"The ground of faith in God and Immortality is not authority, or demonstration, but our own sense of right. It is not God's authority, because that supposes the point in question to be proved. It is to argue in a circle to say that God bids us believe in Him, and therefore that we must do it. It is not the authority of the Bible, for the same reason. To believe on the authority of the Scriptures is to suppose that the Bible is absolutely true, and that requires proof. It is equally strange to say that the Church bids us believe in God, or that our sect does so, and therefore that we are bound to do so. For, in that case, we must believe in the authority of the Church or sect, and these can only derive their authority from God, whose existence is the very point in question. . . .

"In what do I believe? In what do I ask you to believe? I ask you to believe in God the Father Almighty. I ask you to believe in a divine and living Spirit, in whom all Mankind is contained, from whom all men have come, in whose life all men live, to whom all men are, without exception, dear as children to a perfect Father. We come from Him and go to Him; our life is His Life, our noble thoughts and feelings His, our work His work, and divine in Him. There is no life but His, and because we live we are His for ever. . . .

"Yes; God lives. We cannot be divided from His life, we cannot go into Nothingness any more than we can into Eternal Evil. We are all going on, one and all, together to form in the end a complete Humanity, in which for the first time the great cries of Liberty, Equality and Fraternity shall be perfectly realized. For all shall there be members of one body and one of another. Each shall live for all, and the whole shall live for all its parts. The interests of the whole shall be one with the interests of the individual, and the individual shall be sacrificed no more for the whole. There shall be no special class, no special rights, no divisions made by selfishness. One common love shall bind all together into one body, and all shall love one another truly, because all shall worship absolute love, from the least to the greatest. That is what I look forward to night and day, that is what I believe, and it is a glorious thing to trust in, and makes life, even in sorrow, beautiful, and the hardest work divine."

To James Bryce.[1]

"London. July 16, '77.

"When I first saw a day or two ago the death of your father[2] in the paper, I could not believe that it was your father, but as my sister did not hear I came to think that it must be so. I did not write to you at once, for I thought that in so great a shock you would not like letters too soon. But your note to my sister this morning makes me write without fear that you will be pained by a letter. And I wish you to feel how much sorrow I felt for your loss and how truly I sympathize with you. Someway the death and its circumstances affected me very much and I realized very closely how much sorrow it must have given you, and I wished to tell you how sincerely I felt with you. I am so glad to think that there was no pain, and perhaps, dreadful as it was, it may have been the death he would have not disliked to die. It is like an old warrior dying on the field of battle. And when I was most grieved for you the thought that he had died as he had lived in close pursuit of Truth, and in warfare with the secrecy of Nature, and on the field, made me feel the death heroic. Nor did this seem fanciful to me, but true."

[1] The present Viscount Bryce.

[2] Mr Bryce's father died in consequence of an accident which occurred while he was engaged in his favourite pursuit of geology.

BOOK IV

PROPHET AND POET

CHAPTER XVI

SECESSION FROM THE CHURCH OF ENGLAND

1880

" The great motherly authority of centuries—I could never be content with authority of this kind. I admire the great thing, as I admire a nation's great history, but it does not touch me in the slightest. At any rate it is better than the authority of a Book."—(*Diary*, March 21, 1889.)

" When the Queen asked Disraeli to make me a Canon of Westminster, he said, 'I could not appoint a man of his politics.' And when she afterwards tried Gladstone, he said, 'I could not appoint a man of his theological views.' I didn't care twopence to be a Canon."
—(*Diary*, April 14, 1899.)

DURING the nine years of Brooke's ministry at St. James' Chapel his preaching was prophetic, urgent, and impassioned. He dealt freely with social questions. At the same time current theological controversies had their due. He preached on the leading doctrines of the Church, Incarnation, Atonement, Revelation, the Bible, the Person of Christ, Original Sin, Redemption and Justification, and on yet more fundamental problems of religious philosophy. Within the glowing form in which imagination embodied his message there is a framework of doctrine, the result of hard thinking and wide study of thinkers. Throughout the published sermons of the period we can clearly trace a growing emphasis on the human nature of Christ; but the significance of this will be misconstrued unless we remember that there is at the same time a parallel exaltation in the meaning of Humanity, which I think is due, so far as outside influences are concerned, to the writings of Mazzini. Brooke's Christology is becoming a mode of interpreting the Gospel in terms of social ideals. It points less to the salvation of individual souls one by one and more to the creation of a new community founded on the brotherhood of men in Christ. The change that was taking place was more than a process of abandoning particular dogmas. It was a growing revolt against the conception of ecclesiastical dogma as a whole.

At that time he was far from that indifference to theological disputation which marked the last period of his regular ministry and deepened into positive dislike in the closing years of his life. The very title he gave to the best known of his discourses at St James' Chapel —" Theology in the English Poets" (1872) shows that he then regarded theology and poetry as, in some measure, convertible forms of expression. No doubt they were, as he understood the terms; but the conversion did more violence both to the letter and spirit of the Thirty-nine Articles than he was at the moment able to see. Later on he came to recognize that theology and poetry were not so easy to reconcile under the terms which bind a clergyman to recite the formularies; and the result was that he left the Church of England.

HIS SCORN OF THE IRRELEVANT 311

It may be said with some confidence that in theological argument Brooke was never in his element. His ablest opponent on this field was his brother William, who stood firmly on the orthodox side, and with whom, without peril to their deep mutual attachment, he was frequently engaged in theological argument. William's letters have not been preserved and the tenor of his criticisms can only be gathered from Brooke's answers. A study of these leaves no doubt that of the two brothers William was the closer reasoner, the better logician. His argumentation was more sustained; moreover, he saw clearly that the compromise which Brooke had made with orthodoxy in the early seventies could not last in the form in which it then stood.

Mr Chesterton remarks in a review of Brooke's volume on Browning (1902) "one of Mr Stopford Brooke's most characteristic faculties is the faculty of a certain sweeping and scornful simplicity. His power of dismissing things is beyond praise."[1] This remark is true and has a wider application perhaps than its author was aware of. It indicates one of the most striking habits of Brooke in the conduct of his life, as well as one of the secrets of his power as preacher, artist, and critic. He would never linger over an experience longer than was necessary to extract its essence, which done he would dismiss the experience from his thoughts. If a question arose requiring artistic treatment he would brush the irrelevant aside from the outset and deign no more to notice its presence. But when the issue was to be decided by argument Brooke's faculty of dismissing things would sometimes lead him to discharge the argument altogether and replace it with a bold statement of his own intuition. This no doubt

[1] The *Daily News*, September 25, 1902.

is often the most effective way of producing conviction, but it is not what is commonly meant by theology. I remember him telling me of a long argument he had about immortality with Motley the historian in the grounds of Naworth Castle. Motley was not convinced. Finally he turned to Brooke and said, "But do you yourself *really* believe in the immortality of the soul?" "I do!" was the answer. "And that answer," said Brooke, in telling the story, "carried more weight with Motley than the two hours of argument which had led up to it."

Another example among many that might be given occurs in a sermon on Original Sin in the volume "Freedom in the Church of England" (1871). With a somewhat daring logic he identifies "Original Sin" with the temporal imperfection of man as contrasted with the eternal perfection of God, and finds himself confronted, of course, with the old problem of why a perfect God should create as part of His universe so imperfect a being as man. "I answer," he cries, "because God wanted humanity" with its struggle for perfection. Then he sees that this does not solve the problem but only restates it in another form, since it leaves us still asking why the Perfect should want the imperfect, or indeed *want* anything at all. At that point his power of dismissing things comes into action. Instead of answering the question, he proclaims a poetic intuition of the facts. Human life, he says, "is a wild and glorious drama." Who would prefer the "monotony of innocence" to a "struggle so splendid"? "I at least choose otherwise. If God were to offer me perfection . . . I should answer —give me imperfection with the passion for perfection and the power of progress." This may be the right attitude for a prophet, but is not convincing as the end of a controversy. It is deeply characteristic of Brooke's method as a theologian.[1]

The story of Brooke's theological development is one which cannot be told in detail; nor, when once the essential facts are understood, is there any reason why we should wish it to be told in that manner. It is simply the story of a powerful personality passing on to fuller and freer forms of self-expression. All that Brooke came finally to proclaim as the essence of religion may be traced back to his earliest utterances, where it will be found mingled with the orthodoxy in which he had been brought up. This steadily diminished as time went on. As his self-expression developed it became more and more evident that he was unable to do justice to himself through the forms of any accepted system of theology. What we have to watch, therefore, is not the logical growth of one idea from another, but the gradual dropping off of everything which could not be wrought into harmony with his original intuition of Love as the master-principle of life.

[1] The following characteristic letter from Ruskin apparently refers to these sermons:—

"18th Jan., '78.
"Brantwood, Coniston, Lancashire.

"DEAR MR. BROOKE,—I wrote, very soon after your book and kind letter came, to tell you how much I had learned and with how much pleasure from reading the first of its sermons. The letter was mislaid instead of posted. It was so hastily and ill-written that when I found and re-read it, I burnt it, and have been two months proposing to write a letter. In the meantime, I looked further into the book, and came on the sermons about liberty of expression: which, as you perhaps know, is the last liberty *I* would concede to any man. Liberty to knock me on the head, or poison my meat,—reluctantly;—but liberty to howl in my ears or poison my thoughts—'While I live,—*no.*'

"My first lesson to all *my* pupils being: Rule your Heart,—if you can; but at the very least—Rule your tongue: and let that fiery sword not stir from its sheath, till it has God's order, and that clear.

"On the whole, however, I trust these words of yours will do good. I am quite sure of their honest purpose to do it; and am always, faithfully and affectionately yours

"J. RUSKIN."

The six sermons on "Freedom in the Church of England" probably represent the climax of his efforts in the way of doctrinal exposition. They show throughout that his thoughts are struggling with forms which cannot contain them. "I trust," he says in the preface, "that all will recognize in them my sincere adherence to the great doctrines of the Divinity of Christ, of the necessity of a revelation and an atonement for sin." The sincerity of the effort is beyond question, but we may well doubt its success. Assuredly the great truths on which these sermons are based *can* be expressed under the forms of the Divinity of Christ, the necessity of revelation and the atonement for sin. But they can be so expressed only by resort to intellectual accommodations foreign to men of Brooke's temperament; which accommodations he dismissed "with a scornful simplicity" when he found they would no longer serve his purpose. The whole of the sermon on Original Sin illustrates this in a very striking manner. No doubt the doctrine of Original Sin can, by due accommodation, be *made* to mean what Brooke here wishes to convey. But why should the effort be necessary? There are other modes of expressing the meaning which convey it much more simply and which require less apology from those who use them. Why then all this effort to say them thus and not otherwise? Why should a man so impatient of formulæ, so naturally averse to their use, be restricted to one particular formula, and that not a very intelligible one, for saying something which he could obviously say so much better if he were free to put it in his own way? As one reads through the sermon an impression deepens which may be summed up in the words "this cannot go on." A time is clearly foreshadowed when the mind of Brooke

ACCOMMODATION NOT HIS LINE

with its singular faculty of dismissing things, will dismiss the whole class of labours in which, against its proper nature, it has here become involved. This we should infer from a mere reading of the printed page. We infer it with tenfold confidence when we know the man by whom the page was written. There is indeed nothing in these six sermons to indicate that Brooke is contemplating secession from the Church; they are intended rather to justify his remaining where he is. But the indications are far otherwise when the human factor is remembered.

His individuality was too strongly marked and too resolute in self-expression to run a smooth course in the grooves of any system. Had he been a philosopher he would not have followed a school; had he been a politician he would have been no party man. Not through wilfulness, not through pride, not through a supercilious disregard for the opinions of other people, which last was foreign to his nature, but by the sheer impetus of his massive personality he was bound to go his own way. Moreover, there was in Brooke something akin to the wildness of nature which unfitted him for wearing any uniform or repeating the ordered steps of any system.

As a clergyman of the Established Church he associated but little with his own class. Except for Dean Stanley, I know of no clergyman who can be reckoned among his intimate friends in the ten years preceding his secession—unless we include J. R. Green. He took no pains to cultivate close relations with the leaders of the Broad Church party, and even if the whole Church of England had become as broad as he was himself, he would still have held a distinctive position and kept aloof from official programmes and organized propaganda.

316 SECESSION FROM CHURCH OF ENGLAND

Perhaps it may be counted a misfortune that the strength of his individuality thus compelled him to live an independent life. For it not only unfitted him to be the member of a party but disqualified him for leadership as well, leadership, that is, of any organized movement. He could not accommodate himself to the formulæ without which combined action is difficult to most men, nor would he at any time take the personal trouble which has to be taken if a band of followers are to be kept in order. Thus when he left the Church he made not the slightest effort to induce other clergymen to follow his example. He did indeed expect that his example would be followed and was disappointed when it was not. But he made no preparations for such an event and enlisted no supporters. Nor did he seek advice from brother clergymen, with the solitary exception of Stanley, who strongly opposed his contemplated action. Such counsellors as he had were for the most part persons whose point of view lay far outside the clerical world. And when the step was taken he did not follow it up. He seceded, but never attempted to organize secession, never even pleaded that others ought to secede. He had acted for reasons of his own, and left the consequences to be what they would.

How little disposed he was to make his own example in this matter into a rule for other men may be gathered from the following entry in his diary for 1894.

"Mr —— called yesterday and talked over his position in the Church. He is going to stay in till he is turned out. Of course, since he does not believe in the Deity of Jesus, I could not agree with his view; but I held my tongue. Each man must follow his own conscience in these matters .. The *Zeitgeist* will work upon him fast enough."

The character of his friendships, his interests, his studies, and his general mode of life between 1870 and 1880 was such as to enlarge his conception of liberty and to quicken his love of it. He was in touch with a large circle of artists and men of letters—Tennyson, Ruskin, Matthew Arnold, Burne Jones, Holman Hunt, William Morris, the Howards. His literary activity was rapidly increasing. He was preparing himself to write a complete history of English Literature; he produced a volume on Milton; he undertook another on Keats;[1] he planned an edition of Shakespeare's Plays; he made preparations for re-editing the Elizabethan dramatists; he published a lyrical drama, "Riquet of the Tuft;" he made a volume of selections from Shelley and wrote an Introduction; and set to work on a literary Primer of the Bible[2]—a task which he described as "trying to catch a penknife with a hundred blades, all of them open." He was in close relations with Giovanni Costa, the Italian painter, and with the Frenchman Legros. He was steeped in the literature of the imagination; the creative impulse was urgent, and he was constantly writing verse. He was deep in the study of Turner, of Blake, and of the great Venetian painters. He was making collections of works of art. Such was the atmosphere in which at least one half of his life was passed. Can we wonder that his official uniform became somewhat of a misfit? Apart from questions of theology, apart from controversies as to the ethics of subscription, serious enough on their own ground, would not a mind with the artist's perception of congruity find something essentially incongruous between this large free life of the imagination and the weekly recitation of the Creeds which his office

[1] This was abandoned.
[2] It was never completed.

required him to repeat? The two pictures could not be combined into one, and the effort to combine them would have left Brooke divided against himself—a condition which he was the last man in the world to tolerate.

His position in the Church was a barrier which held the prophet and artist asunder, and so prevented the two natures from perfectly reinforcing each other. On the one hand, he was living the life I have just indicated. On the other, he was the preacher to whom great congregations looked Sunday by Sunday for the meat and drink of their souls. He was sure of his audience. Bedford Chapel was full. Immense throngs of people crowded to hear him in Westminster Abbey. Warned by Jowett when he was about to preach in the University Church of Oxford in '73 that he must expect a very thin attendance, he found the place packed to the doors. He was fully alive to his immense responsibilities as a preacher, and threw himself into them with the same passionate ardour which marked the other side of his work. Had the two lives been feebler, or had one of them been the mere pursuit of a hobby, the need for their reconciliation would have been less apparent, and less deeply felt. As it was they claimed an equal freedom. Whether it be true or not that this was ever fully attained, it is certain that the chief barrier which prevented its attainment was removed when, in 1880, Brooke resigned his orders and passed out of the Church of England.

By taking this step he became in form what he had always been in spirit—a free man. This brought him an immense relief, and gave to his subsequent utterance a largeness which enhanced its power. Conscious of this enlargement he left the Church without regret, and never repented of what he had done.[1] His position had

[1] I heard him say when talking to a Broad Church clergyman in

become, to a man made as he was, quite intolerable. Theologically he had abandoned the particular doctrine of the Incarnation on which the Church of England is founded, holding it in a universal form which could not be accommodated to the formularies he had subscribed. Morally his position admitted of a very simple definition —that of a man who week by week publicly declares that he believes what he does not believe; and it is no exaggeration to say that he found the position at this point positively hateful. He was well acquainted with all that had been said and written about the ethics of subscription; but he had a horror of sophistry, and was not the man to balance his soul on a pin-point of logic. He required a broad basis of plain rectitude, veracity, and common sense.

Moreover, he had come to regard the Church in 1880, rightly or wrongly, as on the side of the rich; and he himself stood definitely on the side of the poor. He was in close sympathy with the ideals of Socialism—not those of Karl Marx—and though he believed that the Church and the World were ultimately one, he could not persuade himself that the Church in question was the Church of England to the exclusion of others. On the other hand, he felt no attraction to Nonconformity in any of its varieties, and resolutely refused to ally himself with a sect. Naturally he came into close contact with the Unitarians, and had friendly relations with many members of that body, of whom there were large numbers in his congregation, including the venerable

1905, "Well, if your views had been prevalent in the Church in 1880 I should not have seceded," but this was mere exuberance and would be flatly contradicted next day. In conversation he would often yield to the impulse of the moment, sometimes with astonishingly good effect, but only those who knew him well could say whether his words expressed a passing mood or a settled conviction.

James Martineau and his family. After his secession he preached in their churches and for their associations, and dedicated his last volume of sermons to one of their leading ministers, the Rev. Henry Gow, a beloved friend of his later years. His son was presently to become, for a time, a Unitarian minister in America. But his manner, his style, his ethos, his personality were not those of a Nonconformist. Whenever he preached in their pulpits he was something of a portent, a welcome and salutary portent, but astonishing none the less; and this, I think, would hold true of him when he preached in non-Unitarian places of worship, as in Trinity Church, Glasgow, of which his friend, the Rev. John Hunter, was minister.

Certainly when the cry went forth, as it promptly did upon his secession, that "Stopford Brooke had become a Unitarian," there was much misapprehension. The truth is that when he left the Church he did not pass from the fold of one denomination into that of another, but simply stepped out into the wide world of God and humanity. He "became" nothing that he had not been before, except, indeed, that he became himself in a richer and fuller form. Certainly the Unitarians rejoiced in what he had done, but their rejoicing was based on the fact that he had boldly vindicated the principle for which this body, amid much obloquy and misinterpretation, stands—that of veracity in religious expression. A multitude of congratulatory letters, of which some specimens will be given hereafter, poured in upon him from Unitarian clergymen; but not one of them had the bad taste to welcome him into their denomination. As individuals they offered him the right hand of personal fellowship, and it was a fellowship that was rightly offered and gladly accepted, for other-

BROOKE AT THE TIME OF HIS SECESSION.
From a photograph by Window & Grove.

[*To face page* 320.

wise he would have stood alone. He sometimes called himself a Unitarian, but not in the sense of being a member of the body. And he greatly disliked the name.

It must not be supposed, however, that Brooke's secession took place without causing pain both to him and to others. One of the greatest obstacles he had to face and overcome was the knowledge that what he was about to do would be a bitter sorrow to many whom he loved. His parents were still living in beautiful and venerable old age, and the large circle of his brothers and sisters had been broken by one death only—that of his eldest sister, Anna, wife of the Rev. Thomas Welland, afterwards Bishop of Down and Connor. Not one of them approved of the step he was taking. To his father, most of all, and to his brother William, the event was a catastrophe. Dr Richard Brooke was then too old to accommodate his mind to a situation so out of keeping with his life-long faith and practice, and was unable during the short remainder of his life to overcome the disapproval with which he regarded the action of his son.

Eighteen years afterwards Brooke twice refers to this matter in his diary. Both entries tell the same tale—a clear ratification of conscience mingled with a poignant regret for his father's sorrow. "That," he says in one of them, "is the most painful memory of my life." And in the other he thus writes (June 18, 1898): "I sat down on the grass of [my father's] grave, and read the inscription I wrote for him. And I remembered all he had been, and how I had disappointed him. . . . I was not vext, even then. I knew he would feel in that way. But I was deeply moved and sorry. I did not regret what I had done; I did regret that he had suffered for it. But what else could I have done? A man must do what he must do. I was glad to be there alone with William. Another would not have been in harmony unless it had been Edward."

The fact needs to be recorded, and it throws a strong light on family characteristics, that no breach took place in the chain of affection which held this large group of strongly individualized personalities, brothers and sisters, in a unitary life. On neither side did any coolness, even, develop; the relations were continued as they had existed when they were children together. Nothing divided them till, after many years of close communion, the hand of death began to interpose.

To William Brooke.

"London.
"July 17, '75.

"Have you seen this judgment of Phillimore's,[1] and what do you think about it? I should not like to do

[1] Dean of Arches (R. J. Phillimore) in the case *Jenkins* v. *Cook* (1875).

Henry Jenkins, parishioner of Christ Church, Clifton, was refused the sacrament of the Holy Communion by Rev. Flavel S. Cook, vicar of the parish.

Articles filed against Mr Cook, Feb. 19, 1875. Jenkins had published in 1865 a volume of "Selections from the Old and New Testament." He had sent a copy of this to Cook, who did not look at it till '74. In that month Jenkins wrote to him that the omitted parts were in his opinion incompatible with religion or decency. Cook replied that "the cutting out from the Bible of what is therein written concerning Satan and evil spirits is to me terrible evidence of how far you have allowed yourself to go in mutilating the Word of God"; and gave notice that "while such perversions and denials are not retracted or disavowed you cannot be received at the Lord's Table in my church."

On August 4 Jenkins was repelled as a common and notorious depraver of the Book of Common Prayer and of the Articles (language of Canon 27).

Phillimore sums up the case against Jenkins as (1) denying the eternity of punishment (this charge is taken from a private letter of J. to C., protesting against language which C. had used in the pulpit), (2) denying the existence of the devil, (3) expunging from the Bible anything hurriedly or unadvisedly, but if his reading of the law is confirmed by the Higher Court, it will certainly render my position in the Church of England wholly untenable.

"I should be deeply grieved to leave my old Communion, but I see nothing else to do, if this is law. It is not only the Eternal Punishment business and the personality of the Devil, but the fact, that whether I exercise the function or not, I have the power to repel from the great Christian rite any layman who does not hold these and other doctrines, and to include them under the term of 'evil livers.' It is a power I refuse to endorse by remaining in the Church. It is legal apparently for me to repel such a person—is it illegal of me not to do it? Does the possibility of the first infer the duty of the second? Perhaps next year you will see me in a conventicle. Write to me about it all as soon as you can.

"I was very grateful to you for your letter of the 20th and should have answered it before. I liked it, and was thankful for your loving words, and I was glad you remembered the day when she[1] left us to ourselves, and me to meet life alone. It is in times like these when I feel most her absence, for though she would have said 'stay' as long as she could, she would not have asked me to violate my conscience, if, on mature consideration, I found that there was a *vera causa* for leaving the Church. It is the vile superstition of the thing that revolts me, it is the utter and entire contradiction in it of all the

portions which relate to grave and important doctrines of Christianity. The following is a quotation from the judgment:—

"I am of opinion that the avowed and persistent denial of the existence and personality of the devil, did, according to the law of the Church . . . constitute the promoter 'an evil liver' and 'a depraver of the Book of Common Prayer and administration of the Sacraments' in such sense as to warrant the defendant in refusing to administer the Holy Communion to him, until he disavowed or withdrew his avowal of this heretical opinion, and that the same consideration applies to the absolute denial by the promoter of the doctrine of the eternity of punishment."

[1] His wife.

principles of liberal theology which makes it impossible for me to say any longer, that the law allows these things to be held in the Church of England. I could administer the Sacrament no longer. Practically speaking, half my congregation are subject to excommunication.

".Please write about it, and if, having considered the law, you would publicly write about it so much the better."

To his sister Honor.

"July 13, '80.

"If I finally resolve on this, I shall come over some day next week and see you all, and talk over matters. The real pain of such a step will be the pain it will give at home, and you may be sure I shall not take any final step without talking to my Father about it quietly. . . .

"It is not a question of desirability at all. I know more than any one else how thoroughly disagreeable and painful, at almost every angle of the matter, it will be to me. I don't like trouble, abuse, opposition or pain, and I foresee them all.

"The *only* question is—Can I, in conscience, or in use, stay on? I have not, as you think, acted or thought on this lightly. Five years ago, I talked it all over with Stanley,[1] and at his urgent request I refrained and said I would give it time, because my mind was not fully matured on the subjects in question. Well, scarcely a Sunday has passed during which I have not thought of it, no, not only Sunday, Friday and Saturday, whenever I have written my sermons; and at every point I have been hampered, till at last, it came to this—this year— that I scarcely wrote any sermons at all. I could not touch on any question of doctrine at all, and I longed to do so, for I had so much to say. But I could not say one word without either saying things I should not say,

---

[1] Stanley said, in effect, "The Church is broadening to meet your position." Brooke answered, "Will it broaden sufficiently to admit of James Martineau being made Archbishop of Canterbury?" "Not in our time," said Stanley. "Then I leave the Church of England," said Brooke. This is how Brooke reported the conversation to me.

if I were to be loyal to the widest limits of the Church, or without giving my congregation a false impression—that I believed in things in which I did not believe.

"What am I to do in such a condition? I must either give up preaching altogether, or preach with more freedom than the Church permits. Others may stay in her fold, and deny the miraculous—I cannot. It is a question of individual conscience; and if I stay, on the ground that many people will be disturbed at my going, and go on preaching in an entourage quite false to me— what do you think will become of the good I do? Nor indeed should what others are likely to suffer intrude at all into a question between what seems right and wrong.

"I don't deny that I may lose something in myself by giving up. I see that others lose their judgment and run wild without the sobriety the curb of the Church imposes. But I have thought so long and my whole desire has for so long been towards construction, and not destruction, that I think, without being conceited, I shall not be wild. My heart would be set towards building up people in the faith of Christ. No doubt, the whole thing would at first in the eyes of people seem a movement towards destruction of faith. But I have counted the cost of that, and could wait till people saw with clear eyes what I was really saying. . . .

"I have weighed and weighed motives till I am weary. There is not a thing which may happen disagreeably which I have not looked in the face again and again. What is the use of waiting longer— shivering on the brink any more? The coldest waters are not so cold as the atmosphere in which I live now."

To his daughter Honor.
"July 31, '80.

"I cannot any longer believe in the miraculous element in Christianity, and I do not think it right to stay on in a Church all whose doctrines are built upon that element. It seems disloyal to the Church and disloyal to truth, and disloyal to God and to myself. There are a great many views also in the Church of

England which I disagree with, but owing to the great elasticity of its charter, I could say what I liked about these by stretching the points, but I could not do that when I ceased to believe in miracles. And now that I have resolved on leaving, I am also glad to be no longer forced to *stretch* and *strain* points on the other matters, but able to speak at ease and with freedom. And I hope to show that I am not less a Christian, not the less a believer in Christ as the Master and Saviour of Mankind, than I was before. It will be a new life and probably a lonely one, and it may be a failure. I may lose more than half of my congregation and not make a new one, but I shall retain the Chapel, keep as much as I can of the old Service, and go on preaching as before. And I mean, if I can, to win my day and make success out of temporary failure. I hate failure, and I do not mean to have it. There will be many difficulties, trouble and solitude, but it will be like climbing a mountain, and pleasant, and years hence will be the rest upon the top. And it will be a new life, better than going to America and doing nothing. It is better to get the change I want in the change of labour than in idleness, and the best rest is not sleep but change, change too which I think to be right, which my conscience urges me to, and which is not for the sake of worldly gain or honour, but I hope for the sake of truth. I should like to hear, and with absolute frankness, what you think of it all."

From the Bishop of London.[1]

"Fulham Palace. Aug. 19, 1880.

"MY DEAR SIR,—I have read your letter with the deepest pain. You are, indeed, acting only as I should have expected you to act in withdrawing from the Ministry of the Church after reaching the conclusion which you announce; but it is a conclusion at which I find it very difficult to conceive any unprejudiced student of history arriving. The rejection of the *fact* of the Resurrection (excepting as an unphilosophical a

[1] Jackson.

priori assumption) appears to justify a universal scepticism with regard to all the facts of history : while the acceptance of the fact removes all difficulties in principle to the belief in other miracles. But I had no intention to argue.

"May the Father of lights remove, in His good pleasure, all what may at present be standing between you and truth.—Believe me to be, Very faithfully yours,
"J. LONDON."

From J. R. Green.

"Southampton. Oct. 5, 1880.

"MY DEAR BROOKE,—I am grieved to sail for Egypt before you return to town; or I would have told you face to face how noble and dignified I think your 'Address.' I hope you do not for one moment care for Haweis' letter,[1] it is too flippant and insolent to waste a thought on, and it is as immoral and base as it is insolent. I should have written to tell him so, but I felt that one *could* not bring home to the writer of such a letter what his conduct really was. In every other quarter, public or private, there has been but one feeling as to the course you have taken, a deep regret, but a far deeper respect and regard. Had it been possible for you I should—as I have told you—have been glad could you have withdrawn from the Church unobserved and as a layman, but I cannot question that your decision in this matter has been a conscientious one, and in such a matter (pace Haweis) conscience is the one safe judge. So God speed you in your new career. All that you say now will have the weight that words gain from personal self-sacrifice in the cause of truth. I could not help noting (forgive me for it) how far deeper a tone of simple earnestness there was in your Address than in anything I had ever seen of yours before. You were doing too great a thing to think of pretty phrases. Surely this is an omen of the new depth and force your teaching will gain in the days to come.

[1] Haweis, in a letter to the *Daily News*, had called Brooke's secession " an anachronism."

"You will read this aright, dear friend (and I am now more than ever proud of your friendship), not as words of praise—which would be impertinent—but as a word of sympathy. I never felt so utterly *with* you as I do now. . . .

"Yours affectionately,
"J. R. GREEN."

From the Rev. R. A. Armstrong.[1]

"Nottingham. Sep. 29, 1880.

"DEAR SIR,—Will you allow a stranger to express to you the respectful sympathy and admiration with which he regards the course you have recently pursued, and his cordial hope that your single-minded conduct may lead to the extension and deepening of your influence as a moral and religious teacher? I desire further to express my gratification that you have not elected to join any ecclesiastical body, but retain an unlimited freedom of personal utterance.

"May I point out to you that this is precisely the position of the ministers of those old Presbyterian congregations which have now become independent in Church government and generally Unitarian in doctrine? As one of these, I have never been asked to subscribe or assent to any formula, I am subject to no doctrinal trust deed, I enter into none but purely personal and voluntary relations with any other Churches or individuals, and it is fully recognized by my people that my teaching is to be that which in the development of my own mind may commend itself to me, and that I am to conform to no other standard than that of my own conscience. You have been erroneously described as 'joining the Unitarian body.' This you could not do if you wished, for there is ecclesiastically no 'Unitarian body' in this country, and there is no mode of 'joining' even that group of Churches in which a Unitarian theology prevails, since their communion together is one of sympathy only, and is in no way formulated.

[1] A Unitarian.

"While rejoicing that you then, like us, retain your absolute personal liberty and individual responsibility, I would still express a hope that we may enjoy your sympathy, and that as opportunity occurs your friendship may be accorded to men who are working, with whatever feebleness, for ends identical with your own on the very lines which you have yourself laid down. . . .

"With earnest desire for the blessing of God on your ministry.—I am, faithfully yours,
"R. A. ARMSTRONG."

From the Rev. Brooke Lambert.

"The Vicarage, Greenwich.
"October 18, 1880.

"MY DEAR STOPFORD BROOKE,—So you are back again in London—I thought I would write a line and say how pleased I have been to find no unkind words said about you. Haweis' letter is the only expression which one at all regrets. . . . There is no talk amongst those with whom I meet of the 'lamentable mistake' kind. Unfeigned sorrow that you should have seen it necessary to take the step, admiration of the courage, nothing to pain one. They say the Unitarians are angry with you for not joining them: Wicksteed, the only one I have talked with on the subject, took no such tone. I hope you may find satisfaction in the step which must have cost you much."

From a former hearer in St James' Chapel.

"Paris.
"Oct. 19, '80.

"MY DEAR MR BROOKE,—You will, I am certain, have forgotten my name and existence, but, in this world of ours you can have no more sympathetic admirer than myself, therefore allow me to pay my tribute to you, in expressing my intimate delight at what you have just done.

"As I know your 'Theology of the Poets' by heart,

your remaining in the regular formal Church was the only thing I could not understand.

"I cannot say how I honour you for the step you have taken.

"There are many of your friends who ought to follow your example.

"This perfect freedom of thought and conscience *is the* question of our epoch—it embraces *all* minor ones, and political dissensions are merely a branch of it.

"Here in France the quarrel is a little sharper perhaps, but not half so profound as in England.

"Will you never come over here? France is worth study just now.

"Forgive me for presuming to intrude my prose upon you, but it is a great satisfaction to me to tell you how you are appreciated by us all here."

From the Rev. Charles Wicksteed.[1]

"Croydon.

"SIR,—Is it true that you are about to come out nakedly on the side of Truth? If so—thank God.

"I heard you once. What you said was clever, interesting, earnest, true. But when I put you and the Service and your position together—I said to myself—'that man is not sincere.' Alas! the men that I have seen, and heard and read that might have become Luthers—nay much *better*, if not much greater—and sinking into nothingness, and leaving no personal mark on the history of our kind!

"Look at the men who pass into the shades of our theology—impassive, unimpressive shades!

"Are you going to be of the great, brave few who are remembered as having led away from something false and small and bad, and on to something real and true and good?

"I am shocked at the number of men arriving at the Truth, and not knowing its value, but throwing all their might into existing institutions and forms that are bound to the car of the Untrue.

[1] A Unitarian.

"I know and honour Voysey, although I think him a *mauvais sujet* as regards Christ—he is true as regards God—and would be true as regards Christ if he had not been hopelessly set wrong by the system in which he was brought up.

"Of course Agnostics are all right in their place—but unhappily their place is Nowhere.

"Will you let me see you and talk with you? . . . I write under some excitement of hope. Forgive me and believe me,

"Yours very truly,
"CHARLES WICKSTEED."

CHAPTER XVII

LETTERS TO HIS CHILDREN

1872-1881

"The world of imagination is the only world worth living in. There the sun always shines, and one is always young, and love has no apathy or ennui, and joy no stealing shadows, and there is no winter, and the streams are always clear, and so is the heart."—(*Diary*, October 23, 1901.)

PUBLISHED entire Brooke's letters to his children would present a history of the last half of his life. They would enable us to follow his movements from place to place, his plans and varying phases of his clerical and literary work. They would reveal his friendships, and his passing contacts with men and women. On the inner side we should see his changing moods and his permanent affections; his charm and his seriousness; his playful fancy and his stern resolution; his patient battle with protracted physical suffering; and the constant interweaving of his art with his religion. They would cause us to feel the richness, the variety, the dignity and the rapid movement of his life.

He travelled much, both in England and abroad, and never failed to describe to his children the place in which he was and the things and persons he found there. I have said before, of another group of letters, that they might be used as a guide to the district in which they were written; a guide, that is, for persons who wished to discover the soul of these places. The same may be said of his travels as a whole, as we may follow them in his letters to his children. All the famous towns of Italy, their history, buildings, pictures and the surrounding scenery are described; many towns in France and Germany: Switzerland from a hundred points of view; Ireland; the Scotch Highlands; Wales; England; the scenery of the Lakes; the North-east Coast; the Yorkshire Dales; the cliffs and coombes of Devonshire; the soft landscape of the inland counties; and the smoke-canopied cities—Glasgow, Sheffield, Birmingham, Manchester, Cardiff and many others—places which, as places, his soul abhorred.

The following letters, written to his children while they were young, often show his imagination at play. He delighted, at this time especially, in the making of myths, and could hardly restrain himself from making them. He would pursue them for weeks and months, and as they developed, his interest in them would sometimes become impassioned and serious. The tendency here at work bore rich fruit in his lyrical drama "Riquet of the Tuft," published in the year of his secession.

To his Son.

"Bellagio. Sept. 3, '72.

"My dear Stopford,—I sometimes wish you were here, for you have a sufficient love of what is lovely to be astonished and delighted with the beauty of this place. The lake spreads before our windows, up and down as far as the eye can see, sometimes bright as a silver shield, sometimes blue as Sybil's eyes. Great mountains encompass its shores, terraced with vines, covered with walnut, acacia, chestnut and pine trees, and here and there where white villas stand, a group of dark cypress shoot their spires into the air. But it is the wealth of natural productions which is most wonderful. There are thousands and thousands of flowers, and every flower grows five times as richly and five times as tall as the same flowers in England. There is not an inch of any wall which is not clothed with a garment of moss and ferns and lovely little wild flowers. The maize grows ten feet high; the fig trees cover great spaces of ground, the olives are like clouds in a green sky, and every garden is so thick with luxuriant plants that it looks like the undergrowth of a tropical forest. There are scarcely any birds, and that is a pity, but instead of the birds one has red and green lizards in abundance, glancing over the walls in the hot sun, clattering quickly through the dry grass, and such magnificent butterflies as would do your heart good to see, enjoying life, and in the wildest spirits. Then one can row on the lake and never feel cold, and bathe in its water which is always warm, even at night, when the moon burns like a globe of fire in the depths of the water. You would be so hot, but the heat does not scorch, but makes the heart alive, and even the marrow of one's bones feels it, and is grateful.

"I am so glad to hear that you are enjoying yourself and amusing your sisters to whom you will give one of your boisterous embraces for me. Tell Honor and Maud I often remember their long kisses and sometimes feel them on my lips, and wish to be near them again; and I am always hoping that Evy's tiny little arms may be larger when I come home that I may feel them go round my neck and hold me as tight as possible. Tell her I think of her often, and wish I could see her come into my room to say good night and run away laughing like a silver bell. . . .

"So you are catching shrimps every day. That is a splendid occupation, and how nice for the shrimps who have their own pleasure in the cool sea to be caught by a monster boy and put into boiling water, and then torn asunder and devoured and made into brain matter and turned out finally as Thoughts! But I suppose we must exercise our dominion over the fish of the sea by eating them, and shrimps must die as well as men. Have you

A MYTH

found many fossils—there are quantities at Bognor, but the most are to be found in a low range of rocks which is only uncovered for an hour or so at very low water, and which extends towards the west of Steyne Place. There you will find a great shell like a cockle in abundance. But in order to get them out properly you ought to have a 'cold chisel' as well as a hammer, and this you can buy at any ironmonger's. You know the sort of chisel I mean. I hope you are reading some physical geography with Miss C. and making up your arithmetic, which seemed to me to be in very bad order. No one is educated with Latin and Greek alone, and you must have sufficient energy, when schools are so badly arranged as not to teach English, to read English for yourself, and to add to your knowledge of the past, the knowledge necessary for the present. I want you to know especially all about the forms of government in the countries of Asia and Europe and in America."

To M.[1]

"London. July 19, '74.

" . . . We shall not see one another till October, and then I shall scarcely know my little girls, they will have shot into saplings of the woods, tall and lithe, and swaying with the wind that their own thoughts will make around them. How nice it will be for you to make acquaintance with your former kindred[2] of whom there are a great number in the high meadow near a plantation! There is only one family there, I found out when I was last at Naworth, who originally came from Bagley Wood. I met one dewy morning a very old and gentlemanly rabbit who was frightened when he saw me, and dashed into his hole. But when I went and whispered down to him some of the words of welcome which I had learnt from you, he came out again and we had quite

---

[1] The initials are those of Christian names, and indicate letters to his daughters.

[2] This refers to the "myth" mentioned on p. 422. The child was supposed to have been a rabbit in a former birth.

a long talk. He asked me how I came to know their language, and I told him the whole story. You can scarcely divine his pleasure. 'Why, we came from Bagley Wood,' he said, ' my ancestor, a great great great great great grandfather, was sent north with all his family by his physician, and being always of an aristocratic turn, we set up our hole among the Howards. And the Litha of whom you speak was descended from my ancestor's brother.' It was delightful to hear the gray old fellow talk, and I saw his family—about 100 in all, of whom he was as proud as I am of mine. 'Oh,' he said, 'I wish your girl who was once one of us could call on me.' Do try, dear, then, and find him out; it would only be courteous to pay this little attention to relations, however distant. You will be pleased with them, and you will know them by this—that they all have the right-hand foot black, while the rest are white. I remember you had the same friendly mark when I found you in the trap. They are sportive, chatty, and agreeable, and as I couldn't visit them in their burrow, being too big, I invited them all to a great feast in the courtyard at the castle, promising to shut up all the dogs. They came when the whole household was in bed, about two o'clock on a moonlight night. I gave them fruit and vegetables and some light cakes and rice pudding that I had got from the housekeeper, and a thimblefull of brown sherry and water all round, but to my old gray friend I gave champagne. He made a capital speech in which he told your whole story to his people, so you are well known. I sat on the steps near the hall door, and when I had tied a jasmine flower in the left ear of all of them, they had a great game on the grass, all except the older ones who sat with me and talked about their children. The moonlight was bright, the grass glittered with dew, and as they played, little clouds of dew rose about them, so that soon, they were all seen through a silver mist, and the stillness, and the pearly light, and the pretty movement of the little things in and out of the shadow and the gleam, and the movement being without sound, and yet so gay and glancing, were all the prettier from the contrast of the great gray towers that looked down so gravely on the happy scene. I dare say, if you were to ask them, and wished the little Howards to see it, they would come, only it would be very late, and you would have to ask Mrs Howard's leave. But you might manage it, if you were very courteous and kind to the old fellow whom I first met, for he stands on his dignity, and exacts respect. Remember me to him, at least, but for goodness' sake, don't say that I called him an old fellow.

"Well, my letter is nearly done, but you know how I run on on this romantic subject. I shall never get to the end of it all my days. Your Aunt and I are going to Devonshire on Tuesday morning to such a pretty place where I shall lie on the grass under a tree all the livelong day, and see the sun set over the blue sea. That will be delightful, and you and H. and E. must think of me as enjoying myself, which no doubt will add very much to your enjoyment. . . . I am going to see Stonehenge, a place that no one knows anything about, where big stones, each as big as a thousand Mauds, stand in a circle and talk to one another on stormy nights, a grim, lonely place, where no rabbits ever go."

To E.

"Bideford. July 22, '74.

". . . To-morrow is your birthday. I wish I had something here to send you, but there is nothing to be got in this little town which you would like, but I shall send you some little present soon, which will tell you that I wish you may have as many happy birthdays as you have had smiles on your face to-day and yesterday, and if you live as many years as you have had smiles, you will die a great-grandmother. We did not go to the place where the big stones[1] were after all, for I wished so much to get away from towns and their noise that I ran away as hard as I could to this place, where we came

[1] Stonehenge.

last night, and where I heard nothing at all, as I leant out of the window and looked at the bright stars and a moon as thin as yourself, but the chattering of all the little fairies that live in the leaves of the trees, and who waken up whenever the wind goes by, and say, 'Who is that naughty fellow?' and then go to sleep again.

"This morning it is raining and blowing from the South, and I feel inside, because the air is so damp, exactly as you feel when you have been crying for ten minutes, if you ever cried so long in your short life. I am sitting at the open window, and a broad river runs by to join the sea, crossed by a long bridge, some ships float in the water and others are drawn up along the shore, and men are mending them, and the noise of the hammer comes across the river. Here comes a little bird to the ledge of the window, a young swallow, who has been travelling in England. I must stop to hear what he has to say, for you know my fairy godmother gave me a ring, which made me understand the language of birds and beasts and flowers.

"Well—I have had a pleasant talk with him. He is a cheery, active little fellow, and has seen a great deal of the world already, though he was only born a few months ago. 'Have you been in Cumberland?' I said. 'Yes,' he answered, 'and I visited Naworth Castle.' 'Oh,' said I, 'did you happen to see a little girl there whose birthday is to-morrow?' 'Do you mean,' he said, 'a girl called Evelyn, with fair hair, thin, a nice-looking little thing, who is fond of being with herself?' 'Yes, yes,' I answered, 'that is my child.' 'Yours—indeed! then I am sure you ought to be pleased with her. I liked her, I carry her picture here,' said the bold bird, touching his heart with his wing. 'I fell in love with her; she was walking in the garden on a grassy path between the roses, and a strawberry in her hand; smiling to herself and quite alone. The sun shone on her hair and eyes, and I was so pleased with her that I flew round and round her, dipping and turning on my wing, and playing all sorts of pranks in the air, that she might see I liked her, and she clapped her hands, and said

"Pretty bird," and held out the strawberry to me. I dashed at it and took a tiny bit, but the foolish girl was frightened, started back and ran away to some other little girls on a seat in the garden.'

"'Oh, swallow,' said I, 'fly north again, and give her my love, and a long kiss, for to-morrow is her birthday, and my letter will be late, and I want her to know that I have not forgotten her, and I will tie round your pretty leg a lovely thread of golden silk.' And the swallow said he would, and I tied in a true lovers' knot a golden thread near his ankle and made him the proudest and happiest bird in England. Off he flew, and this afternoon he will come to your window and give you my message. Only I am afraid you will not understand it, though I am sure you will be much happier, even without knowing it, because a swift and pretty bird loves you well. But he can't love you better than I, who am your loving Father."

To E.

"[Donegal]. August, '74.

"Have you forgotten me, for I have not had from you any real message from yourself? I have heard that you sent me your love, but that is very little, isn't it? And I want to hear some long, big, large message, as huge as an elephant, and holding as much love in it as Talkin Tarn holds water, and with as many kisses flying about it as there are birds in the sky. And till I get this I shall have no peace, nor shall I smile 'at all, at all,' as they say in this country. Will your eyes dance when they see me, you little fairy, will they dance like a sunbeam on the water? Oh, say they will and make me happy. And then you will put your arms round my neck and hug me as tightly as the tiny black bears that have just been born in the Zoological Gardens. And then I shall scream, but I shall like it all the same, and even if I am half-choked I shall be pleased, and say, 'Do it again.' . . ."

To H.

"Belfast. Sept., '74.

". . . I have had no adventures since I was at Ilfracombe. Not a Dryad, not an Oread, not a sea-nymph has come near me, and I am very sorry. My sea-princess would have come, I know, but it would be no use whistling for her, for neither she nor any of her family are allowed, for reasons of state, to visit Ireland. It is death for any one of them to touch the Irish Coast; they shrivel into a strip of white seaweed. Twice on Belfast Lough I heard her crying bitterly far out at sea because she could not get in to speak to me, and I believe she would have come in and died, had I not fortunately met a black-backed gull, whom I begged to fly out and tell her that within a fortnight I should leave Ireland, and see her in some English Bay. I saw her receive the message, and smile sadly, and then dive beneath the waves. Her white foot flashed for a moment as she went down, a stray sunbeam touched it, and I was glad to see anything so pretty."

To M.

"'Dunfanaghy,' or 'The End of the World.'
[The Coast of Donegal.]
"Sept. 10, '74.

"It is . . . the very end of Ireland, and because Ireland is the whole world to an Irishman like myself, it is the end of the world where I am staying. It was nice to-day to look over the edge of the world where it goes down in a black wall of rock into an endless deep for ever and ever, and to see the stars in the sky down below at the other side of the earth, while the sun was above my head. I saw with a good telescope the soles of an Australian's shoes, who was standing at his end of the world and looking out from it. Here is a beautiful picture with the things marked for you. [A drawing follows.] There I am. I wish I could have put in my pipe, but the scale is too small. There is the Australian savage, Jacky is his name, and he carries a spear. There are the stars above his head. It is very pretty. I dare say if you look in a map of Ireland you will find Horn Head, a peninsula in the shape of a square lozenge with its edges bitten away by the sea. It was over a great part of that that I wandered to and fro to-day for eight or nine hours. It blew a gale, and the wind was so strong that many times it shut my eyes as I looked into its teeth. Indeed, once, when I opened my mouth like a fool, it turned my tongue right round and nearly made me swallow it. The sea brings up so much sand that it has piled it up, helped by the wind, over a great part of the place and drifted it like snow. . . . Then I went to see a hole in the rocks called McSwynes' Gun. The sea was very high, and the white waves came leaping over the black rocks which were torn and splintered terribly. There was one narrow passage between two walls of rock into which the foaming waters rushed, and at the end of the passage there was a cave into which they threw themselves. The cave was about as long and as high as the hall at Naworth. Fancy the sea racing into the hall and filling it, and thumping furiously at the end with a noise like the going off of a great cannon. And then fancy a big hole in the roof of the hall. What will take place? The sea unable to get out will burst up through the hole in a shattering sheet of white water, and will leap twenty or thirty feet into the air. This is just what does take place. There is a big hole in the roof of the cave, and the sea is thrown up through it backwards, and then when it gets up is carried away over the rocks and the grass in a great travelling curtain of white spray. The tremendous roar it makes is the reason they call it a 'Gun,' and it is called McSwynes' gun, because the McSwynes in old days were the chiefs who ruled this place. I went quite close and tried to peep into it, thinking that the wind would blow the spray away from me; but I was a goose, for a very big wave came in. I felt the rock shake under my feet, and in a moment I was wrapped in the foam and water and wet through. I laughed and shook my hair, for my hat was in my pocket, and ran back up the rocks to a safer place, where I sat down and watched this fine thing for an hour. . . .

"I am taking your Grandmother about with me to see the places where she was a little girl, and I saw yesterday the place where I myself was born and the tree planted the day on which I was born.[1] It is now a stately silver fir, and looking very healthy."

To H.

"Naworth. Oct. 2, '74.

"Great things and great deeds have been done here yesterday, and an endless panorama of muscular and magnificent merriment marches before me whenever I close my eyes and see over again what I saw yesterday. . . . There was a tent on the exercise ground—two tents— and in the tent were tables, and on the tables were bread and butter and a very dark cake—and I regret to say whiskey—and milk and sugar, and there was a big iron brazier under the trees, like that the old Howards and Dacres roasted Jews on for their money. It held kettles and not Jews now, and the kettles made tea. About 300 vassals assembled and were received by 'Lady' Howard in a heavy shower of rain. After a time the sports began : first, leaping over a stick, placed between two uprights, with a pole. They jumped nine feet nearly. Then there was a quarter-mile race, and then another race, and then the wrestling of light weights began—a light weight is about a ten-stone man. That was very interesting, and when the heavier men began to wrestle, it was still more so, because the struggle rarely lasted more than five minutes, and into that five minutes was put all the strength and practice, skill and science, and quickness of intelligence which the two men had been gaining in wrestling ever since they were boys. It made me clench my teeth, and set into firmness and excitement every muscle and nerve in my body, so that one followed [it all], just as one follows music within one, all that was done. There is no time to get tired, it is over so soon : and so much is put into the few minutes that the excitement is very great.

[1] See his description of it on p. 6.

"Every half-hour a rolling pile of dark clouds came up over the trees, and the rain slashed down on the crowd and the wrestlers, and the wind cut through and through one's body like a dagger. Everybody looked blue, but then everybody was good humoured and happy. ... It grew very dark at the end, and the storm waxed loud and the hurdle race was run without enough light. Then there was a great dinner; the whole hall was filled —two rows of tables, thousands of candles, hundreds of geese and turkeys and sirloins and partridges and veal pies, plum-puddings, pastries, jellies—soups, fishes, and millions of potatoes smoked on the board. When the rage of hunger and thirst was satisfied, all the prizes were placed before Mrs Howard. There were tankards with three, two, and one handles, barometers, clocks, opera glasses, teapots, penknives, boxes of knives and forks, watch-chains, and other things, to be given to the 'successful competitors' as they called them. They marched from the end of the hall, and received these things amid thunders of applause. The oaken roof rang, the tapestry waved, the glass in the windows shook, and some of the pictures on the wall smiled and some frowned. Then Mr Howard made a speech and proposed the health of those who got prizes, and then a man called Shuttleworth proposed Mrs Howard's health, and then all the tables were hurried into the courtyard and the hall cleared for dancing, and they danced and made merry till the candles burned to the socket, and the band that played in the chimney had their throats as dry as a bone. And so they went away across the park, the band playing all the time in the wind, some of the horns playing of their own accord, and the day was over, and so is my letter."

To E.

"Naworth. Oct. 12, '74.

"... If you remember Naworth when any sun is shining on it you would scarcely know it now. We seldom see the sun, and it is not only that, but the mass of clouds is so thick that hides it, that scarcely any light gets through, and the continual gloom over all things is, when I am tired, which is sometimes, very depressing. Have you ever felt as if a black cloak were being let down over your head and shoulders like an extinguisher over a candle? That is the way I feel when the days pass by and there is no sun, no colour, no life or light in anything in the garden or the glen.

"The floods have been great. You know Mr Howard's sentry box—I mean bathing box, near the river where the rocks stretch out into the water. Well, the river rushed up to its doors, and hid the rocks entirely, and roared like a bull as it hurried by to the Eden and the sea. And all the banks were strewed with boughs of trees, and torn grass, and leaves and straw and dead things. I went down to see it, and found the path by the stream in the glen covered with yellow water and had to wade. But the most sorrowful sight I saw was as I went by the Quarry Beck. There on a green little bit of meadow, not bigger than this paper, on which a rare ray of sunshine fell, lay two drowned fairies, a fairy boy and girl, folded in each other's arms, their lips pressed together, and their blue eyes half closed. The rough stream had been kind to them, for it had done no wrong to their beauty, and they lay as untouched by the cruel rocks or fierce waves as they had been in their beds of fern far away in their home in the moor that they should never see again. Poor little things, they had been sitting together on a leaf of woodbine that hung over the stream on the edge of the moor, wondering at the angry water, and saying how much they loved one another, when a tall wave rose and carried them away. They lived long enough to clasp one another, and to kiss one another a last kiss, and to be glad that they died together. And when the stream saw that they loved one another so well, it was sorry it had been so cruel, and it laid them gently on the tiny patch of meadow where the sun shone.

"And when I saw them I was very sorry, but I was glad also that I was there, for it was so pretty to see them, and then I could love them for the pity of their death in life, and for their love in death. So I lifted them tenderly in a great leaf and brought them to the garden, and I plucked a yellow rose, and opened its centre and placed them in it, and folded the scented leaves over them, and buried them in the deep moss that grows in the fork of the apple tree and planted an oak over them, and bid them good-bye. And I thought I would tell you this story and that you would like it."

To M.

"London. July 7, '75.

" . . . I do not want you to knit your brows over a letter and to write it as if it were a task. A letter ought to be gaily written, and quickly, and should go to and fro like a swallow over the surface of things, but then it should go gracefully—and it should use pretty phrases, and the writer should care about putting them in a pretty, half-poetical, or glancing way, in order that the reader may be charmed. You can do this, or more of it than you do, if you like. But neither in your letter to me nor in your letter to O. did you like much to do it.

"That is enough of scolding, only it is not scolding, my little woman, it is a bit of literary criticism, two big words your grandfather will explain to you."

To M.

"Richmond, Yorkshire. '75.

" . . . We saw all there was to be seen in Wensleydale and walked twelve miles a day, not very much, but enough for a lazy man like me. Your Uncle William is enjoying himself. . . . He has told me often about all the fun you had in the boat and on the sands. I wish I could see you and Honor and Evelyn and Sybil and Olive and Baby—what a number of names—paddling. You must look like Nereids, who were beautiful women, the daughters of Nereus, who lived in the sea and came out sometimes on sunshiny mornings to play in the breakers just as you play. Only they wore no clothes at all, it was so warm in the Grecian seas that they did not need them, and there were no dressmakers in the sea. They cost nothing to their Father, which was a very good thing."

To E.

"Rome. March 19, '76.

"My dear little Girl,—Rome is a big city, and has lived much more than a thousand years, but yet I do not forget a small child called Evy who has lived, I believe, only 10 years. That is wonderful, is it not, but you see that is owing to the force of love and because I am more of a father than an antiquarian, that is a man who loves all ancient things and especially old walls and cellars and broken pillars, and all kinds of ruins. If one digs anywhere for half a day one finds arched rooms underground or dark passages; in every street bits of the new walls are made of stones which people cut out of the quarries a thousand years ago. The fields where corn grows are full of broken bits of marble which lined the walls or were the pavement of palaces. You will have great fun when you come here making out where all the old Romans who did so much had their dinners and their baths and their bedrooms. All their rooms except where the slaves lived were painted with pretty figures and birds and fishes and trees and flowers, and little pictures of city life, men and women walking and shopping and dancing. You would have made a very neat little Roman girl, and as they were for the most part a dark people, dark hair and eyes, you would have been a phenomenon, which is a very wonderful thing indeed. . . . There are delightful gardens here belonging to the palaces of the rich families of Rome. They have walls all round them, and many of them are as long as Kensington Gardens. Great tall pines with green tops like umbrellas grow in them in groves, and at their feet are lovely meadows so full of white sheets of daisies and of blue anemones and hyacinths that I could scarcely see the grass. And there are avenues of evergreen oaks quite dark-leaved, and under them fountains playing, and statues standing in the shade. And often there is a glorious bright sun shining over all. But for three days now there has been rain and wind, and to-day it is snowing fast and the hills are deep in snow, and it is all very ugly and dirty and cold."

To H.

"Rome. March 7, '76.

". . . If you are interested about the stars, there is a map of them in the big atlas in the schoolroom. I used once to know all about them, but like many other things it is all now gone out of my head. When I come back you will teach it me. I well remember my excitement when I first saw one of the stars which only rises to dip again almost immediately. I had watched for it for several nights, and one very clear night I just caught it, and lo! it was gone. Then I chose one of the stars as my star, the star that ruled my destiny, and I remember the very night I chose it. It was Capella: a star you will easily find, and a very beautiful one. It would do you good in life to choose a star for your own, only you must not choose mine; it is preoccupied. I think you and Maud had better choose the two great stars in the Twins. You will both like to have to do with Castor and Pollux, who were very nice young persons, and whose fountain I saw yesterday, where they washed their steeds after the battle of the Lake Regillus. It has remained dirty ever since. . . .

"The word you use about Titian's portraits—that they have 'power' is just the right word. You will find by and by that it is a word used by people who talk about pictures in a very reckless way. They look at the portraits by Titian and Reynolds, and Guido and Bellini and Raffaele, and half a dozen others, and they say of them all, 'What power!' That is real want of power in them to make distinctions, and in saying the right word about the special quality in each man's work consists true criticism, which is being able to *see* and to *say* that which is the most excellent quality in a man's work, and how he has best expressed that quality. Very few portrait painters have *power*. Titian has, and some time or other I will tell you in what it is shown."

To H.

"London. July 20, '76.

"You have written me a very charming letter, full of pretty description and of interest. I am always glad to hear anything about places of which I am so fond as I am of the glen and garden of Naworth, of the Celt and the Tarn. I like to know how they are looking and what they are doing, to amuse themselves. For the whole glen, you know, is alive, and the beck is its soul, and there is not an atom of it that does not rejoice in its own special life, and make the most of its joy all through spring and summer and autumn. And then when decay comes in October and death in winter, it decays and dies thinking of the beautiful resurrection it will have when the west wind blows from the moors and awakens it to life again. Indeed, it does not die, but sleep, and dream, and the winter is made beautiful to it by dreams. All the leafless trees and undergrowth and all the roots of the grass hear the beck roaring in the rain, or trickling through the icicles, and they say to themselves, we sleep, but our soul waketh, and we shall wake again. Then they curl themselves up in their soft beds and rest in peace.

"I hope that will be our fate when we grow old; but it is hard for human hearts to rest."

To M.

"May 30, '81.

"DEAREST COMPANION,—I was glad to get your letter, and I read it with great pleasure. I felt instantly impelled to answer it, but I missed the moment of impulse, especially as you were goose enough to say you would write again, and more than a week has now passed away, but the impulse has now come again, and here is a letter to you. I am glad you enjoyed your journey. I enjoyed mine, and I enjoyed you. I was rather afraid I should not, for I have not travelled alone with a woman since I used to voyage with your mother; but it was just the contrary. I had a delightful time with you, and

I was very fond of you, and you were very charming. I think it will be very nice for your husband when you have one; only I hope he will be younger than I, as you told me; and gayer and brighter; able to take you to theatres, and interested in something beyond hymns.[1] The hymns have been again gone over, and I have added a few to them. Were it possible to dedicate hymns, they should be dedicated to you. Is your hymn written? I am waiting for it. . . ."

To V.

"Florence. Sept. 26, '81.

". . . It will be your birthday, I believe, on the twenty-ninth, therefore I write to-day that you may get this note on that most auspicious and magnificent of days in the whole year. I offer to you, like flowers on an altar, my fondest wishes, congratulations, hopes, joys, graces, wonders, desires, thoughts, feelings, all sweet, fresh, bright-coloured, gay and splendid. How old you are, I do not know, I do not know how old anybody is, except, alas! myself; but you are too young to think of how many years you have passed in this world, and I hope that all the years to come that you will have will be most delightful to you and full as a chocolate shop of all things nice. That is a wish, if all the girls here say be true, which you will understand most thoroughly. I have a present for you, but you must wait till I come home. Then you will come to me and say, Father, where is my present? And I will say, What do you mean? And you will say, Oh, you know! And I will say, Do I? And you will say, It is naughty to keep me waiting any more. And I will say, Little girls are made to wait. And you will say, Ah, cruel father! and burst into tears. And then I will burst into tears also, and when we have wept our fill together, enough water to turn a mill, I shall remember what the present is, and where it is, and bring it out, and our tears will be made into pearls of joy. At present I am sitting in the cloisters

---

[1] His collection of "Christian Hymns" was made while travelling with this daughter among the cathedral cities of France.

of Santa Maria Novella, near a well, among the grass, and the sky is blue, and the sun shining, and soldiers are marching outside to gay music, and the little wind is soft and warm."

To M.

"London. Dec. 1, '81.

". . . . Picture me lying on the floor in my bedroom in front of the fire with my leg lifted up very high on a cushion, and with the old hateful order in my ears, 'Do not, on any consideration, put your foot to the ground.' And it is only a day ago that I was running over London like a deer, and feeling as if I were a boy. I am half inclined to be impatient. The thought of four or five months of enforced quiet is not pleasant to me. And then there are all the disagreeable chances! Still, what comes must be borne, and all one has to do is to bear it as kindly as possible and to make it as little of a worry as can be to other people. I hate illness; it is so very unpleasant to folk in good health, and to tell you the truth, I have not very much hopes of getting well soon. I don't *feel* like it. And what to do with my work, is utterly beyond my powers of guessing at present."

END OF VOL. I

PRINTED BY WILLIAM CLOWES AND SONS, LIMITED, LONDON AND BECCLES, ENGLAND.

Lightning Source UK Ltd.
Milton Keynes UK
UKHW021828311022
411410UK00003B/304

9 780526 976935